International Perspectives on Aging

Volume 17

Series editors

Jason L. Powell
University of Chester, Chester, United Kingdom

Sheying Chen
Pace University, New York, New York, USA

The study of aging is continuing to increase rapidly across multiple disciplines. This wide-ranging series on International Perspectives on Aging provides readers with much-needed comprehensive texts and critical perspectives on the latest research, policy, and practical developments. Both aging and globalization have become a reality of our times, yet a systematic effort of a global magnitude to address aging is yet to be seen. The series bridges the gaps in the literature and provides cutting-edge debate on new and traditional areas of comparative aging, all from an international perspective. More specifically, this book series on International Perspectives on Aging puts the spotlight on international and comparative studies of aging.

More information about this series at http://www.springer.com/series/8818

Steven L. Arxer · Maria del Puy Ciriza
Marco Shappeck

Aging in a Second Language

A Case Study of Aging, Immigration,
and an English Learner Speech Community

 Springer

Steven L. Arxer
Department of Sociology and Psychology
University of North Texas at Dallas
Dallas, TX
USA

Marco Shappeck
Department of Teacher Education
 and Administration
University of North Texas at Dallas
Dallas, TX
USA

Maria del Puy Ciriza
Department of Spanish and Hispanic Studies
Texas Christian University
Fort Worth, TX
USA

ISSN 2197-5841   ISSN 2197-585X (electronic)
International Perspectives on Aging
ISBN 978-3-319-57608-4   ISBN 978-3-319-57609-1 (eBook)
DOI 10.1007/978-3-319-57609-1

Library of Congress Control Number: 2017938552

© Springer International Publishing AG 2017
This work is subject to copyright. All rights are reserved by the Publisher, whether the whole or part of the material is concerned, specifically the rights of translation, reprinting, reuse of illustrations, recitation, broadcasting, reproduction on microfilms or in any other physical way, and transmission or information storage and retrieval, electronic adaptation, computer software, or by similar or dissimilar methodology now known or hereafter developed.
The use of general descriptive names, registered names, trademarks, service marks, etc. in this publication does not imply, even in the absence of a specific statement, that such names are exempt from the relevant protective laws and regulations and therefore free for general use.
The publisher, the authors and the editors are safe to assume that the advice and information in this book are believed to be true and accurate at the date of publication. Neither the publisher nor the authors or the editors give a warranty, express or implied, with respect to the material contained herein or for any errors or omissions that may have been made. The publisher remains neutral with regard to jurisdictional claims in published maps and institutional affiliations.

Printed on acid-free paper

This Springer imprint is published by Springer Nature
The registered company is Springer International Publishing AG
The registered company address is: Gewerbestrasse 11, 6330 Cham, Switzerland

Preface

The baby-boom generation began turning 65 in 2011 and by 2030 they will all be aged 65 or older. By 2050, approximately 83 million Americans will be 65 or older (U.S. Census Bureau 2007). At the same time, the United States is projected to become more racially and ethnically diverse in the years to come. The Hispanic population is projected to be one of the fastest growing groups, increasing from 55 million in 2014 to 119 million in 2060 (U.S. Census Bureau 2014). By 2060, almost 30 percent of the United States is projected to be Hispanic (U.S. Census Bureau 2014). Similarly, the rate of growth of foreign-born individuals is expected to outpace that of natives, particularly among those 65 and older. Acknowledging these demographic changes is important, especially when one considers how the coming nexus of aging and diversity will require a greater degree of attention and analysis in order to provide policy solutions for this group in the United States.

Those who pay attention to Hispanic older adults have done so in part because they want to improve the quality of life of older adults, reduce racial and ethnic disparities in society, enhance accessibility to social institutions, or help minority elders to be empowered in their own aging. These motivations are what guided our own research agenda and were instrumental in the development of a multi-year family literacy program in the public library system. The stories and experiences gathered from this program are the basis of our book and allow us to explore the relationship between aging, immigration, and second language learning. With *Aging in a Second Language: A Case Study of Aging, Immigration, and an English Learner Speech Community*, we seek to inform public conversations about minority aging and shape how both public and private initiatives are framed with older adults in mind so as to promote successful language resocialization. Our title highlights two important themes: the intersectional character of aging which includes issues of race, ethnicity, and immigration, as well as our focus on capturing the voices of minority elders about their journey to learning a new language. Many older adult immigrants face real challenges in accessing material and social resources critical for second language acquisition. And yet we know that a more diverse aging population will mean more complex and multifaceted challenges and opportunities. The exponential growth of the Hispanic population and cyclical nature of migration suggest a need to identify processes that play a role in the second language acquisition of older adult immigrants. In the coming decades, it will be important to gain a better understanding of how aging and immigration intersect to impact language disparities in our older population.

Central to understanding these processes will be to place into context the everyday experiences of elder minority immigrants and identify the protective and risk factors that create different language development outcomes. We relate this research focus to a unique set of in-depth interviews we conducted with Hispanic older adult immigrants enrolled in a multi-level English second language (ESL) program. Over the course of 4 years, we gathered their voices and now share their experiences on a range of issues on how language learning shapes family relationships, the workplace setting, and notions of self-identity. Most important, we show how ESL classroom socialization helps older adults to create strategies, networks, and capital resources that facilitate target language learning. By creating a sense of *place* in the literacy program, our ESL older adults demonstrate the everyday challenges and affordances to learning a second language in old age.

Our book's goal to center the life stories of minority elders comes at a historical period when demographic and cultural changes are capturing the attention of academics, policymakers, social activists, and the general public. In these changing times, millions of individuals will find themselves in need of institutions and services that are responsive to them in old age. This is particularly the case for non-English speaking older adults who will have to find ways to successfully communicate with healthcare practitioners, social service workers, and other professionals. Bringing to light how older adults can learn a second language in a more effective and meaningful way has significant implications for how we as a society care for our elderly.

Dallas, TX, USA Steven L. Arxer
Fort Worth, TX, USA Maria del Puy Ciriza
Dallas, TX, USA Marco Shappeck

References

U.S. Census Bureau. (2007). Facts for features: Hispanic Heritage month 2007: Sept. 15–Oct. 15. Press release CB07-FF.14, Issued July 16, 2007.

U.S. Census Bureau. (2014). An aging nation: The older population in the United States. *Current Population Reports*. Retrieved from https://www.census.gov/prod/2014pubs/p25-1140.pdf

Acknowledgements

This book is the product of the active collaboration with city partners engaged in a Dallas Public Library family literacy program. We are particularly grateful to our library friends. Thomas Finley, adult services manager at the Frisco library, first introduced us to the opportunity to start a family literacy program. We are especially thankful to Ann Beaver and Pauline Stacchini, who as managers of the Hampton-Illinois branch library prepared and trained staff to assist in the practical management of the program in one of the busiest branch libraries in the city of Dallas. Their continual support made it possible to offer a family literacy program in Southern Dallas by providing personnel and classroom resources. Additionally, we appreciate the work and financial support of the Dallas Public Library. Jasmine Africawala, the Community Engagement Administrator, and Cynthia Perez, ESL coordinator, included our family literacy program in a city-wide initiative to offer literacy programs for adults and children. Their efforts provided classroom equipment, instructional materials, and evaluations tools.

We also recognize our community partners. As board member of the Oak Cliff Foundation, Brian McKay helped to spearhead a successful fundraising campaign at the Texas Theater. Ana Rodrigues of the Hispanic 100 Foundation also made a generous donation. Both funds were used to develop classroom instruction materials for students and teachers.

This project would not be possible without the many volunteers who assisted in teaching ESL classes. We are thankful to our University of North Texas at Dallas student volunteers, many of whom are undergraduates majoring in teacher education and sociology. Their passion, compassion, and dedication made the family literacy program a reality.

Finally, we would also like to recognize the guidance of Janice Stern, Senior Editor, along with Jason Powell and Sheying Chen, Series Editors at Springer. Their peer review and feedback were instrumental in keeping the book focused and us on track.

Contents

1. Introduction: Aging, Immigration, and Second Language Learning in the Hispanic Population 1
2. A Case Study of an English Learner Speech Community 17
3. Minority Aging in an Immigrant Context 31
4. Late-Life Second Language Acquisition: Cognitive and Psycholinguistic Changes, Challenges, and Opportunities 47
5. Social Constructivism and the Role of Place for Immigrant Language Learners 69
6. Building Emotions for Self-Identity and Learning 87
7. Practicing Safe Language Socialization in Private and Public Spaces 105
8. Language Resocialization and Gender Allies. 119
9. Conclusion: Aging, Second Language Acquisition, and Health 135

Index 149

Chapter 1
Introduction: Aging, Immigration, and Second Language Learning in the Hispanic Population

After exchanging the last set of good-byes Marta turns to join her family, who has been waiting patiently near the exit door. She says to them, "I can't believe it. I did it!" Marta, a 61-year-old woman who emigrated from Mexico some 15 years ago, has just graduated from level-2 English second language (ESL) class and is eager to hug her student peers and instructors before leaving the classroom. With a glowing smile on her face that marks the feelings associated with a major accomplishment, she picks up her belongings, taking special care of her graduation certificate, and exits the public library classroom where she has spent the last year learning English. Marta's commitment to moving through a multilevel ESL program is both memorable and transformational at a personal level. As she puts it:

> I am so happy. I can't believe that I finished. I didn't think I would be able to do it, especially at my age. I've learned so much…made many new friends who I have come to rely on very much. I feel more confident about my ability to learn and speak English. It has changed my life. I still have a lot of work to do but this is important for me and my family. It is something I've been wanting to do for a very long time.

This Mexican American grandmother receives her motivation to be engaged as a second language learner from a wide range of individuals, such as her family and now increasingly her classroom peers. She also looks to herself as a way to identify and confirm her strength and ability to learn English as an older adult. Marta spoke about the role of personal reflections and self-awareness in her journey toward second language acquisition (SLA).

In addition to the gains associated with improving her English speaking and literacy skills, Marta clearly expresses the significant impression that her classroom peers and instructors have made on her. Waking up early every Saturday morning to encounter an unfamiliar language is not easy and requires a degree of stamina that is fueled in large part by the support of her fellow classroom peers and teachers.

> All the people that I have met have really helped me along the way. I would always say that I was too old to do this but they would say, "No you're not!" That really motivated me to keep going…the professors were so helpful, giving me homework and ideas for how to improve. It was actually a lot of fun and I'm sad that the class has ended.

Here Marta realizes that building student-to-student bonds and forming open lines of communication with instructors have been critical pieces in her language development. Marta is sure that the relationships she developed in the classroom have made learning English not only a pleasant experience but also established practical resources for her success and continued involvement in ESL.

Marta notes how important these social support systems are in light of trying many times to learn a second language as an older adult immigrant. She is reminded that while acquiring English is a desire held by many who immigrate to the United States, the pressures of immigration and subsequent life transitions in one's later years often frustrate persons' best intentions.

> I know many people, young and old, that would like to speak English but simply don't have the time or know how to. I've tried taking classes before but have had to stop because of my obligations to family and because it was very difficult to find the time and the means. People also become comfortable knowing that they can just speak Spanish to their family and close friends. But we need to learn English in order to live in this society.... My grandchildren speak more English and I don't always know what they are saying.

This story shows us that elder immigrants in society today must navigate an increasingly complex set of values, goals, and pressures as they aspire to make a transition to their life in a new country. On the one hand, they acknowledge the value of SLA for their well-being as older adults as they come to interact more with English speakers both in their families and communities. Marta also draws attention to the barriers posed to immigrant elders who must manage family obligations that impact availability to learn a language, social expectations related to being an older adult, pressures to remain monolingual in their community, and a lack of resources for language learning. In many ways, Marta's story is wrapped up in fundamental questions of what it means to be an immigrant and the various social, cultural, and political tensions associated with this reality.

In recent years, the immigrant population in the United States has grown rapidly, rising to over 40 million (U.S. Census Bureau 2011). Perhaps not surprisingly, immigration has become a key political issue, with the President and Congress regularly debating major immigration reform. Most recently, this issue has become salient due to the contentious 2016 Presidential election and President Donald Trump's well-known campaign promise for a wall to be built along the United States–Mexico border and his assertion that there are some "really bad hombres" in the United States (The Washington Post 2016; The New York Times 2016). These debates signal the real divisions over immigration among policymakers.

Attitudes about what it means to be an immigrant are ingrained in the American public consciousness. Scholars have worked to understand the public's attitude toward immigration and immigrants. Research shows that Americans have defined "successful" or "good" immigrants as those who are educated and in high-status jobs, but look unfavorably on those who enter the United States without authorization, are unemployed or underemployed, and do not speak English (Hainmueller and Hopkins 2014). Hainmueller and Hopkins (2014) refer to this defining perspective as the "hidden American immigration consensus." These definitions of and attitudes toward immigrants, however, have major limitations that can impact information and policies on immigration.

Scholars argue that the nature of immigration and the acculturation experience can be quite different depending on the country of departure, age of arrival, socioeconomic competition, ethnocentrism, and immigration policy (Portes and Rumbaut 2006). Nevertheless, at the heart of the "hidden American immigrant consensus" is the assumption that in the face of such challenges individualistic values of hard work and perseverance ultimately explain individual life outcomes. Sociologists have described this as a form of modern "symbolic racism" (Shin et al. 2015), in that real bias toward certain immigrant groups goes unexamined because attitudes reflect the presumed neutral symbolism of free market individualism.

What some researchers have coined as the "Hispanic paradox" may point to a more fruitful approach to understanding the real opportunities and challenges that lead to differential life outcomes for immigrant groups (Markides et al. 2007). Data shows that despite their comparatively low socioeconomic background, Hispanic immigrant groups compare favorably to or are even better than other non-Hispanic groups who have immigrated to the United States on a range of quality of life indicators, such as life span (Palloni and Arias 2004). At the same time, researchers note that Hispanics' advantages as newly arrived immigrants decrease as the duration of their residency increases (Markides et al. 2007). This is thought to be primarily due to the process of acculturation (Gonzalez et al. 2009). As will be discussed in later chapters, the Hispanic immigrant context includes strong, close relationships with family into old age. What is significant in terms of language resocialization is how these familial and community connections act as a protective factor in providing social and economic support and resources, and also functions to isolate non-English speaking Hispanic immigrants from language socialization with English interlocutors. Hispanic immigrants, particularly older adults, experience a degree of dependency on kin and close non-kin members that limit their access to language resocialization and their ability to benefit from resources found in formal and informal English language settings. Understanding these dynamics is important for placing into context the Hispanic immigrant experience, but also for developing knowledge that can inform policy and programmatic strategies to aid older adult language learning.

In this book we consider the connection between aging, immigration, and language to be complex. A wide range of factors tied to the aging and immigration process—age of initial migration, nature of formal and informal social networks, access to target language interlocutors, to name a few—create various second language development trajectories. Marta's story shows us that immigrants from a wide range of education, income, or citizenship status backgrounds, do value language learning. However, those with cultural and material resources promotive of language resocialization can more easily make gains in this area. In the United States, positive attitudes are often accorded to immigrants who arrive with high status and who already can speak English. This book shifts from an individualistic explanation of language outcomes to a focus on the relationships that promote immigrants' self-conception as a language learner, the various bonds emergent in language resocialization, and resources available in sites of language learning. We argue that efforts to change the trajectory of SLA among Hispanic immigrants, and of elders in particular, is linked to initiatives that encourage a self-as-learner identity and of structured places of learning that build the types of social and cultural capital associated with language acquisition.

By using older adult immigrant firsthand accounts that we have collected over several years, we show the ways structural, cultural, and interpersonal forces impact older adult immigrants' conception of themselves as second language learners and their practical ability to move toward English language attainment. These examples also highlight the important role that places of language learning have in transforming self-identify and generating pathways for individuals to make language gains. Our stories capture a group of older adults from diverse immigrant contexts to help us better understand what the constraints are and affordances under which they attempt to acquire the English language. Our approach assumes that insights can be gathered by knowing just how much room may be available in the everyday lives of older adult learners to maneuver within the social and political terrain of immigration. Insights regarding language identity formation and local implementation of language resocialization can be the critical pieces for developing strategies and programs used to transform the acculturation experience of older adult immigrants and, thereby, change conventional attitudes and perceptions of immigrants in the United States.

Language Matters for Aging Hispanic Immigrants

As we move further into the twenty-first century, the population of the United States and many other nations will continue to age at a growing rate. According to the U.S. Census Bureau (2014), demographic changes suggest that by 2050 the population of age 65 and older is projected to double to 83 million individuals. These demographic shifts are due to various compounding factors, such as high immigration and improvements in life expectancy. The rapid rise of the aging population is also marked by racial and ethnic diversity. By mid-century, the overall number of non-Hispanic whites aged 65 and over will double, the number of blacks aged 65 and over will more than triple, and the number of Hispanics aged 65 and over will increase 11-fold (U.S. Census Bureau 2008). As Angel et al. (2012) point out, "the coming nexus of aging and diversity faced by the United States will require a greater level of scrutiny and analysis if we are to provide policy solutions" (p. 1). A diverse aging population is a matter of importance because the issues, challenges, and opportunities for older adult Hispanic immigrants will be complex and multifaceted in nature.

This book seeks to draw attention to the aging Hispanic immigrant population given the continuing demographic changes taking place in the United States and the Americas, as well as the transmigration of older populations that impact access, resources, and social networks related to language resocialization. Compared to the United States, Latin America's population is younger, but the number of individuals over the age of 60 is growing rapidly. In a few short decades we will see many more countries in the Americas, such as Mexico, rise in the number of elders and match levels found in the United States (U.S. Census Bureau 2004). Similar to the United States, the effects of improved nutrition, living conditions, and decline in fertility have meant a constant growth in older adults in Latin America (Lopez et al. 2002). Thus the topics addressed in this book are designed to aid scholars and practitioners to respond effectively to a diverse aging population and related language and communication needs.

Scholars have argued that the interconnectedness of the United States and Latin America requires a better understanding of how the aging of older immigrants in the United States shapes policies and social service delivery (Angel 2003). The aging of populations in the Americas has implications for a range of economic, social, political, and health care issues. For example, high rates of poverty in countries such as Mexico and gaps in Medicare coverage in the United States for those who cannot afford supplemental policies or do not hold legal status means a lack of full access to quality health care (Frank 2010; Gross et al. 1999). Social Security has helped the lives of older Americans, especially minority elders who hold fewer wealth assets in retirement than non-Hispanic whites, but many older adult immigrants may qualify for very little due to having fewer working years in the United States or may not qualify at all as illegal immigrants. Security also continues to be a dominant issue as it relates to immigration policy. Given high levels of immigration to the United States, the fact that many Latin Americans will age in the United States can give rise to more extreme political positions that view elder immigrants as a threat and drain to the economic security of the nation (Angel 2003). The aging Hispanic immigrant population will grow in the coming decades, as will the challenges tied to the care and well-being of these, and all, elderly.

Language matters in this context because a growing Hispanic aging population brings greater cultural and linguistic diversity (U.S. Census Bureau 2003). One-third of the United States' population identifies with a racial/ethnic minority group and these percentages are expected to increase substantially over the coming decades (U.S. Census Bureau 2002). When one thinks of the major life transitions brought on by immigration, language is foundational to how elder minorities experience social and cultural integration in the host country. Approximately 18% of the population in the United States (46 million people) speaks a language other than English in the home (U.S. Census Bureau 2007). Several states already have more than 25% of their respective populations speaking a language other than English at home (U.S. Census Bureau 2003).

The Hispanic population is an important group to pay attention to since they are currently the largest and fastest growing racial/ethnic minority group in the country (U.S. Census Bureau 2007). Spanish is the most common non-English language spoken in the United States. At the same time research shows that a majority of Hispanics report speaking Spanish in their homes (U.S. Census Bureau 2003). And while over half of this group reports speaking English "very well," these data rely on self-reports which can obscure the varying degrees of lower levels of English language fluency, particularly among older adult Hispanics.

Elderly Hispanics often lack economic and political power, which further problematizes English language fluency. Older adult learners face considerable obstacles related to access to economic, education, and public resources. Especially for recent immigrants, older adults' age and work status place them outside target language speech communities. Scholars note that without being able to access formal schooling and bilingual relationships in public spaces, such as at work, older adults are limited in interactional opportunities in the target language (Brown 2006; Ellis and He 1999). Learners in an immigrant context, particularly those who are not United States citizens, are on the periphery of many "normal" and normalizing forms of social participation that foster second language resocialization. Research shows that new speakers' sense of being peripheral to target language speech communities impacts their self-conception, emotional positioning, family relationships, and non-kin social networks (Norton 2000). This means that this group is at risk of being marginalized from key institutions that shape older adults immigrants' social integration and well-being.

Researchers have produced a wide range of theoretical and empirical analyses that frame discourses about later-life second language development. Conventional views refer to a "critical period hypothesis," which assumes language learning aptitude to decline, or simply cut-off, during aging (Paradis 2004). Aging is understood to weaken the cognitive pathways related to procedural memory important for learning language. The idea that types of learning are available to young children but limited to older adults is not new and works to frame broader discourses about aging and immigration.

Within the heavily divisive issue of illegal immigration, age has been a driver of new laws and policy initiatives directed at educational programs for immigrants. This is perhaps best encapsulated in the DREAM Act, which helps give students who entered the United States before the age of 16 conditional residency and then permanent residency after meeting further qualifications (The White House 2010). This legislation was drafted by both Republicans and Democrats in order to assist young immigrants with their educational pursuits. The idea is that supporting the education of younger immigrant students would be good for the economy and security of the nation as these individuals would be more able to contribute to the country in their later years (The White House 2010). But while the spotlight is on youth, older adult immigrants find themselves outside a future-oriented political discourse and challenged to locate formal means for language education. The U.S. Department of Education estimated that in 2000 there were approximately 1.1 million adults enrolled in federally funded ESL programs throughout the country (Vang 2003). In the wake of the Great Recession, however, older adults have found it more difficult to access adult literacy programs as budget cuts in public libraries and adult learning centers have reduced the number of free or reduced cost courses (Tung 2010). Fewer teachers and fewer classes have meant that older adult learners face real obstacles for moving forward with their language learning.

Nevertheless, the demographic profile of immigrants is increasingly made up of older adults. The rate of growth of foreign born individuals is expected to outpace that of natives, particularly among those 65 and older (U.S. Census Bureau 2014). In the United States there is degree of policy "silence" on elder Hispanic immigrants who will make up a larger proportion of the population and who will need to find ways to navigate a broad range of English-dominant institutions as they age. Elderly immigrants do not fit the youth-based cultural expectations that associate learning and development with younger individuals. Existing policies and future initiatives will need to rethink the usage of conventional approaches that restrict their scope, as well as require a rethinking of the important role of language development for older adult immigrants, given the major demographic changes facing the United States.

Increasingly, though, scholars, practitioners, educators, and workforce employers who interact with older adult immigrants are recognizing the need for and benefit of programs that address older adults' second language resocialization. Conventional theoretical approaches and long-standing cultural narratives may still portray older adults as too cognitively disadvantaged to learn a second language, but recent evidence shows that many professionals are trying to get more involved in older adult ESL, particularly with immigrant populations. For example, given the growing number of workers whose first language is not English, employers are beginning to see the need for work-based ESL classes for immigrant workers (Burt and Mathews-Aydinli 2007). Similarly, major education foundations are promoting the importance of locally available ESL classes for immigrant adults as a way to support the educational pursuits of immigrant youth and reinforce intergenerational family arrangements (Vang 2003).

In contrast to national debates, "on the ground" professionals who direct community programs and work with older adult and immigrant populations have their perspectives enriched by first-hand experience. These researchers and practitioners point to how language resocialization is relevant to older adults' lives and important for addressing issues related to broader social issues. As educators and directors of a community-based family literacy program, we also take the approach that policies and programs need to be more responsive to older adult learners. Often, ESL classes may be the only consistent or primary contact older adult immigrants have with English speakers. A central thread that runs throughout our book is the presentation of older adults' personal stories and experiences. Our hope is that by placing a spotlight on their narrative accounts as ESL learners, elderly immigrants' experiences can be the foundation for future SLA policies and programs.

Framing Our Study

We rely on broad theoretical frames—the self-identity work of older adults and the role of place in shaping older adults' experiences as language learners—to situate our participants' stories in perspective and emphasize ways to foster successful second language resocialization among elderly Hispanic immigrants. We utilize these frames to uncover the opportunities older adults have or might have to participate in English language socialization, while also considering the practical constraints in their everyday lives. The purpose is to show how an in-depth exploration of their narratives sheds light on the circumstances that shape later-life language learners and reveals ways to design more effective ESL programming.

Later-life language learners' experiences are linked to their sense of self in old age and their surrounding environment that define their perceptions, feelings, and actions at home and in public settings, such as in workplaces and in their communities. While programs that assume older adults have the potential to succeed in language resocialization offer a positive view of the elderly, ageist realities emerge in everyday life and are structured within institutions and ideologies that set expectations, roles, and resources associated with being old in society. The intersection of aging and immigration serves to further create an uneven trajectory that disadvantages elderly minority immigrants who already have minimal access to target language resources.

In this vein, we adopt a viewpoint that sees older adult learners' experiences as a dynamic interaction between self-activity and the conditions provided by place. Here we rely on Holstein and Gubrium's (2000) definition that understands the "self" to be principally "agenic and culturally circumscribed" (p. 12). Identities represent interpretive constructions that are simultaneously embedded in particular circumstances, such as already established agendas, discourses, and resources. In our study, selves represent the individual constructions that emerge amidst the circumstances of the places in which older adults find themselves. According to Gubrium and Holstein (2000), these places (e.g., social institutions, organizations, local spaces) carry a set of "going concerns" that are "relatively stable, routinized, ongoing patterns of action and interaction" (p. 102). Especially important this suggests that the social construction of selves emerges out of "the *interplay* between circumstantial demands, restraints, and resources, on the one hand, and self-constituting social actions on the other" (Gubrium and Holstein 2000, p. 9). The construction of subjectivities implies the dual workings of social context and personal agency in their formation. Subjectivities draw from a context of going concerns, such as an ESL classroom, and its discursive resources, demands, and constraints in the construction of self-identities.

In our study, we wanted to ensure that our older adults were not presented as simply passive actors and overly determined by the pressures of social structures. We sought to emphasize what Norton (2000) refers to as the "right to speak" and demonstrate the agency of older adults in their own journey toward language resocialization. In this case, Holstein and Gubrium (2000, p. 12) clarify that the self is not a passive recipient that principally absorbs or consumes an environment for the purposes of constructing an identity; the self is far more active and should be appreciated as "artfully agenic." Put differently, individuals must still interpret, negotiate, and give meaning to the going concerns within social settings. Using this perspective to study older adults, it becomes important to see their interpretive work as they make self-identities under the conditions of various places—such as an ESL classroom, family, workplace, and community. Furthermore, this approach suggests that older adults, while circumscribed by social conditions, remain agenic as they actively interpret and negotiate their context. Scholars point out that a dynamic view of the self-identity recognizes that "discursive environments set the conditions of possibility for constructions of self while also assuming an ethnomethodological view that regards self as continually produced" (Broad 2002, p. 320).

It was important in our study to recognize how the production of selves happens in the context of local cultures and places that are relevant to older adult immigrants. And so we paid attention to how selves are made "in accordance with local relevancies" (Holstein and Gubrium 2000, p. 104). Specifically, local spaces possess cultures and "the set … of regularized ways of assigning meaning and responding to things that is collectively derived and available for application within proximate circumstances" (Gubrium and Holstein 1997, p. 172). To the extent that selves are constructed in concert with going concerns, the ESL classroom is a relevant local space where family, friends, and community members all met. This location provided important discursive resources for the production of selves. With regards to our older adult population, we consider the ESL classroom an important site for self-production because it offers conditional, narrative resources for older adult learners' identity work. As was mentioned earlier, these contextual conditions are not just "directives" pointing to older adults' mere "embeddedness" or integration into the functioning of the larger collective identity of the ESL classroom (Broad 2002). If this were the case, a passive view of self-identity would subsume the self into the collective and ignore the role of human agency. Instead, we embrace Broad's (2002) qualitative conceptualization of self:

> It is the *production* of selves through interpretive practice that is embedded in the working of organization and collectives as they continually create themselves—the interplay between constructions of self and social movement (collectivity). Thus the production of a social movement self … is the interaction between discursive possibilities and constitutive activities of identity work (p. 321).

Conceptualizing selves as the result of an *interactive* dynamic between self-production and local culture, such as an ESL classroom, provides a unique and promising means of examining our older adults' self-identity as learners and how local contexts are critical resources for their learning.

Older adult's identity is tied up with the "the constellation of procedures, conditions, and resources through which reality is apprehended, understood, organized and represented in the course of everyday life" (Gubrium and Holstein 1997, p. 114). In our study, identity work is seen as containing two moments that correspond to and link up the "concrete and representational" facets of the self. First there are those cultural discourses in use in older adult learners' environment which constrain meaning making, in that they are already in place and functioning locally. The idea is that individuals make meaning out of discourses already in play in their surroundings to construct a sense of self. Older adults' identities are thus bound to the dominant discourses that address their aging in a second language.

A second moment of identity work relates to how older adults come to interpret and negotiate with these going discourses. Broad (2002) underscores the point that a full accounting of selves "must examine the processes and procedures by which selves are accomplished in addition to the narrative resources that comprise what a self might be" (p. 326). This means exploring how older adults make choices about dominant discourses on aging and language learning, as well as how these choices impact the actual trajectories of second language acquisition. We center this agenic side of self-production by looking at how identity is "actively crafted in light of biographical particulars, using culturally endorsed formats." Older adult learners make choices about dominant discourses found in their surroundings, such as norms about aging, in accordance with their biographical backgrounds. In this case, we show how older adults' personal biographies allow them to put into practice a learning self-identity. Our participants describe themselves in light of their roles as grandparents, as gendered men and women, as student peers, and as members of a community of language practice. These personal characteristics offer adult learners both cultural and material ways to reframe dominant discourses regarding learning a language in old age and to deploy resources to more fully participate in language resocialization.

Thinking in terms of older adult immigrants, although they are circumscribed by the going concerns of their life circumstances, they are also actively constructing their identities through interpretive work done in the space of ESL classroom. Throughout our chapters, we make use of illustrative stories from our older adult language learners to capture the process by which they *do* self. At heart, showing the interactive process that produces a *self-as-learner* identity is a central focus of our book, which considers more closely minority elders' experiences within their local community to identify shortcomings and opportunities for language resocialization.

Organization of Book

A recurring theme in our chapters is the idea of being responsive to older adults' everyday experiences with English language learning and exploring the ways immigration shapes this process. Key questions guide our analysis of the various issues relevant to Hispanic older adult immigrants. How are older adults' views on second language acquisition part of the structure of their family and larger community? What are older adults' vulnerabilities, needs, goals, challenges, and opportunities as minority immigrants? How do social networks—both kin and non-kin—impact Hispanic elders' access to key language resocialization resources in an immigrant context? How do older adults manage and negotiate the transition to a new country and the process of language acculturation? How is the participation and experience in ESL learning structured differently for women and men? We now present an overview of our chapters, which include conversations with a wide range of Hispanic older adult immigrants about the circumstances that constrain their language learning and how participation in an ESL program generates conditions that promote second language acquisition—namely, motivation, confidence, affective positioning, social support, and language resocialization capital.

Chapter 2 introduces our Dallas area case study of Hispanic older adult English second language learners. Our 4-year case study data of an English second language literacy program reveals the relevance of place and safe language socialization in mediating the acculturation process. Our analysis draws upon focus group interviews and participant observations with a core sample of 40 Hispanic older adult ESL students. Participants were recruited through a face-to-face announcement in our ESL family literacy program located in a predominantly Hispanic community in Dallas, Texas. Our longitudinal data set allows us to explore a wide range of issues associated with the complex and transitional nature of older adult immigrant second language socialization. We utilize a qualitative, active interviewing approach that has the advantage of producing insights about meanings, contexts, and processes related to older adult immigrants' unique experiences and their efforts toward language resocialization.

Chapter 3 focuses on placing elder minority language acquisition in the context of immigration. Acknowledging demographic changes in the United States, we focus on the risk factors associated with immigration and acculturation. Specific attention is given to the economic, social, and cultural effects of immigration on Hispanic immigrants. Exposure to a new country can negatively affect older adults in particular, as poor and economically disadvantaged populations are disproportionally excluded from key institutions and resources. Sociocultural factors profoundly impact minority aging, since acculturation and assimilation are linked with socioeconomic status. We thus examine the cultural and structural factors that uniquely impact Hispanic elders in an immigrant context. The unique barriers for older immigrants are well documented. Institutional disadvantages exclude immigrants from the type of resources and social networks important for language acquisition and, in turn, impact larger indicators of well-being and language performance.

Chapters 4 and 5 introduce current literature on language acquisition and emphasize the key factors scholars have identified as critical for later-life second language development. In Chap. 4, conventional approaches in linguistics are examined for their work on the relationship between aging and language learning. Of particular interest to these traditional approaches is the role of cognition in the development of language. We emphasize, however, the call by social linguists who study how "safe" encounters mediate pressures experienced during second language socialization and empower older immigrants in their cross-cultural engagements. Chapter 5 follows this contemporary work by introducing what is known as the "social turn" in second language acquisition theory. We argue that older immigrant language socialization is shaped by the social bonding and cooperation present between the novice learner and other interlocutors. We recognize that functioning in English-dominant spaces may generate cognitive and social challenges for older immigrant language learners and isolate them from positive socialization encounters with English-dominant interlocutors. In this context, age-related beliefs, behaviors, and self-representations emerge from the backdrop of recurrent social interactions. From this perspective, we emphasize that safe places of interaction promote linguistic resocialization for otherwise culturally isolated older immigrants. What can be called "right to speak" zones help to address concerns of feelings of inadequacy, inhibition, and low self-esteem during target language acquisition. Older immigrants are forced into the cognitive and social complexities of acculturation and adaptation in ways that early-life migrants are not. We argue that research is needed that identifies the practical ways places of language resocialization mediate and reduce these risks and limitations.

Chapter 6 begins our book's examination of how language capital is structured by various formal and informal spaces, such as family, work, and within the ESL classroom. More specifically, this chapter focuses on the important process of affective positioning and how ESL socialization impacts the framing of emotions. A language socialization paradigm suggests that emotions not only mediate the learning experience, but are themselves negotiated and constructed within interaction. From a practical viewpoint, affective stances are important because they help to align language members and communicate sociocultural information that regulates participation in a speech community. Older adult immigrants are usually exposed to a pre-established, often stigmatized, set of evaluative commentary and affective positioning in mainstream socialization that carry a narrow range of language styles and practices. To the extent that the index of appropriate and inappropriate behaviors is limited within mainstream institutional interaction, older immigrants may seek to minimize "errors" by withdrawing from language socialization. This coping strategy may alleviate fear, anxiety, and shame related to their linguistic behavior, but it also restricts their language practice. We highlight how socialization within the ESL classroom serves to build positive affective positions and encourage English language practice. Here older immigrants participate in a linguistic community based on a more diverse index of linguistic behaviors. Linguistic deviations are shared by the group, which destabilizes the social privilege usually assigned to particular social identities, such as being proficient in English. In the absence of these stigmas, older immigrants are free to reinterpret and feel different about their language behavior. This, in turn, promotes continued engagement with cross-cultural encounters.

Chapter 7 centers on both private and public spaces to uncover the ways language capital is generated by older adult learners. Older adult immigrants typically face several challenges tied to the effects of later-life immigration. In their private, domestic life they may experience a reversal of typical age-based language socialization roles. For older second language learners, their immigrant children and grandchildren are often positioned as linguistic "caretakers" for their parents and elders. This involves a counterposing of the normative political economy and status in the family. Typically, young novices are socialized by adult "experts" of the family's native tongue. In the immigrant context, this authority and responsibility no longer belongs to the native-speaking parents, but rather to the children. This role reversal of language caretakers within a household may lead to poor sociopragmatic and linguistic input for older language learners if children withdraw from socializing with them in English or offer narrow linguistic input. Older adults may also find themselves in similar role reversals in public settings where they do not have language authority, such as at work. We explore the ways resources tied to conventional family and societal roles are shored up and redeployed with the aid of ESL language resocialization. The ESL classroom offers a range of symbolic and material resources to support older immigrants to regain capital lost due to the rearrangement of familial and public social roles. Interaction within an ESL classroom provides a location-specific way to identify horizontally based networks built on peer-to-peer status language resocialization. These networks not only generate new forms of cultural and social capital but also alternative ways to invest in a learning self-identity. In this chapter we emphasize the ways "low-risk" learning during ESL socialization affords older immigrants a testing ground to practice their linguistic, cultural, and communicative competence. The effects of this approach are assessed, with data pointing to older immigrants developing increased confidence which fosters continued encounters with proficient interlocutors within family, work, and other public spheres.

Chapter 8 investigates how language socialization in the immigrant context cannot be separated from gender roles and their associative sociolinguistic practices. Exclusionary interactions that emanate either from the dominant or immigrant community have the potential to limit both women and men's mobility and their access to native-speaking interlocutors. This is the case for many immigrant mothers who are responsible for domestic and childrearing work. Studies in immigrant gender identities link potential changes in social position to the simultaneous shifts experienced by immigrants in a new economic context. While shifts to wage labor could result in greater autonomy and equality for women, changes to traditional gender practices within the kinship structure are rarely accomplished in a single generation. For men, English socialization is deemed unnecessary since a large majority of men immigrants create friendships and employment relationships with non-English speakers. For women, enrolling in formal language classes is interpreted as problematizing their domestic roles. Participating in formal language resocialization may deviate from expected gender roles and may be discouraged by family and friends. As our data show, however, the ESL classroom space can be a site where older women and men renegotiate gender norms to become gender allies in the process of second language acquisition.

Our chapters bring in rich, in-depth qualitative data to better understand the nature of immigrant aging and how language resocialization shapes the chronic issues facing the Hispanic immigrant population in the United States. Our final chapter presents recommendations for improving elder language resocialization. Current literature highlights the growing need to build cultural and linguistic competency among older adult immigrants and those who will work with this population. However, there is also a need to find successful and practical strategies to assist aging Hispanics immigrants in their language resocialization. Assuring equal access to quality care, services, and setting will require that aging immigrants are themselves empowered and competent during second language socialization. Successful aging for Hispanic immigrants will depend on research and policy efforts that explore how to bridge the cultural and linguistic gulf between the aging population and those that will work with them in the home or social institutions. In this way, the experience of Hispanic older adult immigrants is representative of the demographic heterogeneity of and issues affecting the aging community at large.

References

Angel, J. L. (2003). Devolution and the social welfare of elderly immigrants: Who will bear the burden? *Public Administration Review, 63*(1), 79–89.

Angel, J. L., Torres-Gil, F., & Markides, K. (Eds.). (2012). *Aging, health, and longevity in the Mexican-origin population*. New York: Springer.

Broad, K. L. (2002). Social movement selves. *Sociological Perspectives, 45*(3), 317–336.

Brown, H. D. (2006). *Principles of language learning and teaching*. New York, NY: Pearson ESL.

Burt, M., & Mathews-Aydinli, J. (2007). Workplace instruction and workforce preparation for adult immigrants. *CAELA Brief.* Center for Adult English Language Acquisition/Center for Applied Linguistics.

Ellis, R., & He, X. (1999). The roles of modified input and output in the incidental acquisition of word meanings. *Studies in Second Language Acquisition, 21*(2), 285–301.

Frank, J. (2010). The global health system: Strengthening national health systems as the next step for global progress. *PLoS Med, 7*(1), e1000089.

Gonzalez, H., Ceballos, M., Tarraf, W., West, B., Bowen, M., & Vega, W. (2009). The health of older Mexican Americans in the long run. *American Journal of Public Health, 99*(10), 1879–1885.

Gross, D. L., Alecxih, L., Gibson, M. J., Corea, J., Caplan, C., & Brangan, N. (1999). Out-of-pocket health spending by poor and near-poor elderly Medicare beneficiaries. *Health Services Research, 34*(1 Pt 2), 241–254.

Gubrium, J. F., & Holstein, J. A. (1997). *The new language of qualitative method*. New York: Oxford University Press.

Gubrium, J. F., & Holstein, J. A. (2000). The self in a world of going concerns. *Symbolic Interaction, 23*(2), 95–115.

Hainmueller, J., & Hopkins, D. J. (2014). The hidden American immigration consensus: A conjoint analysis of attitudes towards immigrants. *American Journal of Political Science, 59*(3), 529–548.

Holstein, J. A., & Gubrium, J. F. (2000). *The self we live by: Narrative identity in a postmodern world*. New York: Oxford University Press.

Lopez, A. D., Ahmad, O. B., Guillot, M., Ferguson, B. D., Solomon, J. A., Murray, C. J. L., et al. (2002). *World mortality in 2000: Life expectancy for 191 countries*. Geneva: World Health Organization.

Markides, K. S., Eschback, K., Ray, L. A., & Peek, M. K. (2007). Census disability rates among older people by race/ethnicity and type of Hispanic origin. In J. L. Angel & K. E. Whitfield (Eds.), *The health of aging Hispanics: The Mexican-origin population* (pp. 26–39). New York: Springer.

McCain, R., & Bromwich, J. E. (2016). "Nasty Woman" and "Bad Hombres": The real debate winners? *The New York Times*. Retrieved from http://www.nytimes.com/2016/10/21/us/politics/nasty-woman-and-bad-hombres-the-real-debate-winners.html?_r=1

Norton, B. (2000). *Identity and language learning: Gender, ethnicity, and educational change*. London, UK: Longman.

Palloni, A., & Arias, E. (2004). Paradox lost: Explaining the Hispanic adult mortality advantage. *Demography, 41*(3), 385–415.

Paradis, M. (2004). *A neurolinguistics theory of bilingualism*. Amsterdam: John Benjamins.

References

Portes, A., & Rumbaut, R. G. (2006). *Immigrant America: A portrait*. Berkeley, CA: University of California Press.

Shin, H., Leal, D. L., & Ellison, C. G. (2015). Does anti-Hispanic bias motivate opposition to non-English languages? *Sociological Inquiry, 85*(3), 375–406.

The White House. (2010). The DREAM act: Good for our economy, good for our security, good for our nation. *DREAM Act Fact Sheet*. Retrieved from https://obamawhitehouse.archives.gov/blog/2010/12/01/get-facts-dream-act

Tung, L. (2010). Budget cuts reduce English classes for immigrants. *Gotham Gazette*. http://www.unhny.org/_blog/News_and_Resources/post/Gotham_Gazette_Budget_Cuts_Reduce_English_Classes_for_Immigrants/

U.S. Census Bureau. (2002). Census analysis tracks 100 years of change. Press release CB02-CN.173, Issued December 17, 2002.

U.S. Census Bureau (2003). Language use and English-speaking ability: 2000. *Census 2000 Brief*. Retrieved from http://www.census.gov/prod/2003pubs/c2kbr-29.pdf

U.S. Census Bureau. (2004). *Global population at a glance: 2002 and beyond*. Washington, D. C: Demographic Programs, International Population Reports. Retrieved from http://www.census.gov/ipc/prod/wp02/wp02-1.pdf

U.S. Census Bureau. (2007). Facts for features: Hispanic Heritage month 2007: Sept. 15-Oct. 15. Press release CB07-FF.14, Issued July 16, 2007.

U.S. Census Bureau. (2008). Table 10. Projected life expectancy at birth by sex, race, and Hispanic origin for the United States: 2010 to 2050 (NP2008-T10). Population Division.

U.S. Census Bureau. (2011). Fact finder. Retrieved from www.census.gov

U.S. Census Bureau. (2014). An aging nation: The older population in the United States. *Current Population Reports*. Retrieved from https://www.census.gov/prod/2014pubs/p25-1140.pdf

Vang, C. Y. (2003). *Language acquisition and acculturation efforts for immigrants and refugees in Minnesota*. Report prepared for The McKnight Foundation. Retrieved from https://www.mcknight.org/system/asset/document/111/full-report-adobe-acrobat-format-264kb.pdf

Woodward, B., & Costa, R. (2016). Trump reveals how he would force Mexico to pay for border wall. *The Washington Post*. https://www.washingtonpost.com/politics/trump-would-seek-to-block-money-transfers-to-force-mexico-to-fund-borderwall/2016/04/05/c0196314-fa7c-11e5-80e4c381214de1a3_story.html?utm_term=.80f0e48d4dec

Chapter 2
A Case Study of an English Learner Speech Community

As we started to study older adults' thoughts and feelings about their experiences as second language learners, we understood we were entering a large field of research. For several decades, linguists, sociologists, and educators have made efforts to answer key questions about the development of second language proficiency, but less has been done to study how learning experiences are related to community spaces, or how language acquisition is shaped by identity work, the process by which people weave together biographical and interactional strategies to develop a learning-self. This book's foray into the subjective lives of a Hispanic older adult immigrant community offered a way to study the role of place and identity in SLA.

Social scientists have adopted various approaches in the study of SLA. And while research has examined the cognitive, psycho-social, and cultural dimensions of SLA, few researchers have chosen to explore the identity formation of language learners from within the social spaces of a community or to observe this identity work as process over time. The relative absence of longitudinal research on a community of older adult learners led us to assume that there was much to be gained by capturing their stories and experiences. Consistent with a qualitative framework, we have considered the relationship between investigators and community as important to the research process. We therefore kept in mind the significance of not only the types of questions that were formulated, but argued for using sensitizing methods for in-depth interviewing about personal topics related to late language learning, such as acculturation, social stigma, and role conflicts. Our methodological choices are relevant to those researchers and social service actors who seek to communicate and work with immigrant community members.

We hope that this project offers insights that may assist others in their own research and clinical work with second language learners, particularly those in an immigrant context. Because the way in which qualitative in-depth interviewing is done impacts data analysis, researchers can benefit from reviewing the methodological decisions we made and issues that emerged from our research. Both quantitative and qualitative researchers seeking to create survey and interview questions may want to consider how the points we raise can inform their project development. From a clinical perspective, social service providers may also find new opportunities to talk in-depth with community members about their needs, concerns, and resources in an immigrant context. The value of our methodology will be more evident when we focus on specific issues important to researchers and professionals studying and working with older adult immigrant communities.

We also emphasize in this chapter the interconnections that exist among various levels of the research process—namely, a study's purpose, data collection process (such as formulating the focus group interview guide and ways to recruit and secure participants), and data analysis. What follows is a discussion of the theoretical and methodological considerations that help to contextualize our overall research design and the substantive techniques used to carry out our project. We present the specifics that guided our data collection and analytic processes. We also explain the way in which we worked to capture and represent the voices of our participants in light of current literature on SLA and aging.

How (Older Adult) Second Language Learners Have Been Studied

Most SLA research has focused on the role of "the age factor" and the idea of a critical period (Hernandez et al. 2005) in native language acquisition. As Hernandez, Ping, and MacWhinney point out (2005), "the idea of a biologically determined critical period plays a pivotal role not just in linguistic theory, but in cognitive science as a whole" (p. 220). A penchant for cognitive and neurobiological approaches to SLA emphasize the effects of processes interacting in the development of language proficiency and the declarative/procedural dimensions widely acknowledged in cognitive science (Paradis 2004; Ullman 2001). The development of fluency is understood as a sequence, wherein initial declarative knowledge (the knowing of facts) is transformed into procedural knowledge (the knowing of how to perform something). In this way, knowledge of language rules is processed in an automatic fashion and language operation occurs progressively more quickly. The classic example is that of driving a car, where the procedures that first monopolized consciousness become more routinized and minimized in importance over time.

This approach is often referred to as the "information-processing model" since it describes inputs mediated by various cognitive, psychological, and social factors to produce a language output. The critical period hypothesis draws upon the assumption of an "implicit linguistic competence" (Paradis 2004, p. 59). Decline in procedural memory for language leads late second language learners to rely on a cognitive system that is different from that which conventionally supports native language learning. Some studies suggest that the biological plasticity of procedural memory for language gradually decreases with age, with some estimating particular cut-off ages (Skehan 1998; Paradis 2004). Other scientists argue for a continuous decline, rather than a specific cut-off point (Hakuta et al. 2003). In either case, aging is understood to weaken procedural memory in older adult learners and increase the reliance on conscious declarative memory for learning in general and learning language in particular. The critical period hypothesis claims that natural language acquisition is available to young children but limited in older adults. While a more thorough theoretical discussion of this debate is forthcoming in Chaps. 4 and 5, a cursory methodological review of the literature is instructive here as it contextualizes how and why second language learners have been studied with particular methodologies in mind. It also informs the sampling, data collection, and analytic choices we made in our research design.

Since the 1980s, there has been a call to researchers to explore the age factor in SLA. This has meant looking into older adults' ultimate attainment of language, the differences between early and late-start language programs, and whether native proficiency is accessible to second language learners after a presumed critical age period. Most research has sought to assess the relative strength of the age factor in the context of SLA. The early and seminal work of Johnson and Newport (1989), for example, used grammaticality judgment tests to evaluate speech fluency. Today, many studies go beyond the traditional grammatical approach and incorporate a variety of methodologies and data collection strategies, yet still retain a focus on evaluating the effect of age in language learning. A large number of studies adopt a quantitative framework that combines experimental methods, formal tests of competence, and measures of performance. Research using these and other data, for example, has used late speech samples of late SLA learners to compare native to nonnative older adult speakers.

In an experimental study, Marinova-Todd (2003) examined the profiles of 30 post-puberty learners of English from 25 countries and speaking 18 languages. These second language learners were compared to a control group of 30 native speakers with similar academic backgrounds. Other scholars have conducted similar research with English as a foreign language population and looked at factors such as education in the host environment, length of exposure to English, and age upon arrival (Urponen 2004). Data were collected with the use of formal tests and a narrative task to demonstrate oral and written proficiency. Formal tasks included a range of standardized tests on vocabulary, reading, and speech. These experimental studies have done much to document some of the factors that support second language attainment, such as having more years of study of the second language before age of arrival to the host environment (in these case studies it was mainly the United States) and more years of general education, more years of reading, and more focus on accuracy and communication skills (Bongaerts et al. 1997; Urponen 2004). However, the quantitative and experimental structure these studies use makes it difficult to reveal the social psychological processes implicated in SLA. How learners perceive and express themselves in light of biographical characteristics, such as their age, culture, and gender are important. Positivistic-based studies are ill-equipped to uncover how individuals construct and assign meaning to their various experiences.

Recent focus group studies and qualitative interviews have begun to supplement experimental research and build on our understanding of the social psychology of SLA (Marinova-Todd 2003; Moyer 2004; Nikolov 2000). These qualitative studies, still guided largely by an interest in the age factor and ultimate language acquisition, have contributed to our understanding of the role of motivation, self-esteem, self-confidence, and emotions. They have also shed light on the ways individuals make sense of and negotiate their self-beliefs and intentions in SLA.

Researchers have attempted to triangulate their data by applying a mixed methods approach. Their studies utilize interview data and self-assessments, along with performance measures (Bongaerts 1999; Bongaerts et al. 1997; Moyer 2004; Nikolov 2000; Urponen 2004). In two parallel studies conducted on late language starters, data on participants' background was collected using structured interviews, narrative tasks asking participants to describe different emotional moments in their life, and speech tasks in the target language (Nikolov 2000). Emergent from these studies is the interaction between speech behavior (false starts, paraphrasing, and hesitation) and the social psychology of second language learners. Self-confidence and notions of self-esteem play a role in the SLA of nonnative speakers. Moyer's (2004) study explored the language attainment of 25 well-educated immigrants to Germany from multiple countries. The study adopted a mix of survey-questionnaires on social psychological experiences, controlled and semi-controlled experiments on production tasks, and semi-structured interviews. Findings suggest that age of arrival and length of residence in the host environment had a similar influence on ultimate attainment, whereas psychological factors (personal interest in fluency and satisfaction with attainment) accounted for a majority of the variance in attainment. Moyer's study emphasizes the context of SLA and the effect of age relative to other social psychological factors that impact language learning. It also documents that successful language learners share a motivation in the target language and a particular self-consciousness of their development and achievements leading them to find opportunities for language socialization.

While the above studies integrate a more qualitative dimension to the research process and have helped to expand knowledge of SLA, they have their own set of limitations. Many fail to account for the interactional nature of SLA and how subjective experiences take place within a dynamic social context. A body of language socialization literature has been developed to address this deficiency. A central feature of the language socialization paradigm is a focus on how speakers are socialized through language and interactions to become competent members of a specific speech community (Englebretson 2007; McEwan-Fujita 2010). What is critical here is that through interactions sociocultural information is generated that serves to help interlocutors manage speech behavior with others. The thrust of the language socialization perspective is that language development (if not all development) occurs through a "peer-based social control" process, since it is within social interaction that persons assign, learn, and negotiate meanings related to language competence (Goodwin and Kyrtizis 2012, p. 381). Efforts have been made to understand language learning from within its formative social milieu. A number of studies have used focus group interviewing and ethnographic methods to uncover the intricate ways language socialization occurs in literacy-focused contexts—most notably, classrooms (Menard-Warwick 2005; Soto-Gordon 2010; Wrigley 2007). The qualitative approach of Soto-Gordon (2010) on a multilevel ESL classroom shows speech competence is a cooperative venture tied to emotive positioning, impression management, and social capital distribution.

The range of survey, experimental, and qualitative research on SLA has provided us with insights that have informed our methodology. On the one hand, research has increasingly moved to problematize an overly cognitive and neurobiological view of SLA. Even factors such as aging are conditioned by the social environment of language learners and are tied to the ways in which individuals give meaning to themselves and their surroundings. In this way, our work is part of what in later chapters is referred to as the "social turn in SLA" (Block 2003), which adopts a constructivist approach. Previous studies, however, have been limited in their methods to address key questions in language socialization literature.

First, studies have highlighted the importance of viewing the learning process as a trajectory, marked by the learner's personal history (Delgado-Gaitan 2001). This is particularly the case for Hispanic immigrant communities because of the range of sociopolitical factors, such as immigration laws, citizenship status, and access to education, employment, and government resources, which have individual and generational effects. Using an ESL classroom as a sampling site, our study uniquely follows the same Hispanic community, and in several cases the same family unit, for over 4 years. There is a paucity of longitudinal case studies of this type that document the trajectories of immigrant language learners through time. Moreover, working with and within the community over time allowed us to investigate the important role of *place* in shaping SLA learners' social identity, social-cultural resources, and speech community development.

Second, while language socialization is understood as a life-long and social process, research has tended to focus on children or adult learners, with less attention to elderly language learners (Bayley and Schecter 2003). As was mentioned in Chap. 1, the population of older adult Hispanic immigrants in the United States is growing, but in-depth studies are lacking that examine the formative process of identity work among this group within their local (e.g., family) and larger (e.g., community) environments. With this in mind, we sampled Hispanic older adult immigrants so as to gauge the unique experiences of this population with respect to the broad array of language acquisition resources and interactional opportunities deemed critical for language development.

Finally, while studies seek to explore fully the complexity of the conceptual or empirical terrain associated with language learners' social identity, they tend to adopt conventional qualitative strategies that are limited. To the extent that sociocultural and language socialization approaches do not see language learning as a simple accommodation to target language norms, data collection must be sensitive to how communicative competence is marked by a process directed by forces of interaction over time—namely, meaning making, negotiation, and power. This means attending to the dual and interrelated dynamic of biography and social environment. To this end, our study employs an active interviewing data collection strategy in order to capture the individual and social movement action endemic to language socialization. The following section takes a closer look at the details of our sampling and data collection procedures.

Study Sample

Several theoretical and practical considerations informed our sampling of Hispanic older adults. Language socialization scholars have noted the mismatch between Hispanic immigrant learners' motivation and expectations regarding SLA, as well as the structural challenges confronting second language learners (McEwan-Fujita 2010). Older adult language socialization is complex and often includes a renegotiation of a learner's self- and social identity. Multiple social spheres (family, workplace, community) are implicated. Our study examined this issue through the perspectives and experiences of a community of older adult immigrants.

We wanted a sample of second language learners that were not too far removed from the time when they first immigrated to the United States. We wanted to ensure that we had the opportunity to talk with them about their immigration experience and how being an older adult impacts language resocialization within this context. We reasoned that this group would provide us with insights about the "immigrant effect" among Hispanics, particularly how enclave communities promote functioning in old age but also complicate language resocialization (Hill et al. 2012). Our participants would be able to share about a wide range of community relationships, including the transitional experiences and turning points in their lives that involved their language identities. It would also offer opportunities to uncover the dual dynamic of how older adults reinvent and modify their SLA *identity* as they encounter language socialization experiences in various *places* (at home, in their community, and in the classroom).

To improve the inclusion of this group, we used both purposive and theoretical sampling strategies, which select participants by using conceptual criteria, and recruited individuals in various ways. Our discussion is based on our core sample of 40 Hispanic older adults. Because our primary goal was to gather theoretical and empirical knowledge about older adult immigrants' subjective experiences as language learners, we did not seek to use a random sample. Instead, our data collection concluded when interviews did not offer any additional conceptual data. This approach was consistent with designing an in-depth qualitative study, as it "permit [ed] the deep, case-oriented analysis that is the raison d'être of qualitative inquiry" (Sandelowski 1995, p. 179).

We used selective site sampling not with the intention of establishing the basis for examining statistical differences among profiles but to ensure that we could get to know members of a specific community, in-depth, and over time. Our study sample site was a multilevel ESL family literacy program. The ESL family literacy program was organized, funded, and managed through the literacy outreach department at the Hampton-Illinois branch of the Dallas Public Library. As university professors who developed a service-learning project with our undergraduate students, we took a leadership role in teaching and planning activities for two adult language classes in the public library. In a separate part of the library, free childcare was provided for the children and grandchildren of enrolled ESL students. Our own subjective experiences as second language learners guided our commitment to developing the family literacy program and informed our sensitivity to the role of identity and place in language acquisition. Two of the authors are second language learners of English, and one is a second language learner of Spanish. From our own personal experiences, we could appreciate how language resocialization is tied up with one's identity and the places that (de)capitalize a sense of self. In this way, our own biographical characteristics served as theoretical tools for the development of our research questions and the data collection site.

All interviews were conducted between April 2011 and May 2015. We audiotaped focus group interviews and conducted 36 weeks of participant observations with our sample of 40 Hispanic older adult ESL students. Participants were recruited through a face-to-face announcement in our ESL family literacy program located in a predominantly Hispanic community in Dallas, Texas. In terms of ethnic composition, our sample participants were from Mexico (n = 34), El Salvador (n = 3), Honduras (n = 2), and Guatemala (n = 1). The majority of the Mexican participants had emigrated from the Western states of Guanajuato, Jalisco, and Michoacán, though a third of the participants had left their homes in San Luis Potosí, Zacatecas, Guerrero, and even the Eastern state of Tamaulipas. Our participants consisted of 26 women and 14 men. Participant ages ranged from being in their early 50s to early 70s. The reason for including participants under 65-years-old was to theoretically sample individuals who were nearing the age of 65 and held a self-conception of themselves as an older adult learner. Interviewees were employed in a range of low-wage occupations that included automotive services and technicians, carpentry, construction, housekeeping, and caregiving. Others held office positions as administrative assistants. The interviews primarily focused on Hispanic older adults' second language acquisition and the turning points in their identity relative to their relationships both inside and outside the ESL classroom. At times, we reference the voices of our ESL teachers and younger ESL students to further contextualize classroom experiences. Interviews were transcribed from Spanish to English by the researchers and we used the constant comparative method that emphasizes an iterative process of data analysis by comparing incident with incident, category with incident, and category with category. Our study is consistent with a grounded theory approach, which includes conducting simultaneously data collection and analysis. Immediately after conducting each interview, the researchers prepared extensive theoretical, methodological, and personal memos. Below is a discussion of the theoretical assumptions that guided our interviewing.

Interviewing Strategies

Our study utilizes the approach to interviewing described by Holstein and Gubrium (1995) as "active interviewing." Using active interviewing was a means to focus attention on Hispanic older adults' situated identity work. In particular, active interviewing fosters a view of the interview as a dialogical, discursive, and active process. In addition, active interviewing can provide insight into how intersectional biographical characteristics (e.g., age, gender, race, culture, and other dimensions) are negotiated and produce older adult learners' sense of self in community. As Holstein and Gubrium (1995) note, interviewees are "multivocal," in that they hold multiple positions and perspectives. This recognition is used to uncover the multiple layers of experience that intersectional analysis suggests exists for Hispanic older adults. In all, active interviewing challenges the supposed "passive role" of the interviewee (and interviewer) and we viewed this approach as a useful way to delineate the active identity work of Hispanic older adults. A brief overview of this perspective is given in this section, with special attention to its differences from so-called "traditional" interviewing and its benefits for studying how older adults socially construct their attitudes, emotions, and behaviors relative to second language acquisition.

Before moving into an exploration of the active interview approach, it is important to clarify why a theoretical discussion of this data collection technique is part of our study's methodology. After all, is not interviewing more of a methodological consideration? It is important to note that Holstein and Gubrium (1995) discuss "the active interview" primarily as a perspective and not simply as a methodological tool. In short, active interviewing makes epistemological comments on the interview process itself.

This book presents a perspective (an implicit theory of interviewing) and not just an inventory of methods. Thus, active interviews are more than a distinctive research tool; instead, we use the term to emphasize that all interviews are reality-constructing and sites where interpretive work is being done. In this section, we present a social constructionist approach to interviewing that "considers the process of meaning production to be as important for social research as the meaning that is produced" (Holstein and Gubrium 1995, p. 4). As will be discussed, active interviewing focuses our attention on both the substantive features of meaning making (what is being constructed), and on interpretive work (how meaning is made). This provides an interview approach that attends to the "whats" and "hows" of meaning making.

The interview as a means of knowing (i.e., to describe, interrogate, assist, test, evaluate) is so pervasive that it is practically a "universal mode of systematic inquiry" (Holstein and Gubrium 1995, p. 1). Qualitative researcher, however, now see interviews as more than neutral tools for gathering data; they are fundamentally active interactions between two (or more) people wherein information and meaning are negotiated and constructed (Holstein and Gubrium 1995). Increasingly, the focus of interviews is not just on the traditional whats (substantive descriptions of everyday life) but also the hows (the active work to make meaning and order in everyday life) (Gubrium and Holstein 1997; Holstein and Gubrium 1995; Silverman 1997).

According to Holstein and Gubrium (1995), the conventional image used to describe interviews is that of a "search-and-discovery mission, with the interviewer bent on finding what is already there inside variably cooperative respondents" (p. 2). The primary challenge of the interviewer is to extract information as directly as possible. This conception of interviewing is distinctly positivistic, in that research is assumed to begin with an empirical referent (the interviewee). This point of departure is supposed to represent the so-called "real world" embodied in the subject-respondent, as opposed to particular standpoint(s) being articulated.

To begin a study in this manner, interpretive judgments must be excluded as much as possible from the interview process. Although researchers are only supposed to "reflect nature," perceptual errors are always possible. Thus while a key methodological approach in the social sciences is observation, it is only after rigorous training that perception can be trusted to discover truth though interviewing. Because the interviewer and interviewee may be unreliable, the interpreter of data must be trained to analyze data in a particular way. It is the very fact that interviews represent "conversations" that they are also "framed as a potential source of bias, error, misunderstanding, or misdirection, a persistent set of problems to be minimized" (Holstein and Gubrium 1995, p. 3). This issue has often been described as emerging from human errors, such as "response effects" or "nonsampling errors" (Bradburn 1983). For example, error in the data may result when the respondent has faulty memory or deliberately tries to please the interviewer by providing a "socially desirable" response; these factors can prevent the researcher from learning something from the respondent (Bradburn 1983, p. 291). According to this conventional view of interviewing, the researcher must learn to counter the effects of situational exigencies in order to enhance the prospects for discovering knowledge from respondents.

Due to this requirement, data collection in interviews becomes highly instrumental. Logistical refinements are thought to lead to a more a "natural" generation of data. As Holstein and Gubrium (1995) note, "the literature on interview strategy and technique remains primarily concerned with maximizing the flow of valid, reliable information while minimizing distortions of what the respondent knows" (p. 3). One response to this problem has been to increase methodological sophistication so as to neutralize the interview process. To the extent that the interview process is understood as a "pipeline for transmitting knowledge," various techniques are introduced to standardize the conversation and ensure the study is not replete with bias (Holstein and Gubrium 1995, p. 3).

In structured interviews, the interviewer asks all respondents the same series of pre-established questions with a limited set of response categories. There is usually little room for variation in the responses, except where open-ended questions (which are usually infrequent) are asked. Moreover, the interviewer records responses according to coding schemes already developed by the project director. By heavily controlling the pace of the interview, standardizing both questions and answers, and repeating these processes for all interviews, the interview context is supposed to allow the interviewer to play a neutral role. In behaviorist fashion, the structured interview proceeds under a stimulus-response format that assumes that the respondent will truthfully answer questions previously determined to reveal satisfactory indicators of the variable in question. Subjects are considered essentially passive in this scenario, representing "vessels-of-answers." Survey and conventional interview instruments tend to be structured in this manner.

Because conversations take place largely in the situational everyday worlds of societal members, interviews should reflect this type of contingency and spontaneity to better capture the way the world actually works (Douglas 1985). For this reason, we argue against "how-to" guidelines in conducting interviews, suggesting that interviewing and interviewers must be "creative" by adapting themselves to the ever-changing situations they encounter. Standard survey and structured questions create an overly detached interviewer and present an almost nonhuman subject to respondents; this approach usually only touches the surface of experience and is unable to tap into the "emotional wellsprings" underneath. "Creative interviewing," on the other hand, establishes a climate of mutual disclosure in which the interviewers' deep disclosure elicits reciprocal actions on the part of respondents. Getting respondents to share deep feelings and emotions requires more than simply "probing" them, since mutual understanding requires that the "researcher…know thyself" (Douglas 1985, p. 51).

We sought to adopt a more dynamic view of the interview process, one that goes further than a neo-positivistic stance. While it is important to move beyond traditional formulae guiding interviews, it is also important to question the positivistic idea of respondents constituting a pure empirical referent that the researcher need only access. While interviews do require "99% perspiration" in the form of developing mutual disclosure, care must also be taken to not assume subjects contain "wellsprings" of experience and researchers act as prospectors who tap into this rich resource. "Thus the subject behind [the] respondent remains an essentially passive, if creatively emotional, fount of experience" (Holstein and Gubrium 1995, p. 13). As Holstein and Gubrium (1995) point out, discussions of interviews often center on "the characteristics and aims of the interview process, with little attention paid to how interviews differ as occasion for knowledge production" (p. 7). What is missing, in other words, is the recognition that interviews, or conversations, construct data, as much as they are a source of information.

Because of the penchant for methodological sophistication, researchers ignore the most basic of epistemological questions in the interview process: "Where does this knowledge come from, and how is it derived?" (Holstein and Gubrium 1995, p. 2). For no matter what form the interview takes, whether highly structured, standardized, quantitatively oriented, or free-flowing exchange and creative, "all interviews are interactional events … constructed in situ … [and] a product of the talk between interview participants" (Holstein and Gubrium 1995, p. 2). This contrasts with the traditional "vessel-of-answers" approach which assumes that the subject behind the respondent is passive. In other words, respondents are viewed as merely "containers" that hold information that can be extracted by the researcher in an unbiased manner so long as certain measures are taken (Holstein and Gubrium 1995, p. 8).

The typical "vessel-of-answers" approach fails to recognize that both the interviewer and interviewee are always and unavoidably active; each is involved in "meaning making work" during the interview. The point is that meaning is not simply extracted by "asking the right questions" because meaning is constructed through the actual interview. The interviewer and interviewee are collaborators that assemble knowledge together. Interview data are unavoidably collaborative and thus attempts to strip interviews of their interactional ingredients will be futile. Instead of adding to the long list of methodological constraints under which interviews should be conducted, Holstein and Gubrium (1995) "[propose] an orientation whereby researchers acknowledge interviewers' and respondents' constitutive contributions and consciously and conscientiously incorporate them into the production and analysis of interview data" (p. 4). In this way, active interviewing represents a "theoretical stance toward data collection and analysis" (Holstein and Gubrium 1995, p. 73).

Consistent with language socialization research, an active interviewing approach is well-suited to address the "social turn" in studying language learning. Knowledge can never be collected in a disinterested manner, since "knowledge itself is a product of interaction … [and] is created from the action taken to obtain it" (Holstein and Gubrium 1995, p. 3). Given the epistemological stance by language socialization researchers, the traditional methodological image of the interview situation is ill-equipped because it obscures the basic fact that "interviews fundamentally, not incidentally, shape the form and content of what is said" (Holstein and Gubrium 1995, p. 3). This approach to interviewing informs our study of Hispanic older adult learners in a number of ways.

Active Interviewing with Hispanic Older Adult Second Language Learners

First, treating respondents as a "passive vessel of answers" denies their active involvement in the production and maintenance of social reality. Consistent with our theoretical frames discussed in Chap. 1, interviewers must be cognizant that language learners do not possess a static set of meanings (e.g., motivations, attitudes, emotions, behaviors) about SLA, but rather they construct themselves through interpretive actions within language socialization. In this vein, active interviewing reaffirms the idea presented in contemporary SLA literature that older adult learners' identities are fundamentally interactional constructs and reflect the dynamic interplay between selves and their context. Traditional interviewing techniques and analyses amount to systematically grouping and summarizing descriptions and offering a coherent framework to explain these details of the social world. Put differently, the "objective whats overwhelm the hows" (Holstein and

Gubrium 1995, p. 79). In contrast, "active interview data [is gathered and] analyzed to show the dynamic interrelatedness of the what and the how" (Holstein and Gubrium 1995, p. 9). Consequently, in presenting findings the goal is to reveal what identities are present and how they are constructed. In practice, researchers should focus on dialogue or how conversation establishes meaning about the self as learner. Certainly a better understanding of the formative development of second language learners' identity involves examining the ways they talk about themselves, their ideas, and relationships with others during language resocialization.

Second, active interviewing offers a means of capturing the role of intersectional and biographical issues. A primary goal in active interviewing is to cultivate the respondent's narrative activity: "this means that the respondent's positional shifts, linkages, and horizons of meanings take precedence over the tacit linkages and horizons of the predesigned questions that the interviewer is prepared to ask" (Holstein and Gubrium 1995, pp. 76–77). In this sense, the interviewer may want to promote multivocality and shifts in narrative positions to expose the potentially multifaceted answers of respondents. For example, we asked study participants to move from the position of parental authority figure to a classroom student and to consider how age factors in their language socialization across multiple settings. Multivocality allows for the possibility of "narrative linkages," which illustrate the multiple ways respondents are connected to one another and even to their own selves (Holstein and Gubrium 1995, p. 69). Fostering multivocality is useful for revealing the various dimensions of experience and attending to intersectionality.

And third, active interviewing alerted us to "narrative linkages" that "demonstrate the reach of the political into areas typically assumed to be personal" (Reinharz 1992, pp. 249–250). Consistent with Smith's (1987) idea of "institutional ethnography," the goal is to reveal the relationship between personal experiences and larger social structures. A theme of central interest to us is the relationship between language learning, power, and inequality. While early SLA research tended to treat cognition and other learning factors as independent of interactional context, indicators of interpersonal relationships (such as economic and social resources) are main determinants in language learning. Research suggests that SLA is fundamentally shaped by social relationships and the sociopolitical dynamics that result from these interpersonal and larger interactions (Dewaele 2005; O'Grady 2005). An important finding relates to how the social status and position of learners influence ultimate language attainment (Moyer 2004). DeVault (1999) writes that "[i]nstitutional ethnography is always concerned with institutional connections, with relations across and among various sites of activity, and with the coordination of these sites with ruling regimes" (p. 49). Active interviewing can provide a way to show "relations of ruling," wherein cultural and social prestige shape SLA learners' consciousness of their achievement, work on their language proficiency, and access to extensive opportunities for communicating in the target language.

The goal of our research design is to offer researchers and social service providers a senstsized view of the individuals they study and with whom they work. Both in theory and practice, the way we develop research agendas, construct study and interview questions, how we approach the data collection process, and who we are all impact the research event. From our read of the epistemological and methodological shifts in SLA literature, we understood our methods as being well-suited to appreciate the fundamentally social character of second language learning. The in-depth and longitudinal nature of our investigation led us to suspect that we would acquire novel and socially relevant conceptual and empirical knowledge of Hispanic older adults' learning of a second language.

References

Bayley, R., & Schecter, S. R. (Eds.). (2003). *Language socialization in bilingual and multilingual societies*. Clevedon, UK: Multicultural Matters.

Block, D. (2003). *The social turn in second language acquisition*. Edinburgh, UK: Edinburgh University Press.

Bongaerts, T. (1999). Ultimate attainment in L2 pronunciation: The case of very advanced late L2 learners. In D. Birdsong (Ed.), *Second language acquisition and the Critical Period Hypothesis* (pp. 133–159). Mahwah, NJ: Erlbaum.

Bongaerts, T., van Summeren, C., Planken, B., & Schils, E. (1997). Age and ultimate attainment in the pronunciation of a foreign language. *Studies in Second Language Acquisition, 19*(4), 447–465.

Bradburn, N. M. (1983). Response effects. In P. H. Rossi, J. D. Wright, & A. B. Anderson (Eds.), *Handbook of Survey Research* (pp. 289–328). New York: Academic Press.

Delgado-Gaitan, C. (2001). *The power of community: Mobilizing for family and schooling*. New York, NY: Rowman & Littlefield.

DeVault, M. (1999). *Liberating method: Feminism and social research*. Philadelphia, PA: Temple University Press.

Dewaele, J.-M. (2005). Investigating the psychological and emotional dimensions in instructed language learning: Obstacles and possibilities. *The modern language journal, 89*(3), 367–380.

Douglas, J. D. (1985). *Creative interviewing*. Beverley Hills, CA: Sage.

Englebretson, R. (2007). Stancetaking in discourse: An introduction. In R. Englebretson (Ed.), *Stancetaking in discourse: Subjectivity, evaluation, interaction* (pp. 1–25). Philadelphia, PA: John Benjamins.

Goodwin, M. H., & Kyratizis, A. (2012). Peer language socialization. In A. Duranti, E. Ochs, & B. B. B. Schieffelin (Eds.), *The handbook of language socialization* (pp. 365–390). New York, NY: Blackwell.

Gubrium, J. F., & Holstein, J. A. (1997). *The new language of qualitative method*. New York: Oxford University Press.

Hakuta, K., Bialystok, E., & Wiley, E. (2003). Critical evidence: A test of the critical period hypothesis for second-language acquisition. *Psychological Science, 14*(1), 31–38.

Hernandez, A., Ping, L., & MacWhinney, B. (2005). The emergence of competing modules in bilingualism. *Trends in Cognitive Sciences, 9*(5), 220–225.

Hill, T. D., Angel, J. L., & Balistreri, K. S. (2012). Does the "healthy immigrant effect" extend to cognitive aging? In J. L. Angel, F. Torres-Gil, & K. Markides (Eds.), *Aging, health, and longevity in the Mexican-origin population* (pp. 19–34). New York: Springer.

Holstein, J., & Gubrium, J. (1995). *The active interview*. Thousand Oaks: Sage.

Johnson, J., & Newport, E. (1989). Critical period effects in second language learning: The influence of maturational state on the acquisition of ESL. *Cognitive Psychology, 21*(1), 60–99.

Marinova-Todd, S. H. (2003). *Comprehensive analysis of ultimate attainment in adult second language acquisition* (Unpublished doctoral dissertation). Harvard University.

Menard-Warwick, J. (2005). Intergenerational trajectories and sociopolitical context: Latina immigrants in adult ESL. *TESOL Quarterly, 39*(2), 165–185.

McEwan-Fujita, E. (2010). Ideology, affect and socialization in language shift and revitalization: The experiences of adults learning Gaelic in the western isles of Scotland. *Language in Society, 39*(1), 27–64.

Moyer, J. (2004). *Age, accent and experience in second language acquisition*. Clevedon, Avon: Multicultural Matters.

Nikolov, M. (2000). The CPH reconsidered: Successful adult learners of Hungarian and English. *International Review of Applied Linguistics, 38*(2), 109–124.

O'Grady, W. (2005). *How children learn language*. Cambridge, UK: Cambridge University Press.

Paradis, M. (2004). *A neurolinguistics theory of bilingualism*. Amsterdam: John Benjamins.

Reinharz, S. (1992). *Feminist methods in social research*. New York, NY: Oxford University Press.

Sandelowski, M. (1995). Sample size in qualitative research. *Research in Nursing & Health, 18*(2), 179–183.

Silverman, D. (1997). *Qualitative research: Theory, method and practice*. London: Sage.

Skehan, P. (1998). *A cognitive approach to language learning*. Oxford: Oxford University Press.

Smith, D. (1987). *The everyday life as problematic: A feminist sociology*. Boston, MA: Northeastern University Press.

Soto-Gordon, S. (2010). *A case study on multi-level language ability groupings in an ESL secondary school classroom: Are we making the right choices?* (Unpublished dissertation thesis). University of Toronto, Toronto, Ontario, Canada.

Ullman, M. (2001). The neural basis of lexicon and grammar in first and second language: The declarative/procedural model. *Bilingualism: Language and Cognition, 4*(2), 105–122.

Urponen, M. I. (2004). *Ultimate attainment in postpuberty second language acquisition* (Unpublished doctoral dissertation). Boston University.

Wrigley, H. (2007). Beyond the life boat: Improving language, citizenship, and training services for immigrant refugees. In A. Bellzer (Ed.), *Toward defining and improving quality in adult basic education* (pp. 221–239). Mahwah, NJ: Erlbaum.

Chapter 3
Minority Aging in an Immigrant Context

At the end of her second semester as an ESL student, Rosa openly talks about the challenges she faces as an older adult second language learner. While she feels confident in her decision to attend English classes, she expresses deep concerns and frustrations with how being a second language learner impacts important aspects of her family life.

> I want to learn [English] because I have a family. I have a granddaughter who is in 5th grade. And at the school she attends, they only speak English. But this has changed our lives. I want to be part of her life. I want to help her with her homework and talk to her teachers. But I can't read the papers she brings home. I am very frustrated so I want to learn English to help me with these things.

Rosa, a 62-year-old Mexican women, struggled during the semester trying to make time for ESL class. She mentions having to juggle family and work responsibilities, while still having time in her day to come to class. Rosa's busy schedule heightened her awareness of her immigrant status and the challenge to attend English classes.

> I didn't work when I first arrived [to the United States]. But I needed to work to help my family. I work part-time but it was difficult to make it to class. I was fortunate that the instructors allowed me to come to class late sometimes and leave early if I needed to. I felt bad that I couldn't be in class longer. I also felt bad because I enjoy being in class and interacting with everyone. But what am I supposed to do? I need to work to have money and I want to learn English. What am I supposed to do as someone learning English?

Now seeing herself as "someone learning English," Rosa describes her life as fundamentally changed. She is seeking to restructure everyday activities, including the way she interacts with friends and family.

> This [learning English] has completely changed my life. I now think about what I'm going to do. Do I come home and watch television or movie? I think about how I need to be working on my speaking. Even when my family calls me to visit or do something, I say I can't. It's like my friend says, "ha cambiado el estilo de vida" [my lifestyle has changed]. I now see things differently. My friends have begun to change because I look for people who can speak English or want to learn English—like the people here in this class. It isn't easy…. I feel like I'm out of my time…as if I'm too old to learn something new. I need to lose my fears in order to move ahead.

Her transition to assuming a new social and cultural identity means casting aside a previous lifestyle in order to become committed to learning English. This has meant rethinking friendship and family relationships. Like many second language learners, Rosa also reports being scared about the learning process, but she is encouraged by a new perspective on life and future possibilities.

Rosa's story provides us with insight into the relationship between aging and immigration. Aging immigrants adjust to living in a new land, as they learn and negotiate a new cultural and social landscape that differs from their own. Roscow (1967) developed his classic definition of social integration as it relates to aging in his book, *Social Integration of the Aged*:

> Integration…concerns how the person is tied into the webs of beliefs and action in his society. The integration of individuals into their society results from forces which place them within the system and govern their participation and patterned association with others. This network of bonds has three basic dimensions: (1) social values, (2) formal and informal group memberships, and (3) social roles. Thus, people are tied into their society essentially through their beliefs, the groups that they belong to, and the positions that they occupy (pp. 8–10).

Similar to the lifelong effects of culture, the process of immigration generates pervasive and intense influence on older immigrants' lives.

Rosa's narrative also highlights the challenges and related pressures of interacting with new cultural frameworks, normative rules, and social interactions. Scholars have long claimed that acculturation—"the process whereby individuals learn about the rules for behavior characteristics of a certain group of people"—is not easy or uniformly experienced (Corsini 1987; Padilla et al. 1982). This can be seen in the wide array of terms used to describe the social and psychological stress related to the impact of adapting to a new culture, such as "culture stress," "culture fatigue," "culture shock," and "language shock" (Smalley 1963). Whether it is immigrants contemplating their identity prior to arriving to the host country, navigating the complexities of unfamiliar social and cultural interactions, or deciding how to integrate with their new environment in their daily lives, the meanings immigrants attach to acculturation can affect their decisions and experiences in many ways.

We think an important step in understanding older adult immigrants' experience in language acquisition is to first explore the contours of minority aging and how an immigrant context shapes the experience of aging in unique ways. As was mentioned in Chap. 1, our approach emphasizes the importance of the identity of the older adult language learner, as well as the role of location in situating the process of identity formation. In this chapter, we broadly highlight the circumstances faced by those living at the intersection of aging and immigration. To understand aging in the context of immigration, we turn to a critical social gerontology that appreciates the social construction of aging. This means examining the connection between structural, macrolevel forces and the identity, micro-processes of minority aging (Estes et al. 2003). In short, we focus on how individual factors and larger environment shape the life trajectories of Hispanic older adult immigrants, while revealing the links between inequalities in later life.

Transitions and Immigration

Some of the most fundamental ways in which minority aging is shaped is through what Paykel (1974) refers to as "exit" events—situations that symbolize loss. Those working from a life course perspective focus on how chronological age, social relationships, life transitions, and critical points of social change define people's lives over time (Cowan 1991). By examining the ongoing shifts in older adults' life circumstances, we gain an understanding of the critical markers that shape their language learning.

The notion of "transitions" is important throughout our analysis because it suggests something distinct in the experiences of Hispanic older adult immigrants as it relates to their language learning. As Cowan (1991) states, individual and larger group transitions may be seen as long-term processes that result in qualitative reorganization of both inner and external behavior. For a life change to be designated as transitional, it must involve a qualitative shift from the inside looking out (how the individual understands and feels about the self and the world) and from the outside looking in (reorganization of the individual or family's level of personal competence, role arrangements, and relationships with significant others) (Cowan 1991, p. 5). Transitions help to establish adjustments in the mindset of Hispanic older adults as they deal with the "before" and "after" nature of immigration. Transitions also alert us to the behavioral changes undertaken by them to manage and negotiate these new realities.

These events emerge from structural conditions and individual perceptions that lead to significant life changes and which impact critical life chances (Wilmoth and Chen 2003). Experiences of loss and lack of access to key resources are of course specific to the individual, but are also tied to a larger structural background that determines group level outcomes (Tummala-Nara 2001). The immigrant grandmother who leaves her home to live in a new country may make a successful transition if she gains the social support of her family but also will need additional social interactional resources to develop English language skills.

Transitions occur from specific events and at specific times. The changes resulting from the multiple intersections of aging, immigration, race/ethnicity, and gender can lead to significant shifts in self-identity. These identity adjustments are also tied to individuals' sense of themselves as learner of a second language. It can also direct their behaviors toward language acquisition and socialization.

Scholarship focuses on the dynamic between social structures and culture that condition the life transitions of elderly minority immigrants, as well as its impact on the acculturation process. Some have examined the way structural and sociocultural factors play a key role in the experience of aging and access to important resources. Scholars emphasize the dynamic impact of these forces on the life trajectories of individuals and their developmental pathways (Elder 1994). In the context of immigration, acculturation involves a variety of processes of change, including assimilation, integration, and marginalization as a result of immigrants' encounter with a host culture.

The Structure of Minority Aging and Immigration

Social scientists point out that minority aging is shaped by a variety of structural factors linked to immigration, geographical proximity, nativity, age of arrival, education, and employment (Padilla 2002). In their seminal book, *Latin Journey*, Portes and Bach (1985) argue that not all migration experiences are the same. Geographical proximity facilitates migration, as is the case for Cubans who migrate to South Florida or Mexicans who settle along the Southwestern United States. However, Cubans and Mexicans historically encountered different degrees of reception and accommodation linked to education, economic class, and race. This, in turn, has facilitated greater levels of acculturative success among Cubans. Due to political circumstances in Cuba coming to the United States has been described more as an escape than an immigration, particularly for those included in the early waves of migration in the late 1950s and early 1960s (Portes and Bach 1985). The political context of migration afforded many Cubans a unique pathway for legal entry.

The story is different for many other Latin American immigrant groups, such as Mexicans, Hondurans, and Dominicans. Over the past 30 years, the total number of undocumented immigrants in the United States has grown from an estimated 2.5 million in the late 1980s to a little over 11 million today (Passel and Cohn 2010). Scholars explain this demographic trend as the result of a confluence of factors that include border policies meant to slow undocumented immigration (Nevins 2010) and transnational, circular migratory flows that link individuals to social networks across national borders (Cornelius and Lewis 2006). In reaction to the financial costs and dangers related to making multiple migratory trips back and forth in the 1990s, there has been increasingly more illegal immigrants making the United States their permanent home.

Immigration law and circular migratory flows interact in ways to produce specific meanings and experiences depending on persons' age of arrival. Illegal immigrants may withdraw from seeking important resources for fear of being reported to Immigration and Naturalization Services. This can particularly impact older adults. Their older age places them at a disadvantage to access public and social resources, such as formal education, that are directed to other immigrants and youth. In all, undocumented older adults go through transformations that impact their self-identity, social bonds, goals, and expectations, as well as their social and economic status.

Daniel is 63-years old and settled in the United States over 10 years ago from El Salvador. He spoke about his family's experience of moving to the United States. Daniel's experience mirrors that of many others whose transnational social networks condition their migration.

> Well…I didn't plan to live in the United States. My whole life was in El Salvador. My cousins and lifelong friends are still there. My son first traveled to the United States and then over time we all came over. I like it here but it's completely changed my life. I feel a

> bit more isolated now since my lack of English makes it hard to communicate. It was hard at my age to leave El Salvador.

He also alerts us to how being undocumented structures marginalization in subtle ways.

> I have it easier since I'm now a citizen but there are many people I know who are not. Things are difficult for them. They are scared to talk to people because of what could happen to them. Even coming to these [ESL] classes... I tell them to come but they are nervous even though it would help them.

Fear of deportation leads to a well-known stress-response where illegal immigrants withdraw from social interactions and institutions (Viruell-Fuentes 2011).

As Viruell-Fuentes (2011) notes, exposure to implicit and explicit messages about legal status also reproduces inequality by "differently locating[ing] individuals within the ethnoracial hierarchy of the United States" (p. 46). Nativity, or country of birth, is highly related to the acculturation process (Rodriguez and Kosloski 1998). Immigration to the United States from Latin America is colored by the effects of racial discrimination. As Espin (1987) states,

> When a migrant comes from a country where she belongs to the racial majority, or where, as in Latin countries, racial mixtures are the norm, the experience of turning into a minority in the United States and encountering overt racial discrimination becomes a disorienting experience (p. 493).

A wide variation in skin color is common in many Latin American countries. In the United States, however, the historical use of a "white frame" has led to racial dichotomization and discrimination of the basses of skin color (Feagin 2010). Thus, darker skinned, Latin American immigrants have had a distinctive acculturative experience because they have needed to deal with the labeling and prejudice that accompanies racism in the United States.

Dora, a 60-year old who emigrated from Mexico, casts light on the pernicious effects of race.

> I really didn't think about it too much in Mexico. I mean...we are all have different colors...some darker and other lighter. But we are all a family. When I got to the United States it was different here. The news and everywhere talked about skin color. I began to think that I was different because I'm Mexican and have dark skin.

While Dora reflects on a new self-awareness of a racial identity, scholars have theorized the intersections between immigration, the racialization process, and inequalities. White racial framing functions to define certain immigrant groups as "inassimilable others" (Sanchez 1997), shaping who qualifies for citizenship along racial lines (Chavez 1998). The process of "othering" produces marginalization and social exclusion, leading to "discriminatory practices which exclude Mexican American's from participating fully as citizens" in key areas of social life that are important for language resocialization (Padilla 1980, p. 51).

One key area is education. Education is a central resource for reducing inequality in the United States. However, education levels vary more significantly for older adults than for younger persons. Recent reports describe that 77% of all elders had a high-school degree and approximately 21% of all elders earned a bachelor's degree or higher (AOA 2010). The statistics are more troublesome for minority elders, particularly Blacks and Hispanics. On the whole, minority elders have lower education levels than non-Hispanic whites (AOA 2010).

Juan explains the challenges he and others face as elder immigrants in the area of education, particularly language acquisition.

> You hear from people that we [immigrants] don't want to learn English and fit in. I can tell you that we do. I do want to. I've been in the United States for many years but it has been very difficult for me. My grandchildren know more English than Spanish now. They go to school and learn and watch TV in English. Where am I supposed to learn? That's why these [ESL] classes are so important because they are a place we can go for free and better ourselves.

As formal institutions for language learning and socialization, schools generally support young immigrants' acculturation more than older individuals. As Juan points out, having access to places to learn the English language are not as obvious as they are for children. The conventional locations of school and media are often off limits to older adults. Juan also speaks about the possible intergenerational differences that occur at the level of cultural assimilation. His grandchildren are already speaking greater amounts of English, which can make communication a challenge. Indeed, as will be noted in later chapters, these generational fault lines can also reorganize the structure of family roles (Escobar et al. 2000).

Yet another important factor that shapes minority aging is employment type and status. Clearly, both of these are associated with education. The skill level of Mexican migrants to the United States, for example, is a key issue of policy relevance. In the past, European immigrants with minimal English language skills had meaningful access to jobs because physical labor was central to the economy. Today, workers are affected by a service and global economy. Once in the host country, those individuals who do not speak English tend to have lower levels of education, do not find employment or are employed in low-paid jobs, and are less well acculturated than others (Suarez and Pulley 1995).

The majority of our study participants were employed in a range of low-wage occupations that included auto mechanics, carpentry, construction, housekeeping, and caregiving. Our study participants acknowledged the links between education and employment. Francisco is turning 60 in a couple of years and works as a mechanic. He explains how important learning English is to his employment.

> I don't have to speak English much at work. A lot of the guys there speak Spanish and we all talk to each other. But the boss is American and I know that it would be good for me to learn more English. I want to make sure that I'm seen as a valuable employee and can talk to customers a bit. Learning a few words has been good and my boss has noticed. That's why I'm here taking English classes...to educate myself and move ahead.

While Francisco's occupation does not require that he be fluent in English, he does highlight the value that language education plays in the future of his career. Indeed, he even points to the growing consumer-centered economy and the increasing role of customer service in job stability.

Sandra, on the other hand, works in an office setting where communication and information require more English. She says that work is becoming more difficult and it has prompted her to seek English classes.

> I need it for my job. I have been here for over 25 years and I focused a lot on my children's education. But now I would like to focus on me. It's what I want…to learn and to get ahead. I want to communicate with those around me, at work. I used to not have to speak any English but now it seems that everything is in English…paperwork, phone calls. They say we need more business. But if I don't [learn English] I will feel like I don't exist. I need to learn English.

Clearly, Sandra is reflecting on the changing landscape of work. For many Hispanic immigrants who have been accustomed to working in exclusively Spanish enclaves, these labor markets have broken open due to competition in a global marketplace. Employers have needed to expand their customer base in order to maintain revenue. This has meant adding new, non-Spanish speaking clientele. And as Sandra points out, there is pressure for employees to retool themselves to fit changing market needs. This has meant acquiring more English skills by enrolling in language courses.

Aging in Culture and Family

In addition to macrolevel factors, scholars have pointed to cultural and social factors that mediate the immigrant experience of older adults. A major area where sociologists, social gerontologists, and others have studied the influence of culture on minority aging is through an examination of informal social systems, such as kin and non-kin networks (Gratton 1987). With respect to kin networks, the structure of family obligations and intergenerational family relations plays a key role in cultural production and self-identity for minority elders (Gratton 1987). The extensive involvement of Hispanic elderly with immediate and extended family has been a central theme in scholarly literature. In particular, this work has highlighted how the family is part of helping older adults manage with the challenges and burdens of aging in American society. The family has also been viewed as an essential mechanism for keeping older minorities integrated in society.

Most commonly known as *familism*, or familismo, this concept refers to the cultural commitment to immediate and extended family relationships (Perez and Cruess 2014). Attention has been paid to the ways in which ethnic minority families place high value on family and maintain a strong commitment to its elderly. Behaviorally, this ethnic family orientation is shown in families living near one another or engaging in common activities. At 63-years old, Dora, who immigrated to the United States within the last 10 years, shares that her family is central to her sense of identity and connection with others.

> My family is everything to me. Without them I couldn't go to stores where they speak English or sometimes to the doctor. They make me feel good about myself because I don't

like not being able to communicate in English with others. I have been here [United States] for 10 years and I'm still learning. So, without my family I would have a difficult time.

Scholars debate about the political implications of associating familism with racial/ethnic minorities. Feminist scholars contend that racial/ethnic minorities share common characteristics in kin structures due to social and economic conditions that encouraged "alternative" family arrangements (Zinn 1994). While not biological, these characteristics represent a socially constructed response to structural conditions that make family bonds a resource in a racist and gendered society. Others argue familism is not uniquely linked to minority families and can now be observed within white families as a result of economic and demographic changes (Franklin 2010). As the middle-class shrinks and the aging population grows, financial, and social network pressures force white families to develop more elaborate kin arrangements that resemble those of minority families.

Studies have also linked familism to minority aging well-being (Campos et al. 2014; Valle and Cook-Gait 1998). Findings from the Mexican Health and Aging Study reveal high rates of co-residence and intergenerational households, although recent studies point to a decline in these rates (Wong and Palloni 2009). Even when generations reside in different households, instrumental support exchanges between adult children and their elderly parents are high (Gomes 2007). Close living arrangements are one of the central ways older Hispanics keep a sense of social connectedness. Multigenerational living arrangements are usually a result of financial and sociocultural pressures. For example, Mexican American older adults with fewer wealth assets are less likely to own their own home (Burr et al. 2011). Co-residence with younger individuals who are more acculturated mitigates the immediate difficulties of language-use and social integration related to later-life migration.

The positive effects of familism for elderly Hispanics have also been tied to social status (Taylor et al. 2012). Familism within Hispanic families is said to emphasize age hierarchy and respect for the elderly (Schwawrtz 2007). Scholarship points to the high status ascribed to elderly in the family (Markides et al. 1983). Elderly Hispanics' status relates to a continuation of authority due to their role in the cultural socialization of children (Boswell and Curtis 1984). Diego, who is in his late 50s but cannot work due to health reasons, confirms the special role allotted to him within the family.

I feel important in my family. I'm somebody because I can help with the kids and encourage them in their lives. Nowadays older people are not as important in the community as they used to be. I feel bad for people who don't have a family or a good connection with them. I'm respected in my family, even though I can't always help.

What is interesting is how Diego describes how high family status does not necessarily translate to social power outside of the family. Diego notes the way family relationships define his sense of duty to his family, triggering his motivation to learn English. At the same time, however, family obligations constrain his second language acquisition.

I don't want to be a burden on people, like my kids. They are very busy with work and raising their children. I haven't been able to work in a while, so I help with smaller things. But it's not easy getting around, especially not knowing English. I want to learn English so that I can be more useful but people around me don't always see why I need to learn at my age...since I can speak Spanish at home and at my stores. I'm old but I'd like to learn English so I can expand my world and what I can do. But I have a lot of responsibilities at home and it's difficult to make time for this [ESL class].

Immigrants' perception of themselves as older adults in the context of life transitions can shape their own trajectories as members of a new host country. Older immigrants' self-perception can inform meanings linked to status and development over time. The most basic choices that older immigrants make involve the interaction between self-identity and their environment. These choices include decisions related to avoiding or pursing a second language, acknowledging or ignoring the challenges to language acquisition, and engaging in or withdrawing from second language socialization. Many of the frustrations and anxieties that older immigrants experience as language learners, for instance, come from their efforts to balance their own and others' expectations about acculturation in later life.

Familial Social Exchange: Benefits and Barriers to Minority Aging

Consistent with Diego's account earlier, social scientists argue the social exchange process of family relationships is an important mechanism that conditions the meanings and trajectories of minority aging. In the context of familism, social exchange refers to the long history of reciprocal exchanges (i.e., giving and receiving) that occurs across generations (Hamilton and Sandelowski 2003). This social exchange process is understood to be a communal obligation to meet the demands of life and to establish social equity (Hirdes and Strain 1995). Driving the social exchange process are factors linked to persons' availability and social roles.

Availability sets the baseline of who can participate to assist in perceived family needs. In the context of immigration, age of arrival to the host country can impact the types of social exchanges available to and required of older adults. Research shows that being of an older age and living for a fewer number of years in the United States has a significant effect on increasing expectations for filial obligations (Biafora and Longino 1990). Immigration alters the timing of life course events and roles can be changed quite dramatically. While older immigrants may have been preoccupied with various obligations outside the home in their previous country, immigration can reorganize their lives in ways that increase their dependence on family. The pressures of acculturation can alter older adults' daily lives due to emerging language barriers, changes to their social networks, and obstacles to economic, political, and cultural resources (Treas 2008). Later age immigration often means the presence of various challenges to the process of settlement that centers the family as a primary resource used to navigate new terrains (Treas 2008).

Environmental changes and limitations to their interactions with the world outside their immediate family and neighbors can also impact older adults' well-being, self-identity, and sense of social solidarity (Treas and Mazumdar 2004). Margarita recalls that early in their emigration from Honduras, she and her husband relied heavily on their children for social support. Though they did not work, they helped by taking care of their two grandchildren and maintaining the house.

> We were already a bit older and knew that it was going to be difficult to start a new life. But it was the best thing for the whole family.... I told my son that I would take care of the kids and the house since I didn't work and didn't speak much English. It has taken many years but now I have more time to come to class and learn more English.

The number of children available in the household and the age of the oldest child also affect the expectations and obligations of older adults to offer familiar care.

Emerging research presents a complex image of the effects of familism for older adult well-being (Gallo et al. 2009). Familism is argued to provide physical and psycho-social benefits by reinforcing social support resources in the areas of health care, financial support, and self-esteem (Perez and Cruess 2014). At the same time, familism may encourage a form of isolation that limits access to behavioral norms outside the family and, thus, increase risks associated with acculturation (Gallo et al. 2009).

In the case of our study participants, older adults did not always have access to successful language socialization with English interlocutors within the family. Maria talked about the tension between fulfilling a sense of responsibility to assist in the raising of her grandchildren and working towards both citizenship and learning English.

> For many years I helped my daughter raise the kids. Taking them to school, preparing meals.... Becoming a citizen has been a longtime goal of mine but it's been hard to do everything I need to achieve it. I'm fortunate now because my daughter has a better work schedule and this class has daycare for kids. Otherwise I don't think I would be able to come to class.

This was a common story told by those that we interviewed. Our participants had great pride in their role as caretakers and expressed gratitude for the affirmation received for their contributions (Johnson and Barer 2003). But they also echoed Maria's feelings about obstacles to fulfilling their goals to gaining full citizenship and developing their English proficiency. They often discussed the familial obligations that made achieving those goals more difficult.

For Maria, as for many other older immigrants, expectations about aging are tied to ideological beliefs about what persons are capable of doing physically and socially. In an interview, Maria noted that she often hears from family that older persons do not need to learn a second language.

> My family sometimes finds it funny that I want to learn English at my age. They think I'm too old and don't need to learn as someone who arrived to this country as an old person. But I feel like I do need to learn to be able to talk to others and even my grandchildren. I used to think I was too old but I look around here [in the classroom] and see other people of my age learning English.

Maria lets us see that aging is inscribed with social meanings related to cultural age-based expectations. Moreover, these notions and expectations are tied to life course events, social roles, and positions that undergo changes due to immigration. For those that immigrate in their later years, filial obligations become an important system of social support that shape older adults' trajectory in the acculturation process. Familial arrangements also structure dominant meanings related to aging, whereby "being old" centers on activities of caretaking and nurturing. And, while these arrangements offer buffers to psychological and social stress linked to immigration, older adults may simultaneously be disconnected from important acculturative resources known to help their language learning efforts.

Social Networks and Neighborhood Context

Beyond the home, Hispanic older adults live within broader social environments—enclave neighborhoods and communities—that provide many sources of social capital and social ties. There is little doubt that immigrants are a large and increasingly ethnically diverse segment of the population of the United States (Grieco 2003). These individuals are likely to live in neighborhoods with a high representation of other immigrants and with individuals of the same ethnic group (Suro and Tafoya 2004). An important feature of minority aging is the nature of Hispanic immigration and neighborhood context.

Immigrant enclaves—neighborhoods with significant numbers of immigrants and immigrants from similar ethnic background—are an important structural feature that shapes the experiences and meanings associated with immigrant aging. Perhaps most significant is that ethnic enclaves carry a range of cultural and economic resources, as well as social networks, that support non-English language speakers (Fernandez and Schauffler 1996). It is through these and other pathways that meanings about aging are constructed and choices regarding acculturation made. In addition to family, the impact of ethnic enclaves on minority aging has been studied through informal non-kin social support networks.

Migration experiences determine the character of non-kin social networks available to older adults. Country of origin and timing of entry are significant factors differentiating the type of social support systems among Hispanics. Studies show that among Cuban Americas, non-kin informal networks (i.e., friends and acquaintances) are used for emotional and other support (Angel and Angel 1992). Mexican Americans, on the other hand, rely more on family members for emotional support, money lending, and information exchange (Becker et al. 2003).

Differences in informal social support systems among Hispanics result from different ethnic enclave experiences. Cubans who immigrated in the 1960s received the benefit of a closed ethnic enclave, which promoted wealth accumulation, political ascendency, and cultural assimilation. In turn, this encouraged Cuban Americans to later on extend their social networks beyond the ethnic enclave into larger society. As Portes and Bach (1985) point out, the experience for Mexicans, and other Hispanic groups, has been different. Indeed, later Cubans migrants—such as those from the so-called "Mariel" wave of the 1980s—arrived to a more open enclave that exposed them to the risks of a larger and more competitive economic marketplace. In this context, Mexicans, and later waves of Cubans, rely on family relationships and fictive kin (i.e., close friendships) as a primary source of social support.

Minority elders are uniquely shaped by the cultural values and norms derived from the racial and ethnic groups to which they identify. A major effect of the ethnic enclave is the preservation of a group's culture and language. The powerful social networks within these enclave communities may help to reinforce cultural norms and rules of behavior that are different from the dominant host culture (Zhou 2001). On the whole, Hispanic older adults are more likely than non-Hispanic whites to possess various form of social support from nuclear family, extended family, and non-kin members that reinforce monolingual patterns (Chow et al. 2010).

Ethnic enclaves, therefore, operate in a dual fashion. On the one hand, they insulate individuals from potentially stressful forces of acculturation and, on the other, they may isolate them further from those outside the ethnic enclave (Portes and Rumbaut 2006). Older Hispanics who rely on nuclear and extended family networks for social support report a high sense of well-being and emotional reward (Martinez 2002). However, these individuals also report feeling more socially isolated (Treas and Mazumdar 2002).

Juan shares a similar view when talking about his interactions with neighborhood friends. Although Juan is very grateful for the emotional connection that goes along with these relationships, he nevertheless stresses the challenges that close non-kin bonds present for second language socialization.

> My friends sort of make fun of me for coming to class. They say, "Why are you learning English at your age…you're too old." I laugh too because I am old for this. But it's something that I've been wanting to do for a long time…. The problem is that all I speak is Spanish with them [Juan's fiends] and I don't have anyone to talk to in English. How am I supposed to improve if everyone around me only speaks Spanish? This is nothing against them. They still support me…but…you know…you need to practice. I can't just go to school, like my grandchild, to learn.

Juan alerts us to the fact that many Hispanic immigrants need meaningful access to non-monolingual socialization. For older adult immigrants who have limited sources of non-kin social support, the benefits of this type of interaction are also not readily available. Some time ago sociologists (Granovetter 1973) called this phenomena "the strength of weak ties," referring to the power of weak-informal contacts to deliver diverse social and economic capital. The nature and composition of social networks can leave some Hispanic immigrants particularly vulnerable, as they are left outside of everyday English social interactions known to offer resources for language learning.

Building Language Capital Through Place

When put together, the narratives we have shared tell of the complex and uneven contours of Hispanic older adults' lives as immigrants. While the intention was not to be exhaustive, these stories emphasize the importance of understanding the ways immigration and aging intersect to generate the transitional experiences of Hispanic older adults, as well as the endemic challenges they face. As we saw, Hispanic older adults are situated in a unique social location that increases their exposure to structural circumstances affecting their vulnerability and stress as immigrants. We also know of the ways in which they adjust to and negotiate with these context factors.

We focused on structural and cultural factors that generate transitions in Hispanic older adults' self-identity, roles, feelings, interactions, and resources. Socioeconomic patterns related to immigration also have negative effects on Hispanic older adults' language development. Pathways to acquire English as a second language are disturbed by a lack of resources that would help immigrant elders deal with the demands of acculturation. Initiatives designed to meet the needs of this population will need to be responsive to the circumstances that minority elders encounter on a regular basis. This means acknowledging the primary transitions in family roles, social support, and capital resources that produce both protective and risk factors for immigrants at a later age.

At the same time, it is important to avoid a view that sees ethnic minorities as a static group. A dynamic approach is needed that recognizes changes in family and larger social relationships. Recent research, for instance, suggests there are generational shifts taking place in Hispanic family values, with younger generations adopting more individualistic conceptions of family solidarity and older generations continuing to value traditional family bonds (Smith-Morris et al. 2013). The composition of language within the family is also changing, with younger generations adopting English as a dominant language. Considering the growing aging population of Hispanics and their reliance on filial social support, changes to values and behaviors related to family solidarity will likely have implications for the well-being of Hispanic elders.

We consider these and other trends as significant for how they may enhance or limit language learning. Our study participants have unique obstacles but all share a set of ideas, feelings, and experiences that together frame a common story of minority aging in an immigrant context. Whether it is a 62-year-old grandmother, like Rosa, who is struggling to maintain a communicative bond with her English-speaking granddaughter; an older man who continues to work as a mechanic, such as Francisco, and desires to remain relevant in the workplace; or Juan, who seeks to expand his social interactions beyond his monolingual peers, each of these individuals highlights their desires and frustrations regarding developing their English proficiency.

Of special interest to us in this study are the forms of human and social capital that are developed *in place*—particularly, in the context of our ESL program. Given the structural, cultural, and social circumstances that frame minority aging for immigrants, we seek to uncover the formative development of language resources available in learners' local settings. Specifically, we are looking for the ways Hispanic older adults develop a "self-as-learner" identity built on modes of thinking, feeling, and acting that promote second language socialization and learning. In order to address the call for a more responsive approach to a diverse aging population, it is important to link life transitions with the forms of human capital that can mitigate the pressures of minority aging. This means paying close attention to the places where human, and more specifically language, capital are produced. This, in turn, can guide strategies for intervention.

We also take the view that interventions may need to be more than one-shot case studies, and instead focus on long-term projects. This is why our study examines a Hispanic immigrant elder community over several years. This helps us to acknowledge the dynamic nature of people's lives and how these changing trajectories influence language acquisition. The next two chapters focus in more detail on the theoretical considerations we kept in mind regarding language acquisition, as well as the significance of place for the language learning process of older adults.

References

Administration on Aging (AOA). (2010). A Statistical Profile of Hispanic Older Americans Aged 65+. Retrieved from http://www.aoa.acl.gov/Aging_Statistics/minority_aging/Facts-on-Hispanic-Elderly.aspx

Angel, J. L., & Angel, R. J. (1992). Age at migration, social connections, and well-being among elderly Hispanics. *Journal of Aging and Health, 4*(4), 480–499.

Becker, G., Beyene, Y., Newsom, R., & Mayen, N. (2003). Creating continuity through mutual assistance: Intergenerational reciprocity in four ethnic groups. *The Journals of Gerontology, Series B, Psychological Sciences and Social Sciences, 58*(3), S151–S159.

Biafora, F., & Longino, C., Jr. (1990). Elderly Hispanic migration in the United States. *Journal of Gerontology: Social Sciences, 45*(5), S212–S219.

Boswell, T. D., & Curtis, J. R. (1984). *The Cuban-American experience*. Totowa, NJ: Rownam & Allanhead.

Burr, J., Mutchler, J., & Gerst, K. (2011). Home ownership among Mexican–Americans in later life. *Research on Aging, 33*(4), 379–402.

Campos, B., Ullman, J. B., Aguilera, A., & Dunkel Schetter, C. (2014). Familism and psychological health: The intervening role of closeness and social support. *Cultural Diversity and Ethnic Minority Psychology, 20*(2), 191–201.

Chavez, L. (1998). *Shadowed lives: Undocumented immigrants in American society*. Orlando: Harcourt Brace.

Chow, J. C., Auh, E. Y., Scharlach, A. E., Lehning, A. J., & Goldstein, C. S. (2010). Types and sources of support received by family caregivers of older adults from diverse racial and ethnic groups. *Journal of Ethnic & Cultural Diversity in Social Work: Innovation in Theory, Research, & Practice, 19*(3), 175–194.

Cornelius, W. A., & Lewis, J. M. (Eds.). (2006). *Impacts of border enforcement on Mexican migration: The view from sending communities*. Boulder, CO: Lynne Rienner Publishers and Center for Comparative Immigration Studies, UCSD.

Corsini, R. J. (1987). *Concise encyclopedia of psychology*. New York: Wiley.

References

Cowan, P. A. (1991). Individual and family life transitions: A proposal for a new definition. In P. A. Cowan & E. M. Hetherington (Eds.), *Family transitions* (pp. 3–30). New Jersey: Lawrence Erlbaum Associates.

Elder, G. H. (1994). Time, human agency, and social change: Perspectives on the life course. *Social Psychology, 57*(1), 4–15.

Escobar, J., Hoyos, N., & Gara, M. (2000). Immigration and mental health: Mexican Americans in the United States. *Harvard Review of Psychiatry, 8*(2), 64–72.

Espin, O. M. (1987). Psychological impact of migration on Latinas. *Psychology of Women Quarterly, 11*(4), 489–503.

Estes, C., Biggs, S., & Phillipson, C. (2003). *Social theory, social policy and ageing: Critical perspectives*. Maidenhead: Open University Press.

Feagin, J. R. (2010). *White racial frame: Centuries of racial framing and counter-framing*. New York: Routledge.

Fernandez Kelly, M. P., & Schauffler, R. (1996). Divided fates: Immigrant children and the new assimilation. In A. Portes (Ed.), *The new second generation* (pp. 30–53). New York: Oxford University Press.

Franklin, D. L. (2010). African Americans and the birth of modern marriage. In B. Risman (Ed.), *Families as they really are* (pp. 63–74). New York, NY: W. W. Norton.

Gallo, L. C., Penedo, F. J., Espinosa de los Monteros, K., & Arguelles, W. (2009). Resiliency in the face of disadvantage: Do Hispanic cultural characteristics protect health outcomes? *Journal of Personality, 77*(6), 1707–1746.

Gomes, C. (2007). Intergenerational exchanges in Mexico types and intensity of support. *Current Sociology, 55*(4), 545–560.

Granovetter, M. S. (1973). Strength of weak ties. *American Journal of Sociology, 78*(6), 1360–1380.

Gratton, B. (1987). Familism among the Black and Mexican American elderly: Myth or reality. *Journal of Aging Studies, 1*(1), 19–32.

Grieco, E. (2003). Migration policy institute policy brief. Washington DC: Migration Policy Institute. Retrieved from http://www.migrationpolicy.org/pubs/MPIPolicyBrief Census.pdf

Hamilton, J., & Sandelowski, M. (2003). Living the golden rule: Reciprocal exchange among African Americans with cancer. *Qualitative Health Research, 13*(5), 656–674.

Hirdes, J., & Strain, L. (1995). The balance of exchange in instrumental support with network members outside the household. *Journal of Gerontology: Social Sciences, 50B*, S134–S142.

Johnson, C. L., & Barer, B. M. (2003). Family lives of aging Black Americans. In J. F. Gubrium & J. A. Holstein (Eds.), *Ways of aging* (pp. 111–131). Malden, MA: Blackwell.

Markides, K. S., Martin, H. W., & Gomez, E. (1983). *Older Mexican Americans: A study in an urban barrio*. Austin: University of Texas Press.

Martinez, I. L. (2002). The elder in the Cuban American family: Making sense of the real and ideal. *Journal of Comparative Family Studies, 33*(3), 359–375.

Nevins, J. (2010). *Operation gatekeeper and beyond: The war on "illegals" and the remaking of the United States-Mexico boundary*. New York: Routledge.

Padilla, A. (2002). Hispanic psychology: A 25-year retrospective look. In W. Lonner, D. Dinnel, S. Hayes, & D. Sattler (Eds.), *Online readings in psychology and culture* (Unit 3, Chapter 3). Center for Cross-Cultural Research, Western Washington University. Retrieved from https://www.wwu.edu/culture/padilla.htm

Padilla, E. R. (Ed.). (1980). *Acculturation: Theory, models, and some new findings*. Boulder, CO: Westview.

Padilla, E. R., Olmedao, E., & Loya, F. (1982). Acculturation and the MMPI performance of Chicano and Anglo college students. *Hispanic Journal of Behavioral Sciences, 4*(4), 451–466.

Passel, J., & Cohn, D. (2010). U.S. unauthorized immigration flows are down sharply since mid-decade. Washington DC.: Pew Hispanic Center. Retrieved from http://www.pewhispanic.org/2010/09/01/us-unauthorized-immigration-flows-are-down-sharply-since-mid-decade/

Paykel, E. S. (1974). Life stress and psychiatric disorder: Applications of the clinical approach. In B. S. Dohrenwend & B. P. Dohrenwend (Eds.), *Stressful life events: Their nature and effects* (pp. 135–149). New York: Wiley.

Perez, K. G., & Cruess, D. (2014). The impact of familism on physical and mental health among Hispanics in the United States. *Health Psychology Review, 8*(1), 95–127.

Portes, A., & Bach, R. L. (1985). *Latin Journey: Cuban and Mexican immigrants in the United States*. California: University California Press.

Portes, A., & Rumbaut, R. G. (2006). *Immigrant America: A portrait*. Berkeley, CA: University of California Press.

Rodriguez, J., & Kosloski, K. (1998). The impact of acculturation on attitudinal familism in a community of Puerto Rican Americans. *Hispanic Journal of Behavioral Science, 20*(3), 375–390.

Roscow, I. (1967). *Social integration of the aged*. New York: Free Press.

Sanchez, G. L. (1997). Face the nation: Race, immigration, and the rise of nativism in late twentieth century America. *International Migration Review, 31*(4), 1009–1030.

Schwawrtz, S. J. (2007). The applicability of familism to diverse ethnic groups: A preliminary study. *The Journal of Social Psychology, 14*(2), 101–118.

Smalley, W. (1963). Culture shock, language shock, and the shock of self-discovery. *Practical Anthropology, 10*(1), 49–56.

Smith-Morris, C., Morales-Campos, D., Alvarez, E. A. C., & Turner, M. (2013). An anthropology of familismo on narratives and description of Mexican/immigrants. *Hispanic Journal of Behavioral Sciences, 74*(2), 312–327.

Suarez, L., & Pulley, L. (1995). Comparing acculturation scales and their relationship to cancer screening among older Mexican-American women. *Journal of National Cancer Institute Monograph, 18*, 41–47.

Suro, R., & Tafoya, S. (2004). Dispersal and concentration: Patterns of Latina/o residential settlement. Pew Research Center. Retrieved from http://www.pewhispanic.org/2004/12/27/dispersal-and-concentration/

Taylor, Z. E., Larsen-Rife, D., Conger, R. D., & Widaman, K. F. (2012). Familism, interpersonal conflict, and parenting in Mexican-origin families: A cultural-contextual framework. *Journal of Marriage and Family, 74*(2), 312–327.

Treas, J. (2008). Transnational older adults and their families. *Family Relations, 57*(4), 468–478.

Treas, J., & Mazumdar, S. (2002). Older people in America's immigrant families: Dilemmas of dependence, integration, and isolation. *Journal of Aging Studies, 16*(3), 243–258.

Treas, J., & Mazumdar, S. (2004). Caregiving and kinkeeping: Contributions of older people in immigrant families. *Journal of Comparative Family Studies, 35*(1), 105–122.

Tummala-Nara, P. (2001). Asian trauma survivors: Immigration, identity, loss, and recovery. *Journal of Applied Psychoanalytic Studies, 3*(3), 243–258.

Valle, R., & Cook-Gait, H. (1998). *Caregiving across cultures*. Oxford: Routledge.

Viruell-Fuentes, E. A. (2011). "It's a lot of work": Racialization processes, ethnic identity formations, and their health implications. *DuBois Review: Social Science Research on Race, 8*(1), 37–52.

Wilmoth, J. M., & Chen, P-C. (2003). Immigrant status, living arrangements, and depressive symptoms among middle-aged and older adults. *Journal of Gerontology: Social Sciences, 58B*(5) (September): S305-S313.

Wong, R., & Palloni, A. (2009). Aging in Mexico and Latin America. In P. Uhlenbery (Ed.), *International handbook of population aging* (pp. 231–252). Netherlands: Springer.

Zhou, M. (2001). Contemporary immigration and the dynamics of race and ethnicity. In N. J. Smelser, W. J. Wilson, & F. Mitchell (Eds.), *America becoming: Racial trends and their consequences* (pp. 200–242). Washington DC: National Academy Press.

Zinn, M. B. (1994). Feminist rethinking from racial-ethnic families. In M. B. Zinn, & B. T. Dill (Eds.), *Women of color in U.S. society* (pp. 18–26). Philadelphia, PA: Temple University Press.

Chapter 4
Late-Life Second Language Acquisition: Cognitive and Psycholinguistic Changes, Challenges, and Opportunities

> I have grandkids. They aren't even 10-years-old yet and they speak English with no problem. I've been here for 32 years and I only know a few words. My friends laugh at me for studying English. They think I'm wasting my time. I tell them that I am learning a lot of English. But sometimes I wonder if they're right. Can older people learn? Can I learn enough to communicate with my grandchildren? I don't know if I can even do it, but I'm still going to try.

As with many adult second language learners, the participants in our family literacy program embodied the conventional language ideology that children learn their second language with ease while adults hardly make any progress despite their tremendous efforts. Pedro, who is 64-years-old, highlights several of these age-related conceptions. Commonly held beliefs about second language acquisition are informed by two generalized forms of information: (1) an observable trend in society where children's ultimate attainment of their second language is native-like while adults typically maintain an accent and (2) summaries and tidbits of neurolinguistics research that highlight the overall "cognitive slowing" of the aging brain.

In the North American context, it is oftentimes assumed that adult language learners will simply have a more difficult time in their second language. The two most recognizable cases are L1 (first language) English-speaking adults who struggle in a foreign language classroom setting and L1 Spanish-speaking adults who speak low-to-intermediate levels of English after having resided in the United States for several years. Sociolinguistic patterns among intergenerational speakers do give the impression that such a societal tendency must be related to the aging mind, especially, when the children of immigrants master English by the time they are in their early teens. However, if we conclude that after a particular maturation stage of human cognitive development (i.e., early adulthood) our genetic makeup does not permit nonnative language acquisition, how would we explain the exceptions? Though it is certainly not the norm, a percentage of adult L2 (second language) learners who after living in the target language society for several years manage to master their second language in a native-like manner.

General perceptions about L2 learning focus on a body of experimental research in psycholinguistics and neurocognition. The perennial refrain is usually employed to explain the process: a child's brain soaks up language input like a sponge; they learn their second language fluently and effortlessly. But is it true? Are children cognitively predisposed to acquire multiple languages? Or are there other environmental factors dealing with socialization practices in society that provide support for younger learners, giving us the impression of a precipitous decline in adult learners' abilities? These questions have been intensely researched, vigorously debated, and wholly controversial over the last sixty or so years of SLA research. Through it all, our understanding of language acquisition has been enhanced, though it may be unsatisfactory for readers to know that these discoveries introduce many more nuanced and complex questions than they unequivocally answer.

In this chapter, we will learn how the hotly contested issues of second language acquisition has been disproportionately focused on children and young adults, the result of which has led to a significant omission: after nearly a century of psycholinguistic research, we know little about the cognitive or social factors influencing older adults' acquisition of a second language. Nearly all SLA research compares children to young adults. When language and cognition is studied in older adults (65+), the subjects are overwhelmingly monolingual and the methodological orientations usually measure linguistic decline and attrition. Nonetheless, we cannot completely ignore the work that has been conducted on the critical period of language learning which is believed to occur near, or slightly prior to, puberty since it is this line of research that has generated multiple discourses about the feasibility of adult L2 acquisition. Certain distinctions in cognitive change between childhood and adulthood will help us focus our discussion on the scant research examining older adult second language acquisition.

Reviewing studies on general cognitive aptitude (e.g., processing speed, working memory, and executive control) allows researchers to draw some speculative connections as to how this may affect an older adult's attempts at learning a second language. Within this discussion, we will report on positive attributes of the aging brain that aid the language acquisition process. Since so much of the research on the aging brain is derived from deficit models ("healthy" adults studied as a control group for research subjects with dementia and Alzheimer's disease), we find it essential to highlight the advantages afforded to older adults' accumulated intellectual knowledge and expertise in response to declines in psychometric assessments of cognitive ability, visual aptitude, and auditory acuity.

Many of the ageist discourses that circulate in our daily interactions seem to make reference to neurolinguistics research and propagate defeatist ideologies of learning and aging. In reality, several significant inconsistencies across disciplines exist in the work that is being published that would color our perception of the aging brain. We highlight some of the more prevalent challenges to producing reliable results when conducting research with this particular population.

We close the chapter by proposing research directions that could be beneficial for a comprehensive understanding of the brain during various responses to particular cognitive changes. However, before we begin discussing the abovementioned topics, a brief review of general linguistic topics will be necessary since much of the research we synthesize frequently examine isolated aspects of language function, namely morpho-syntax, phonology, pragmatics, and the lexicon. The following section reviews six identifiable stages of English question formation along with nontechnical explanations of the grammar rules for such question formation.

Review of Linguistic Areas of Interest for SLA and Aging Research

Question Formation in English (Developmental Sequence)

Several lines of inquiry for both first-and second language acquisition research measures progression through question formation and the developmental sequences learners tend to pass through in their acquisition of the morpho-syntactic rules in English. Pienemann (1989) and Pienemann et al. (1988) outlined a six-stage development that is by and large incremental (i.e., the previous stage is typically mastered or acquired before the next stage). In other words, a learner would rarely master stage six questions before those associated with stage four.

We have taken several of the questions that were formulated during face-to-face oral language activities with our older adult ESL students to illustrate each of the developmental stages. The stages are slightly modified from Pienemann's early work which focused on L1 German speakers acquiring English as a target language. Since our English language learners (ELLs) are L1 Spanish speakers, some of the questions informing the stages in the developmental sequence are specific to the language context. In our examples below, several influences from Spanish are present, though the grammatical challenges confronting speakers at each level are generalizable to all learners of English. As a brief note to the reader, in linguistics and throughout the book, "*" denotes "ungrammatical sentence structures". The declarative clauses are written after some of the questions to highlight *subject + auxiliary verb* inversion that is required by English grammar in many question types.

Stage 1 Questions:

(1) *Hungry? [Hungry.]*
(2) *Two weeks? [Two weeks.]*
(3) *Go to work today? [(You) go to work today.]*
(4) *"Hey, how're you doing?" [You are doing.]*

When adult L2 learners begin to first articulate basic questions, the results found in stages one and two parallel those of L1 English-speaking toddlers. Questions in stage one may be a single word (1), two words (2), predicate question (3), or idiomatic formulae (4). In more advance stages, we will learn just how the structure of (4) requires that the speaker recognize that *are* is functioning as the auxiliary verb and needs to switch with the subject *you* to formulate the question. The interrogative word *how* is fronted in the clause and the auxiliary verb is contracted so that the two words *how are* could be pronounced as one syllable *how're*. According to our own designation of L2 learner development, well-formed question (4) belongs in stage five (see below). We call this an idiomatic question or a formulaic sequence since the learner has memorized the entire interrogative clause as one large lexical chunk that is associated with the speech act of "greeting" or "salutation." It would be quite normal for this speaker to maintain the *how're* even when the subject has changed (**How're Tina doing?*) since the learner has not acquired subject–verb agreement rules yet, but rather has memorized the phrases as if it were one vocabulary word.

Stage 2 Questions:

(5) *You have the truck here?* [*You have the truck here.*]
(6) *Your grandchildren go to school?* [*Your grandchildren go to school.*]
(7) *The children are in the yard?* [*The children are in the yard.*]

Stage two questions are based on the high-frequency structures, such as [Subject + Verb + (Object)] which are many times headed by the highly frequent subject pronoun, *you* (5), a simple noun phrase, *your grandchildren* (6), or *the children* (7). These question types typically rely on utterance-final rising pitch to communicate its interrogative reading. What we do not typically observe in stage two are questions where auxiliary verbs, or *be*-verbs, are inverted with the subject (7) or done so correctly (11).

Stage 3 Questions:

(8) *Is everybody happy?* [*Everybody is happy.*]
(9) **Can she marry with Antonio?* [*She can marry Antonio.*]
(10) *Does she know my brother?* [*She knows my brother.*]
(11) **Are the picture has two planets on top?* [*The picture has two planets on top?*]
(12) **Does she has a shoe on your picture?* [*She has a shoe on your picture.*]
(13) **Does in this picture there is four astronauts?* [*In this picture there are four astronauts.*]
(14) **Where the children are playing?* [*The children are playing there.*]

In stage three, L2 learners of English begin to test "working hypotheses" related to yes/no question formation. If you are a native speaker of English, chances are you acquired the complex grammar rules of various yes/no question types without ever having to think explicitly about them. Here is a brief review: When the main verb of a sentence is some form of *be* (*am, is, are, was, were, being, been, be*) it should be fronted and used as an interrogative marker (8). When a *be* verb is not the main verb of the sentence, the first auxiliary verb of the verb phrase is fronted to form a question, *can* (9). When *be* verbs are not the main verb of the sentence or the verb phrase does not contain any auxiliary verbs, English grammar requires *do* to be inserted, then fronted, and then agree with the subject of the sentence (10).

Language learners in stage three tend to overgeneralize rules that seem to have worked in other contexts. Since they might have had success in fronting *is* or *are* in some yes/no questions, they begin to hypothesize that in order to create a yes/no question, all they have to do is place a form of the *be* verb in the beginning, thus (11). When they have had some success fronting a form of *do*, they will overgeneralize that rule and start other yes/no questions with it, such as in (12). Finally, when there is an existential subject *there* (13), or if the subject is preceded by a prepositional phrase, rules that had already been learned may not be applied correctly. Notice that the speaker should have applied the fronting rule in (8) when forming the question in (13). Fronting the *be* verb with wh-questions is typically not mastered in stage three (14), though it should be noted that all of the ungrammatical iterations (11–14) are necessary for learners to begin to acquire these rules and move to the following stage. In other words, producing ungrammatical questions is a strategy language learners use to test and improve their working hypotheses about the target language grammar and prepare them for more complex question formations.

Stage 4 Questions:

(15) *Do they liked the new school? [*They liked the new school.*]
(16) Are they going to be in Dallas next year? [*They are going to be in Dallas next year.*]
(17) Where is the notebook and the pencil? [*The notebook and the pencil are here/there.*]
(18) *Why he call my brother? [*He called my brother.*]

The insertion of *do*, *does*, *did*, or *done* (called "do-support") when the declarative clause lacks an auxiliary verb requires further analysis by the learner. After a form of *do* is inserted and fronted, it must also agree with the subject if the clause is in the simple present tense. If the clause is in the past tense (15), *did* marks the temporal past and the main verb, *like*, should have been placed in its infinitive form. This is a case where the question is syntactically well formed as the word order does not need to be changed, but the morphological agreement rules have not been applied correctly. As will be discussed in greater detail below, maintaining morpho-syntactic rules clearly organized during the production of a question during speech requires a sufficient amount of short-term working memory. The morpho-syntactic rules found in stage four questions not only challenge the working memory capabilities of ELLs, but even native English speakers who may be experiencing a form of dementia. Inverting the *be*-verb with the subject in a wh-question becomes achievable for English learners in stage four (17). However, wh-questions where *do*-support is required tends to continue to cause problems (18).

Stage 5 Questions:

(19) What does your job do for you and the holiday? [*Your job _____ for you on the holiday.*]
(20) What are you writing? [*You are writing _____.*]

(21) *I'm not sure <u>when should I go to the other table</u>. [*I'm not sure (when) I should go to the other table.*]
(22) *I asked him <u>if would he like a new job</u>. [*I asked him (if) he would like a new job.*]

In stage five, the inversion in wh-questions is mastered and utilized on a more frequent basis (19 & 20). Some ELLs attempt embedded questions, but given the added cognitive load, they are frequently avoided by expressing a similar message with a different construction. Embedded questions are clauses within a longer complex sentence (underlined in 21 & 22). Had the question been freestanding, the rules from stages 1–4 would have applied; however, as question clauses subordinated in a larger matrix clause, subject–auxiliary verb inversion is not needed. For example, *When **should I** go to the other table?* is a well formed question when it is a freestanding clause. Yet, embedded in a larger sentence, the *should* follows the subject *I'm not sure when **I should** go to the other table.* Similarly, in (22), **Would he** *like a new job?* is acceptable as a complete sentence by itself. As an embedded question, the auxiliary verb *would* should follow *he* as in *I asked him if **he would** like a new job?*

Stage 6 questions:

(23) *Thomas went to the school, didn't he?*
(24) *Why don't my grandchildren work and make money?*
(25) *Jose doesn't know <u>what he is reading</u>.*
(26) *Martin wants to know <u>where does your family buy food</u>.*

Embedded questions are one example of complex formations in English, tag questions are another. A tag question (23) begins with a declarative clause (*Thomas went to the school*) and finishes with a brief question that is tagged at the end (*didn't he?*). They are quite complex in that (a) the tag question is negative when the declarative clause is affirmative and vice versa, (b) a subject pronoun must be used in the tag (**Thomas went to the school, didn't Thomas?* is nonnative usage), and (c) all of the rules that apply to movement of auxiliary verbs in other questions also apply to the tag question (i.e., since there is not any auxiliary verb in the declarative sentence in (23), a form of *do* is added and must follow subject–verb agreement rules or mark the past tense). English learners in stage six also achieve full mastery of inversion in wh-questions (24) and embedded questions (25 & 26). Occasional performance errors will occur just as they do with native speakers of English, but the underlying morpho-syntactic knowledge to construct all question types in English is acquired by stage six.

The developmental sequence of English questions outlined above does not predict the rate in which a learner may progress or their ultimate attainment. As can be observed in any L2 speech community, some speakers may communicate effectively using the structures in stages 1–4 and shy away from the embedded and tag questions in stages five and six. They may have a passive knowledge of stage six questions in the sense that they understand when other speakers use them, but it has been observed that L2 learners will find it more efficient to fluently ask stage four questions than slowly stumble through the formation of more complex ones, such as, a tag question.

Four Linguistic Areas Researched in Psycholinguistics

Most of the research in psycholinguistics focuses on four areas of language use: morpho-syntax, pragmatics, phonology, and the lexicon. The movement and insertion of words from declarative to interrogative clauses (5–23) is an appropriate illustration of the relationship of morphology (the way words change) and syntax (the way words are arranged in a sentence). The subject–verb agreement rules related to *do*-support are certainly important, but failing to apply all of the rules does not tend to inhibit comprehension, rather it marks the speaker as nonnative (e.g., **Does you want some gum?*). The change of *do* to *does* is a morphological issue while the requirement to change it is derived from the syntactic rule of subject–verb agreement. Since it belongs to the same grammatical process where the order of the words in the sentence influence how the words themselves change (from *does* to *do*), it is referred to as *morpho-syntactic*.

Although it may pass under our level of consciousness, tag questions have been observed in American English to serve, among other things, as a politeness marker (Holmes 1995). This means that considering the many options a speaker has when forming a question, such as (27), is used more frequently to hedge in a conversation or gently ask or suggest something than in (28 and 29).

(27) *The keys are in the drawer, aren't they?*
(28) *Where are the keys?*
(29) *Are the keys in the drawer?*

The use of any type of grammatical formation (or any type of language style or speech register) to communicate connotational meaning based on the interpretation of the social context is related to the study of pragmatics. The social and interactional norms that are reified, flouted, and/or negotiated in face-to-face speech encounters follow their own type of pragmatic rules in the sense that there is a tendency to speak in a certain way during certain occasions and among certain people. Although it is not prescribed in a formal sense to use tag questions to convey politeness (for example, it is not taught as such in the American school system), it has emerged as an option. For native English speakers, tag questions were acquired naturally and without explicit instruction. Our ability to use them in appropriate contexts to convey politeness or hedge a topic or sentiment, was also acquired below our level of consciousness. Second language learners of English, however, would need to learn the *when's*, *where's*, and *why's* of the pragmatic rules of American English in addition to the already complex grammatical rules. For cognitive linguists, the fact that pragmatic knowledge is stored in a different region of the brain than grammar has a number of implications for other aspects of language use. The decline of working memory in the aging brain raises various questions of how cognitive changes affect linguistic knowledge and at what cost to the other neurolinguistic regions of the brain.

Phonology, the study of the sound system in a language, is indelibly linked to both the perception (acoustic phonology) and production (articulatory phonology) of language and the aging body. As elements of the auditory system begin to age, speech is perceived in a different manner just as the functional range of the jaw, gums, tongue and vocal chords changes and affects speech production. In second language acquisition, the brain uses phonological information as another representation of meaning to aid the cognitive load in working memory (Bigelow et al. 2006). For example, words that have been read and thus visually stored in the brain, rely on only one particular cognitive function to decode and retrieve the meaning of the word. If the visual regions could be aided by another source, such as the sounds of the language, then together visual and auditory information can extend working memory, and give sufficient time for the brain to perform other cognitive tasks related to language (Salthouse 1987; Bigelow et al. 2006). This process is referred to as a "phonological loop" in that the auditory information is looped into other resources in short-term working memory. For this reason, tests on phonology for second language learners and aging L1 speakers have sought to correlate language use capabilities and the level of phonological awareness. As hearing capabilities decrease, speakers can no longer rely on the phonological loop to help the brain process linguistic input and, therefore, other parts of the brain (examining visual cues during speech encounters more vigilantly) will carry more of the cognitive load of meaning making.

Finally, the lexicon, a term used in linguistics for vocabulary knowledge, is one aspect of language that does not decline in old age and in fact has been shown to grow (Burke and Peters 1986; Schaie 1996; Park 1998). The lexicon has been discussed as a separate functional entity from grammar for well over a century. It was even in the 19th century that researchers, such as Jean-Baptiste Bouillaud, Ernest Aubertin, Paul Broca, and Karl Wernicke, theorized the localization of language functions in different regions of the brain. One may wonder why the phonological and morpho-syntactic skills that are learned and mastered throughout life begin to decline in old age, yet the networks in our brain that have been acquired lexical items (i.e., words) do not tends to decline during the various stages of aging. Grammar rules are finite and follow a pattern in which you can plug in different words and use them endlessly. Words, on the other hand, have been learned piecemeal where every single word had to be learned and remembered one at a time, unlike the productively recycled rules of grammar. For this reason, it has been proposed that the lexicon is stored in a separate region of the brain though researchers continue to propose new models of the mental lexicon for L1 and L2 vocabulary development (Wolter 2001).

Research in SLA and Cognition

The Critical Period Hypothesis

> Sometimes we feel that our brains cannot do it. We try to learn English, but we cannot remember words like we did when we were children. You are a professor of language. You read the studies about language and the brain. What do you think? Are children's brains like sponges? Are old people's brains like dirty rags? Where do the words go after I learn them? I cannot seem to find them, you know.

Clara, now in her late sixties, is making reference to what is known as a "strong version" of the critical period hypothesis, which states that a child's brain undergoes a lateralization process during puberty, assigning particular cognitive tasks to the left and right hemispheres. The left hemisphere is considered to be more powerful in a computational sense than the right. The interaction among various levels of linguistic representation requires more mental processing capabilities for which the left hemisphere is more equipped to perform. The right hemisphere, which processes visuospatial information, pragmatics, intonation, and some lexical items, plays a role in decoding texts and interpreting other semiotic cues in communication events; however, the linguistic information reviewed in the previous section (morphology, syntax, phonology, and most of the lexicon), is processed in the highly specialized left hemisphere.

The initial investigations in brain plasticity monitored the capacity this organ has to redistribute particular functions after head trauma or severe brain injury. The work of Lenneberg (1967) demonstrated how a child's brain was typically successful in delegating linguistic functions to other areas of the brain after severe injuries to the left hemisphere known to be related to language perception and production; head trauma to adults usually results in impaired language use. More recent studies would appear to lend support to the critical period hypothesis when language acquisition between adults and children are compared with cognitive aptitude, such as working memory, processing speed, and executive control (see below). The success of an adult learning a second language is influenced by their level of aptitude while children will learn their L2 regardless of difference in aptitude (DeKeyser et al. 2010). These results suggest that at a minimum, children, and adults learn languages differently, and as such, the critical period hypothesis for language acquisition has been connected to Noam Chomsky's ideas of biologically endowed grammar among all humans who are exposed to a baseline of input during critical maturational developments. Therefore, the nativists argue that once the brain has been lateralized, the window of language acquisition closes and every year afterwards the input of a second language is processed less efficiently than in a child's brain.

The critical period hypothesis has gained wide recognition in the research community as well as in the public as can be observed by Clara who likens the adult brain to dirty rags. For bilinguals who reflect on their own language acquisition process, whether during childhood, adolescence, prime-of-life, or old age, the idea that learning was easier during youth is quite intuitively satisfying. When you compare those who started learning their L2 at different stages of their lifespan, the ones who began earlier tend to speak with little to no accent while the adult L2 speakers often times speak with a foreign accent for the rest of their lives.

Interactionalism and Environmental Factors

Interactional psychologists have challenged the strong version of the critical period hypothesis with several compelling observations that would explain the difference in attainment levels, such as foreign accents and native-like pronunciation. Although several essential cognitive developments occur during childhood and adolescence that would give the appearance of an innate advantage, the linguistic environments are strikingly different for children and adults and could help explain the age-attainment relationship among L2 learners.

Children tend to participate in daily L2 interactions at school with teachers whose profession is dedicated to their language growth. They receive several hours of modified speech that is appropriately slowed down and repeated based on their perceived L2 proficiency level. When the burden of speaking in the L2 is overwhelming, children are typically allowed to remain silent either by pretending they are not feeling well, or if they are young enough, entering into an imaginary world of play that is deemed normal behavior for their age. It is after several years of these daily interactions with other peer interlocutors as well as developmentally minded L2 media that they begin to sound native-like and speak fluently.

Adults on the other hand are not afforded such linguistically rich interactions and environments. If they find themselves working with other speakers of their native language, they may not even be exposed to daily L2 input or create relationships with L2 speakers who would take the time to sustain long conversations that approximate to their level of proficiency. Applied linguists characterize this necessary relationship building as "recruiting interlocutors" or in more colloquial terms, "finding friends." Native English speakers, for example, who are learning Japanese as their L2, would not have much success if after having spent a year in Japan, they never created actual relationships with any Japanese speakers. Interactionists maintain that the L2 acquisition process is severely limited if the only input available to the learner is passively watching Japanese TV; the level of Japanese would be too advanced and thereby essentially useless without comprehensible input. Interaction where two speakers are negotiating the meaning of things in the target language is considered to be an ideal environment for language learning. It tends to happen with children at school throughout the day. Yet, it happens less frequently among adult learners. Considering the stark contrast in language environments, interactionists wonder how adults would perform if they had the privilege to live 7–10 years in children's L2 world which is rich with modified (child-directed) speech, patient and playful interlocutors, robust interactional opportunities, and the freedom to experiment with language production without worrying about the stigma of making repeated pragmatic and linguistic blunders.

Language Acquisition and Attrition Among Older Adults

The Paucity of Research on Late-Life Language Learning

When the four language areas (morpho-syntax, pragmatics, phonology, and the lexicon) are applied to research on language and the brain, subjects range from newborns to early adults due to interest in inquiries relating to the critical period hypothesis. A relatively miniscule number of studies have focused on adults 30 years or older. Older adults (65+) are even more understudied. When they *are* invited to participate in a research study, they function as control groups for the speakers with various forms of dementia and other age-related diseases. As such, when non-pathologically aging subjects are included, their results are rarely compared to middle-age adults, another scarcely studied cohort. As a result, a comparatively small number of studies have brought attention to the issues of aging and individual L2 learning (Bialystok et al. 2005). Nearly all of these studies, which amount to few, center on monolingual subjects losing their L1 (native) language. They are not focused on older adults acquiring a nonnative language. Thus, the participants in our study, who are older adults learning their second language later in life, are quite "invisible" in the annals of cognitive aging and SLA research. What we do know comes from correlations between traditional language variables of aptitude tests that have historically linked decreased working memory to both L1 attrition and L2 acquisition.

Language Aptitude in Late-Life L2 Learning

> It's a very difficult topic for us. It scares us to study. Not understanding simple questions, it's terrible. It's ugly. It's a horrible experience. Even if my family says, "Have a better attitude". It doesn't help. It's just ugly. I don't know if I'm able to do this.

At 63-years-old, Irene highlights the issue of the ease and fluidity of learning in old age. This was a theme brought up by many of our older adults as they often interpret their own difficulties in language learning to a "slower brain." Two major cognitive dichotomies have been employed to sketch the general processes of the aging brain: (1) fluid intelligence versus crystallized intelligence and (2) short-term working memory versus long-term memory. Fluid intelligence (which includes short-term working memory, executive function, and processing speed) has been shown to decline starting in the third and fourth decades of life (Craik and Trehub 1982; Salthouse 1985; Cavanaugh 2010). Crystallized intelligence and long-term memory typically maintain, and in some cases increase, levels of functionality in non-pathologically aging brains. We will briefly review the more systematic cognitive declines and how they have been applied in SLA research before addressing the cognitive resiliencies that healthy aging offers the older adult L2 learner.

Fluid Intelligence and Working Memory

The *fluid* in *fluid cognition* makes reference to a person's ability to apply inductive reasoning to learn new information, identify relationships, solve problems in novel situations, and manipulate the surrounding environment. The primary cognitive domains associated with fluid intelligence are psychomotor skills, processing speed, executive function, and working memory. Since acquiring a second language requires a learner to reason and problem-solve in unfamiliar contexts, fluid intelligence has been widely studied as a central factor in L2 development.

Working memory involves retaining elements of information for short periods of time (i.e., less than 1 min or so) in order to process and manipulate this information. Once these elements are used, the information dissipates between 0 and 30s for recency memory and 30–60s for primacy memory. Older adults tend to score lower than younger cohorts on ordering and comprehending series of letters, figures, and numbers (Salthouse et al. 1989). For instance, estimating the total cost for 25+ items in a shopping cart before checking out at the supermarket requires a significant level of working memory capability. Although the task of rounding the prices up and adding them together is an intellectually simple task, a certain level of speed is required so that the running tally is not forgotten. Various kinds of measures have been used to determine processing speed—speed of reacting, speed in behaving, speed in thinking, perceptual speed, movement time—and have been used to test a wide range of common and novel tasks, from tying shoe laces to dialing a number on different kinds of telephones.

In the example of the price estimation tasks in the supermarket, one final cognitive domain interacts with processing speed and working memory to make fluid reasoning function properly: executive function. While adding the prices of 25 grocery items needs to be accomplished quickly for the working memory to process the information before it is forgotten, a certain level of planning, organizing, reasoning, and self-monitoring is essential. If too much time is spent debating whether to round up or round down an item that costs $4.42, then precious time could be wasted. If a buzzing or ringing phone draws your attention away from the task at hand, working memory will probably have erased these digits by the time the task is continued. Executive abilities allow us to engage in purposeful, self-serving behavior that demands mental flexibility in solving problem and producing novel responses.

Fluid intelligence, working memory, processing speed, and executive function all experience systematic neurological declines throughout adulthood and degrade in old age (Grady and Craik 2000; Kemper et al. 2001; Hakuta et al. 2003; Salthouse 2004, 2010). It is important to emphasize once again that the component skills associable to linguistic knowledge center on L1 attrition. More direct processing of meaning occurs when a person's first language is used and for this reason many of the linguistic skills are stored in procedural memory. During the early stages of L2 development, declarative memory is typically maximized until some of the language functions can be automatized and carried out by procedural memory.

Until the brain can organize the L2 knowledge in relation to the emergent interlanguage development, working memory, and memorization continue to function as the main processing mechanism.

The scaffolding of language learning is supported by simpler component skills that build on each other, similar to the developmental stages of English question formation. At the beginning of English language learning, stage one and two questions will require that fluid intelligence to allocate and inhibit attention to morpho-syntactic and phonological rules. With continued practice, less working memory will be needed when these component skills become more automatic and form part of the learner's procedural memory. When subject–verb inversion is mastered, less attentional effort will be required, giving more capacity for working memory to process other high-order component skills such as stage four and five questions which require *do*-support and syntactic movement with larger phrasal constituencies. When working memory begins to decline, the controlled processing of component skills poses a greater challenge for L2 learners and lowers the individual's aptitude (Miyake and Friedman 1998; Craik and Bialystok 2005). Since interaction with other target language speakers is considered ideal language input, lower working memory reduces the learner's ability to benefit from the feedback that is offered by these interlocutors (Ellis 2005; Sagarra 2007; Mackey et al. 2012).

In the following example, Marcela appears to be concentrating on the correct word selection and phonological information in the sentence. Although the instructor is trying to point out a subject–verb agreement rule in English (i.e., *My children come* vs. *My children comes*), she may not have the working memory capacity at this stage of her L2 development to even notice the intention of the teacher's feedback.

L1	Marcela	*My ch-childrens…my childrens many times comes to home*
L2	Instructor	*Your children many times come home…come home and-*
L3	Marcela	*Yes, my childrens comes home tired*
L4	Instructor	*My children*
L5	Marcela	*My children*
L6	Instructor	*My children come home*
L7	Marcela	*My children comes home*
L8	Instructor	*My children come home tired*
L9	Marcela	*My children comes home tired*

With regard to grammar, working memory has been linked to acquiring syntactic dependencies (such as the subject–verb agreement issues in the above example) as well as other morphological dependencies and lexical items (Williams and Lovatt 2003). Several studies have correlated working memory with L2 aptitude since it affords learners the necessary efficiency to perceive, process, and produce language in real time (Horn et al. 1981; Craik and Trehub 1982; Gregpore and Van der Linden 1997; Mackey et al. 2010). L2 learners with stronger L1 literacy skills have been observed to attain higher levels of proficiency and do so in a shorter time period (Bigelow et al. 2006). It is thought that literacy aids how we encode sounds as well as other forms of input by storing the information in alternate formats. Short-term working memory increases when multiple formats can be used to help make information available for working memory to process.

Adults in general are exposed to less qualitative and quantitative L2 input than children who receive ample modified input and output opportunities in school and play settings. In addition to the poorer input, they are utilizing lower powered working memory capabilities. When comparing the mean and standard deviations of working memory among older adults and college aged students, the lowest scores for listening span tasks remain higher than the highest scores for older adults (Mackey et al. 2002, 2012). When Irene and Clara reflect on their own declining capabilities of the working memory features they have been accustomed to using their entire life, they may be accurate in their meta-cognitive assessment, that is, their brain's organization of knowledge is undergoing a type of realignment as they learn English.

Fortunately, working memory capacity is not the only cognitive-based mechanism involved in SLA. Several researchers have found evidence of compensatory strategies that reorganize the functions of particular tasks to better fit processing mechanisms. Based solely on the low working memory scores of older adults, one would predict that they would be quite atrocious at second language learning while in fact their rate of language acquisition and ultimate attainment are not much below the mean of younger adults (Park 1998). In the following section, we review the strengths of the aging brain and the compensatory though effective additional platforms of language processing and retrieval.

Crystallized Intelligence and Long-Term Memory

> My grandchildren bought me a smartphone. I was very scared to use it. I thought I was going to break it or scratch it or something. But then my girlfriend showed me how to download apps. I even figured out how to track my son so that I know what part of the city he is in. I have learned to look up recipes and send emojis with text messages to my grandchildren. I know there are things that I cannot do. That's fine. I use it more than what I ever thought I would.

Another name for crystallized intelligence is "acculturation knowledge," and perhaps it helps describe an aspect of human cognition that covers a wide range of abilities and skills. Lizbeth, who is 63-years-old, reflects on the amazing ability to learn new skills at any age. This makes us aware that one battery of tests accurately samples the breadth and depth of this intelligence which includes: vocabulary, knowledge of language, information about dominant culture, concepts, listening comprehension, esoteric knowledge, as well as knowledge in the sciences, social studies, literature, and humanities. As would be expected, crystallized intelligence accumulates over time and correlates with education, social class, and social networks. Long-term memory, which encodes and consolidates information, refers to the ability to fluently retrieve stored knowledge and is indicative of crystallized intelligence. Similar to recency and primacy measures in working memory, long-term memory examines two periods: information encodes, consolidated, and stored information (1) several minutes and hours (e.g., names of people and characters in story) and (2) many months and years after the event (e.g., concepts, ideas, narratives).

Since life experience plays a central role in developing crystallized intelligence, older adults outperform younger adults on tests that require this kind of knowledge (Salthouse 2012). Having observed more examples of personality types, speech acts, crises, personal growth, and the like, older adults are equipped to make important decisions based on the prior experience and lessons learned (Park 1998). Their increased tolerance to ambiguity and openness to different perspectives helps them manage communication decisions in their second language (Mackey et al. 2012). While children may have greater brain plasticity, a less solidified ego, weaker L2 inhibitions, and more modified input considered ideal for language learning, adults have far superior analytic abilities, more sophisticated pragmatic skills, greater knowledge of the world and human behavior, and a better understanding of the various registers and styles of their native language (Vaid 1986). With improvement of crystallized intelligence into the sixth and seventh year of life (Botwinick 1978; Rabbitt and Abson 1991; Schaie 1996), sometimes into the 80's (Kaufman 1990), we are left to ask two important questions: (1) What is the relationship between crystallized knowledge, long-term memory, and second language learning? and (2) In what ways might crystallized knowledge compensate for the decline in fluid intelligence and working memory as it relates to SLA?

A large percentage of SLA research focuses on ultimate achievement rather than rate of acquisition at novice, intermediate, and advance levels (Snow and Hoefnagel-Hohle 1977). Several studies have demonstrated that both adolescents and adults outperform children in second language learning the first year of exposure to the language (Snow and Hoefnagel-Hohle 1977, 1978; Krashen et al. 1979). Considering that children are charged with learning a language system (both phonological and orthographic representations) and the conceptual knowledge that is conveyed by language, adults are privileged with superior life and world experiences. For instance, adults have been exposed to thousands of stories and are able to predict character development, recognize irony and humor, locate the story historically and geographically, and even describe the genre it may belong. When stories in a second language are presented to adults, they are in a position to hypothesize about the character and the things they might do in the plot. They may fill in the blank when words or meanings are unfamiliar to them and steer their attention to comprehending the overall gist and morale. In contrast, when children find the L2 input too advanced, they may reallocate their attention to details unrelated to the plot or even to the story as a speech event. If the language is understood by them, other details about the characters and background might be novel information and require them to concentrate on semantic content over the representation of the language itself.

Children do outperform other age cohorts (adults of all ages) in the long term. Yet, the first year of exposure to the L2 is more efficiently processed by adults due to their accumulated knowledge. Breaking down the stages of language acquisition sheds light on what we mean by "better" learners. Should we focus on phonological production, such as pronunciation and near-native intonation patterns or will acquisition be measured by particular grammar-based variables, such as particular aspects of question formation? Will speech fluency be weighed more heavily than functional achievements of performing language appropriately in dynamic social settings? Since many learners do not intend to sound like a native speaker, why do we hold all learners to that idealized standard?

The relative weight of crystallized intelligence in SLA remains poorly theorized and under-investigated, though evidence does suggest that older adults develop compensatory skills in lieu of declining ones. Salthouse (1985) examined typists in training from various age cohorts. Older adults scored lower in skills that would appear to benefit typing, such as finger-tapping speed, choice-reaction time, and digit-symbol substitution ability; however, their typing actually matched other cohorts in both accuracy and speed. As it turns out, older adults' relatively longer eye spans allowed them to segment the text into more substantive chunks. Whether Salthouse's work on typing exists as an analogy of the compensatory strategies older adults might employ in learning a second language or as evidence that the aging brain distributes cognitive tasks to different cognitive domains, the results are encouraging. Lizbeth's adaptation to new cell phone technology underscores the importance of learner strategies, confidence, and sensible pedagogy. It was her friend after all, and not her grandchildren, who taught her how to navigate the initial hurdles of smart phone usage. Older adults have proven to excel in leadership positions that demand acumen, precision, and higher order cognitive skills. In light of the declines of fluid reasoning and working memory, either the aging brain restructures to continue development of expertise (Horn and Masunaga 2000) or the cognitive models researchers use to measure features of human intelligence need to be recalibrated.

Challenges and Issues with Late-Life SLA Research

Cognitive health is linked to the use, maintenance, and learning of a speaker's L1 and L2; yet when we examine successful L2 learners beyond the basic cognitive threshold, there lie other factors that influence SLA and L2 performance. Researchers have highlighted epistemological challenges of correlating cognitive aging effects with other sociocultural and extralinguistic variables. In part, the issue is muddied by the very definition of "age" since functional age does not always correspond with chronological age. A person's mental capabilities may function at the level of a 35-year-old even though they may have been born 50 years ago, just as the converse may occur with rapidly aging individuals (Vasunilashorn and Crimmins 2008). Accounting for the rate of functional aging variability has been putatively resolved with larger sample sizes and more responsible statistical applications. Yet, many of these methods that account for functional aging are not applied consistently across studies (Mackey et al. 2012). Furthermore, the effects of early-onset dementia are often times present several years, even decades, before they are properly diagnosed by researchers. Verifying that all of the subjects truly represent the normal, non-pathologically aging brain has been cause for some concern.

Personality characteristics, motivation, interactional styles, and appropriate social conditions for language learning all play important roles in the overall success of acquiring a second language. Different compensatory strategies, such as socio-pragmatic skills, fill in the gap when other, more relied-upon cognitive functions (i.e., fluid intelligence, short-term working memory) begin to decline. In thinking about the larger purpose of communicating in a second language, researchers have reconsidered how "success" in language learning is defined and how we ought to go about measuring "rate of acquisition." The reasons for learning English for older adults may vary significantly from those of younger adults or adolescents. Older adults may hope to simply communicate basic information to medical professionals or playfully interact and care for young grandchildren in a second language. Younger learners, on the other hand, may focus on occupation-oriented speech registers, technical jargon, and mastery of social media to name a few factors. The progress that is achieved in learning particular communicative registers in situated modalities may generate inaccurate results in psycholinguistic and cognitive batteries. For example, even under the cognitive domain of central executive function, older adults show no degradation in their ability to interpret proverbs, retell fables, perceive similarities, and manipulate familiar expert knowledge (Horn and Masunaga 2000). Despite speech production being widely cited as declining in old age, the 80-somethings have demonstrated prime-of-life levels of metaphoric language and complex syntactic structures in retelling the narratives of fables as well as explaining the underlying connotational meanings.

SLA research has at the very least problematized the central questions related to rate, accuracy, and quality of language learning in addition to the methods we use to measure them. Studies on the critical period of language acquisition are proposing an earlier timeframe for phonological acquisition than for morphology and syntax. The acquisition of L1 or L2 vocabulary has no observable critical period and tends to increase throughout the lifespan (Horn and Masunaga 2000). Such insights make it difficult to talk in general terms about the acquisition of a second language since different components may be developed at different rates in the learner's life stages, thus producing variable effects on the entire interlanguage system. With over 20 years of experimental research, researchers have found significant asymmetries between language production and perception; retrieval of phonological and orthographic information decline with age while comprehension and perception remained stable.

It has been noted that adult L2 learners tend to operate from strongly automatized L1 systems (given the decades they have used it for a range of communicative purposes) that may enhance L2 learning (Mackey et al. 2012). Experience in life and accumulated knowledge, variables that would be difficult to measure but can be assumed to accompany old age, have a psychological measurable effect on the brain in that it reduces the need for novel problem solving. Having had numerous similar experiences in life, several activities become an automatized process that requires less cognitive effort for novel problem solving (Salthouse 2004).

Articulating the relationship between older adults' general decline in several cognitive domains and their continued growth of acculturate knowledge continues to prove difficult in most research studies (Park 1998; Horn and Masunaga 2000). The rate of decline in processing speed and working memory, for example, varies more among older adults than in any other age cohort. People age in different ways and at different stages of their lives which complicates the application of results that are based on the statistical means (Hararda 2013). Heterogeneity in rate and onset of cognitive degradation exists alongside other environmental considerations of communicative needs during the different stages of life. In learning a second language, a person can never be said to have reached an endpoint in attaining complete acquisition. As we learn new speech and written registers, technical jargon, emergent idioms, field-specific concepts, and tomorrow's slang words, our internalized language systems reorganize the cognitive functions of perceiving and producing new language for new purposes.

The social turn in SLA has influenced experimental research in psycholinguistics by focusing on the ways in which interpersonal communication and social interaction maintains high levels of cognitive function throughout the development of SLA. Recently, research has begun to focus on the relationship of interactional processes and second language development among older adult speakers (Mackey and Philp 1998; Mackey et al. 2000, 2003, 2010; DeKeyser et al. 2010; Mackey and Sachs 2012). While working memory is assumed to act as the primitive for processing efficiency and cognitive function, it has been more widely accepted to divorce separate intelligences from a single unitary process. Cognitive domains appear to decline at varied rates and timeframes among individuals which suggests that other social factors play definitive roles in how older adults acquire language (DeKeyser et al. 2010; Mackey and Sachs 2012). A number of significant disparities in language learning opportunities exist between younger and older immigrants. The interactions of these extralinguistic variables, though difficult to control in experimental studies, may help explain the heterogeneous rates of cognitive decline and L2 attainment patterns.

Beyond a Deficit-Model

When older adult L2 learners meta-cognitively assess their linguistic aptitude, ideas inculcated through deficit-oriented discourses remains an intrepid catalyst for self-doubt and pessimism. Indirect messages about what older Spanish-speaking immigrants are capable of achieving circulate in numerous spaces throughout their daily lives. Even finding an adult ESL class to attend is rather difficult as they are rarely advertised on the radio, billboards, newspapers, websites, churches, community recreation centers, or assisted living facilities. Most immigrants are not aware that such courses even exist or that they are designed for older learners such as themselves. Coupled with the fact that the cognitive behavior of older adults is characterized by habitual patterns of behavior and overlearned skills (Grady and Craik 2000), learning a complex system such as a new language, age-advanced Spanish monolinguals are confronted with greater obstacles to independent living.

Some of the variability in cognitive ability among individuals of the same age cohort may be attributable to genetic composition. In addition to genetics, other physiological and psychological pathologies, such as auditory and visual deterioration, motor skills related to speech production, and physical mobility, may spur cognitive impairment and decline. Yet, several behaviors and activities have been linked to healthy cognitive aging and are typically cited in public health literatures: eating balanced meals, exercising daily, cultivating social relationships, and avoiding highly stressful environments are usually at the top of the list. In the context of adult ESL programs, developing a credible counter-narrative to an overly cognitive discourse will help reset learners' outlook on the possibility of learning and using a second language. English learners who identify less with the target language culture are typically less motivated to learn the language. A learner's affective position to the target language is also a variable that is rarely measured in experimental research and represents the driving force behind a learner's motivation to seek out new social encounters. In our book, we highlight the benefits of their advanced crystallized knowledge and the role of social-interactional factors, such as their tendency to employ more interactional moves and comprehension checks in face-to-face interactions (Oliver 1998). This allows us to better understand the impact of learners' affective dispositions and social life on SLA efficacy. Subsequent chapters examine the extra-cognitive dimensions to language learning. We argue that a full accounting of the possibilities and challenges to later-life language acquisition requires an in-depth focus on the everyday interactional work done by older adult learners and the contextual spaces in which this social activity takes place.

References

Bialystok, E., Martin, M. M., & Viswanathan, M. (2005). Bilingualism across the lifespan: The rise and fall of inhibitory control. *International Journal of Bilingualism, 9*, 103–119.

Bigelow, M., del Mas, B., Hansen, K., & Tarone, E. (2006). Literacy and the processing of oral recasts in SLA. *TESOL Quarterly, 40*, 1–25.

Botwinick, J. (1978). *Aging and behavior: A comprehensive integration of research findings*. New York: Springer.

Burke, D. M., & Peters, L. (1986). Word associations in old age: Evidence for consistency in semantic encoding during adulthood. *Psychology and Aging, 4*, 283–292.

Cavanaugh, J. C. (2010). *Adult development and aging (6th edition) Boston*. MA: Wadsworth Publishing.

Craik, F. I. M., & Trehub, S. (Eds.). (1982). *Aging and cognitive processes*. New York: Plenum.

Craik, F. I. M., & Bialystok, E. (2005). Intelligence and executive control: Evidence from aging and bilingualism. *Cortex, 41*, 222–224.

DeKeyser, R., Alfi-Shabtay, I., & Ravid, D. (2010). Cross-linguistic evidence for the nature of age effects in second language acquisition. *Applied Psycholinguistics, 31*, 413–438.

Ellis, N. C. (2005). At the interface: Dynamic interactions of explicit and implicit language knowledge. *Studies in Second Language Acquisition, 27*, 305–352.

Grady, C. L., & Craik, F. I. M. (2000). Changes in memory processing with age. *Psychological Review, 103*, 403–428.

Gregpore, J., & Van der Linden, M. (1997). Effect of age on forward and backward digit spans. *Aging, Neuropsychology, and Cognition, 4*, 140–149.

Hakuta, K., Bialystok, E., & Wiley, E. (2003). Critical evidence: A test of the critical-period hypothesis for second-language acquisition. *Psychological Science, 14*, 31–38.

Holmes, J. (1995). *Women, men, and politeness*. New York: Taylor & Francis.

Horn, J. L., Donaldson, G., & Engstrom, R. (1981). Apprehension, memory and fluid intelligence decline in adulthood. *Research in Aging, 3*, 33–84.

Horn, J., & Masunaga, H. (2000). New directions for research into aging and intelligence: The development of expertise. In T. Perfect & E. Maylor (Eds.), *Models of cognitive aging* (pp. 124–159). Oxford: Oxford University Press.

Kaufman, A. S. (1990). *Assessing adolescent and adult intelligence*. Boston, MA: Allyn and Bacon.

Kemper, S., Greiner, L. H., Marquis, J. G., Prenovost, K., & Mitzner, T. L. (2001). Language decline across the life span: Findings from the Nun study. *Psychology and Aging, 16*, 227–239.

Krashen, S., Long, M., & Scarcella, R. (1979). Age, rate, and eventual attainment in second language acquisition. *TESOL Quarterly, 13*, 573–582.

Lenneberg, E. H. (1967). *Biological foundations of language*. New York: Wiley.

Mackey, A., Abbuhl, R., & Gass, S. M. (2012). Interactionist approaches. In S. Gass & A. Mackey (Eds.), *The Routledge handbook of second language acquisition* (pp. 7–23). New York, NY: Routledge.

Mackey, A., Adams, R., Stafford, C., & Winke, P. (2010). Exploring the relationship between modified output and working memory capacity. *Language Learning, 60*, 501–533.

Miyake, A., & Friedman, N. P. (1998). Individual differences in second language proficiency: Working memory as language aptitude. In A. F. Healy & L. E. Bourne (Eds.), *Foreign language learning: Psycholinguistic studies on training and retention* (pp. 339–364). Mahwah, NJ: Erlbaum.

Mackey, A., Gass, S. M., & McDonough, K. (2000). How do learners perceive interactional feedback? *Studies in Second Language Acquisition, 22*(4), 471–497.

Mackey, A., Oliver, R., & Leeman, J. (2003). Interactional input and the incorporation of feedback: An exploration of NS-NNS and NNS-NNS adult and child dyads. *Language Learning, 53*, 35–66.

Mackey, A., & Philp, J. (1998). Conversational interaction and second language development: Recasts, responses and red herrings? *The Modern Language Journal, 82*(3), 338–356.

Mackey, A., Philp, J., Egi, T., Fujii, A., & Tatsumi, T. (2002). Individual differences in working memory, noticing of interactional feedback and L2 development. In P. Robinson (Ed.), *Individual differences and instructed language learning* (pp. 181–209). Philadelphia: Benjamins.

Mackey, A., & Sachs, R. (2012). Older learners in SLA research: A first look at working memory, feedback, and L2 development. *Language Learning, 62*(3), 704–740.

Oliver, R. (1998). Negotiation of meaning in child interactions. *Modern Language Journal, 82*, 372–386.

Park, D. C. (1998). Cognitive aging, processing resources, and self-report. In N. Schwarz, D. C. Park, B. Knauper, & S. Sudman (Eds.), *Aging, cognition and self-report* (pp. 45–69). Washington, DC: Psychology Press.

Pienemann, M. (1989). Is language teachable? Psycholinguistic experiments and hypotheses. *Applied Linguistics, 10*, 52–79.

References

Pienemann, M., Johnston, M., & Brindley, G. (1988). Constructing an acquisition-based procedure for second language assessment. *Studies in Second Language Acquisition, 10,* 217–243.

Rabbitt, P., & Abson, V. (1991). Do older people know how good they are? *British Journal of Psychology, 82,* 137–151.

Sagarra, N. (2007). From CALL to face-to-face interaction: The effect of computer-delivered recasts and working memory on L2 development. In A. Mackey (Ed.), *Conversational interaction in second language acquisition: A collection of empirical studies* (pp. 229–248). Oxford: Oxford University Press.

Salthouse, T. A. (1985). Speed of behavior and its implications for cognition. In J. E. Birren & K. W. Schaie (Eds.), *Handbook of the psychology of aging.* New York: Reinhold.

Salthouse, T. A. (1987). The roe of representations in age differences in analogical reasoning. *Psychology and Aging, 2,* 357–367.

Salthouse, T. A. (2004). What and when of cognitive aging. *Current Directions in Psychological Science, 13,* 140–144.

Salthouse, T. A. (2010). Selective review of cognitive aging. *Journal of International Neuropsychological Society, 16,* 754–760.

Salthouse, T. A. (2012). Consequences of age-related cognitive declines. *Annual Review of Psychology, 63,* 201–226.

Salthouse, T. A., Michell, D. R., Skovronek, E., & Babcock, R. L. (1989). Effects of adult age and working memory on reasoning and spatial abilities. *Journal of Experimental Psychology. Learning, Memory, and Cognition, 15,* 507–516.

Schaie, K. W. (1996). *Intellectual development in adulthood: The Seattle longitudinal study.* Cambridge: Cambridge University Press.

Snow, C., & Hoefnagel-Hohle, M. (1977). Age differences in the pronunciation of foreign sounds. *Language and Speech, 20,* 357–365.

Snow, C., & Hoefnagel-Hoehle, M. (1978). The critical period for language acquisition: Evidence from second language learning. *Child Development, 49,* 1114–1118.

Vaid, J. (Ed.). (1986). *Language processing in bilinguals: Psycholinguistic and neuropsychological perspectives.* Hillsdale, NJ: Erlbaum.

Vasunilashorn, S., & Crimmins, E. (2008). Biodemography: Integrating disciplines to explain aging. In V. L. Bengtson, D. Gans, N. M. Putney, & M. Silverstein (Eds.), *Handbook of theories of aging* (pp. 63–85). New York: Springer.

Williams, J. N., & Lovatt, P. (2003). Phonological memory and rule learning. *Language Learning, 53,* 67–121.

Wolter, B. (2001). Comparing the L1 and L2 mental lexicon: A depth of individual word knowledge model. *Studies in Second Language Acquisition, 23*(1), 41–69.

Chapter 5
Social Constructivism and the Role of Place for Immigrant Language Learners

> When I arrived here 20 years ago I wanted to learn English. I wanted to understand when people talked to me. Then I started to work when I learned a little bit .... I am retired and now all my life I'm around people who speak Spanish. The young people I know are not going to come to me and speak in English. They would say, "What am I going to talk to this old lady about?" .... I want to help my daughter. I want to understand my grandson! Now I come here [to the ESL class] and I feel I am learning. Although, you know, learning at an old age it is not easy.

In this excerpt, Clara, a 66-year-old woman, talks about her experiences learning English. Like other older immigrants in our study, she arrived with her family nearly two decades ago and still depends on her daughter to navigate some parts of her daily life, such as obtaining a state identification card, paying bills, visiting a medical specialist, or interacting with monolingual English speakers in consumer exchanges. During our interview, Clara self-disclosed that her age was a determinant factor for why people would not talk to her, describing herself as "boring" and "uninteresting" to younger interlocutors. These negative stances contrasted with Clara's enthusiasm in the ESL classroom. During a typical Saturday ESL class, she was a sharp, participative, and dedicated student. Clara expressed how her desire to learn English was mainly driven by gaining independence and becoming helpful within the family, especially with her grandson who was growing to use more English than Spanish. Clara's devalued stances about her elderly identity did not negatively influence her weekly attendance at the library which she saw as a "safe space" to interact with other language learners who were in the same situation. Within the ESL classroom she gained confidence about her ability to learn English and overcame the pressures of stereotypes that defined her as "too old to learn." It also allowed Clara to have aspirations for herself and her family. In short, the ESL classroom promoted a new self-concept, built on a conception of self-efficacy about speaking in English-dominant social spaces.

In Chap. 4 we reviewed the neurolinguistic evidence that correlated SLA aptitude with a general decline in working memory during the functional aging process. Experiments that task research subjects to produce "target words when cued by their definition" or "determine if each of a series of letter strings is a word" (Hasher and

Zacks 1988, pp. 193–194) are limited in their approach. The premise would be that "understanding and remembering are substantially impaired for older adults as compared to younger adults when a message is presented rapidly rather than slowly" (Hasher and Zacks 1988, pp. 193–194; Stine et al. 1986). These studies do not tend to control for other variables, such as "intelligence, education, life history, motivation, sensor integrity, mental status and vigor," which have been proven to have "a strong effect on performance in these [experimental] tasks" (Bayles and Kaszniak 1987, p. 152, cited in Coupland et al. 1991). Ignored in these studies is how Clara's social environment, for instance, has an impact on her language learning process together with the cognitive changes that have been observed to take place in aging.

Second language acquisition studies would also consider that psycholinguistic traits such as aptitude, motivation, personality traits, and personal learning strategies would have an effect on her ability to acquire language (Norton Peirce 1995). The experiences of Clara as an immigrant and older adult L2 learner who is trying to convince younger family members to speak in English with her would be obscured by conventional research designs that measure her L2 potential solely through performance levels on experimental cognitive tasks (Coupland et al. 1991).

In this chapter, we focus on the epistemological changes that sociolinguists have spearheaded since the 1990s that move beyond a cognitive deficit model to learning. This shift foregrounds the experiences we share in later chapters of our learner population in their social environment and how interactional stimulation and negotiation in the target language enhances their SLA processes (Block 2007; Norton and Toohey 2000; Pavlenko and Blackledge 2002). Second, we review literature on applied linguistics and aging which points to the significance of communication with the elderly. Socialization in old age is mediated by negative stereotypes and ageist attitudes that perpetuate narrow definitions about old age and intergenerational boundaries.

Socio-constructivist approaches to second language acquisition serve as a framework to our exploration of older adults' "aging in place" (Cutchin 2003). The idea of aging in place has been commonly used to denote the ideal of being able to remain at home during old age (Cutchin 2003). Additionally, environmental sociologists point to the importance of the people, institutions, networks, and resources available in the local spaces of older adults (Golant 2003; Lawton 1986; Scheidt and Norris-Baker 2003; Wiles et al. 2011). Life changes related to decline in physical mobility, the death of friends and close kin, and the need for immediate access to social services are mediated by the environmental places of the elderly. Spaces rich with social and material capital can help older persons' effort and ability at solving day-to-day challenges. Successfully meeting these everyday challenges can inform how persons renegotiate their identities as they manage life changes in old age (Wiles et al. 2011, p. 1).

In our analysis, we situate SLA in the spaces tied to an immigrant context and examine how linguistic barriers emerge in symbolic and structural ways. For example, limited access to local interlocutors presents learners with difficulties in their "right to speak" in everyday family interactions and in larger institutional contexts. As an alternative place, we present our ESL program as an emergent "safe space" where our older adult immigrant learners overcome the negative attitudes related to their marginalized social status and the behaviors of others who operate from the assumption that learning a language in old age is an impossible endeavor. We conclude by exploring the ramifications that attitudes in micro-interactions have on the self-conceptions of old age learners.

Socio-SLA: Social Constructivism in Adult L2 Learning

A critique to cognitive-based models of SLA started to emerge in the mid-1990s in a movement that is now referred to as "the social turn in SLA," an approach that promoted interdisciplinary investigation into how cultural and social aspects affect the various aspects of L2 learning (Block 2007; Norton 2000; Norton Peirce 1995; Pavlenko and Blackledge 2002). Bonnie Norton, the foundational figure in the socio-SLA movement, describes the problem as follows:

> SLA theorists have failed to explore the extent to which sexism, racism, and elitism influence the kinds of opportunities second language learners have to practice the target language and how immigrant language learners are frequently marginalized by members of the target language community (Norton Peirce 1995, p. 2).

Drawing on poststructuralist theory, the socio-SLA paradigm focuses on the challenges adult L2 learners face when trying to create relationships with target language speakers who have the potential of offering them the necessary linguistic input to practice, maintain, and improve their communication skills. Sociocultural approaches to language acquisition emphasize how in the immigrant environment social inequality between target language learners and native speakers shape the learning processes and outcomes of an individual (Norton Peirce 1995). For socio-SLA, the focus is on the interactional context and sociopolitical dynamics between immigrant groups and mainstream society. Examining the linguistic interactions between learners and native speakers at a local level allows researchers to demonstrate how L2 learners construct and subvert their identities.

Socio-constructivist perspectives, an offshoot of poststructuralist theory, complements our study of minority aging by centering the role of language socialization in older adults' learning. Socio-SLA studies contend that social challenges for immigrant language learners is more overwhelming than previously described and unsuccessful attempts at relationship building with target language speakers isolates learners from critical socialization opportunities (Norton 2000). L2 aptitude, defined as cognitive skills, such as working memory, may be an ineffectual predictor of L2 attainment if the learner is not exposed to modified input or given space to perform and modify output with advanced target language speakers. Drawing from Bourdieu's (1977) concept of the "right to speak" and the richly contextualized ethnographies of Canadian immigrants, Norton (2000) illustrates how L2 learning was marked by how others positioned themselves during routinized speech acts. In their narratives, immigrants depicted their interactions with native interlocutors as delegitimizing encounters; their low social status, accent in English, and communicative styles produce, at best, condescending foreigner talk and, at worst, a complete avoidance and no engagement at all. Language as a political practice moves beyond the delivery of encoded phonemes for denotational interpretations of meaning; a speaker's utterance is valued by their affiliation to particular social groups and the connotative or associable meaning that these groups embody for the interlocutor (Norton 2000). Social approaches to SLA also yield reconceptualizations of traditional cognitive notions, such as "motivation," "affect," and "personality types," which had been examined only through a psycholinguistic lenses. For Norton (2000), the cognitive basis of "motivation" does not capture "the complex relationship between relations of power, identity, and language learning." Using the term "investment," Norton Peirce (1995) reveals "the socially and historically constructed relationship of the individual to the target language and their sometimes ambivalent desire to learn and practice it" (p. 17).

From this perspective, language learners are conceptualized as having "complex identities" and "multiple desires" to learn the language that related to integrating themselves into target language networks, assimilating into the larger society, or even finding a job. The desire to learn a second language is also shaped by the language learner's own personal experiences, roles within the family structure, sense of self-efficacy, and need to adequately articulate ideas. As Darvin and Norton (2015) note "a student may be a highly *motivated* learner, but may not be *invested* in the language practices … if the practices are racist, sexist, or homophobic" (p. 37). In other words, learners need to feel comfortable, accepted, and understood in the communities in which they participate, and if the learner's identity is threatened the individual may halt the learning process. Thus, the speaker's investment in language learning becomes an investment in social identity (Norton Peirce 1995; Norton 2000).

Building on the intersections of elderly identities and investment, we sought to describe the processes that impact older immigrants' claim to a right to speak. In fact, considering that friends and family members may ridicule older adult learners' decision to learn English, often deeming it a waste of time, we wondered what motivated older adults' investment in ESL instruction. More than monitoring the linguistic (and usually grammar-centric) achievements of our learners, our focus group and interviewing practice revealed other extralinguistic features. We could not deny, for example, that in fact many of the older adult language learners were attending class for important exchanges about resources and information. In the following sections, we depict in greater detail our ESL community as it relates to the formation of a learner-identity and investment in target language acquisition.

Applied Linguistics and Aging

Scholars in the field of sociolinguistics have started to focus on the ways older speakers discursively construct elderly identities as well as patterns of intergenerational communication. In more traditional structuralist research, sociolinguistic variation was studied by correlating large sets of linguistic data (e.g., phonological, lexical, and morpho-syntactic variants) with macro-social categories, such as age, gender, education, and social class (Labov 2001). Coupland (1997) noted how in the case of language and aging many sociolinguistic studies during the 1990s primarily focused on "how people of different ages speak." For sociolinguistic variationists, the primary objective is to monitor how certain linguistic features are used across age cohorts and document patterns of language change. Little emphasis is placed, however, on how language learners discursively construct an "aging identity" that includes their stances toward old age, strategies during intergenerational speech events, and assessment of younger speakers' conversational norms (Coupland 1997).

In 1991, the publication of the monograph entitled *Language, Society, and the Elderly*, by Nikolas Coupland, Justine Coupland, and Howard Giles, presented the first premises of the "sociolinguistics of aging" with the aim of examining aging and communication from a sociocultural perspective. In the volume, the authors criticized how the existing literature of language and communication was depicting elderly speakers from a "deficit paradigm," describing aging as a "progressive, inevitable, unwanted decline" (Hepworth 2003, p. 89). Coupland et al. (1991) argue that neurolinguistic perspectives tend to typecast the interpersonal communication problems of the elderly as a consequence of inherent "homogeneous cognitive decline" with little regard to social variables, such as the precipitous decline of quality opportunities for reciprocal and productive speech encounters (p. 56).

Coupland et al. (1991) concentrated on the interactions between women in their 70s and 80s and women in their 30s by recounting turn-taking strategies and conversational management between dyads. Younger interlocutors, for instance, chose different approaches when managing discursive moments of "painful self-disclosure," that is, when elderly "reveal personal and intimate information about ill health, bereavement, immobility, loneliness and so on" (p. 22). They tended to be either "over-accommodative" by showing emphatic sympathy for the older person's painful disclosures or "under-accommodative" by shifting or even switching topics so that the older person would discontinue the painful disclosure. Conversely, older speakers used "self-handicapping" strategies to indicate that future tasks may not be performed well due to illness or other kinds of mishaps. It is their way to save face and, at the same time, communicate their potential vulnerability, seek comfort, and help others understand their situation.

These types of routinely communicative speech acts, where the older person speaks about painful self-disclosures and the younger person acts as a "therapist" through "supportive talk," was found to inhibit older speakers from building a positive identity by constraining the roles they could take during the interactions. By recursively orienting themselves to these types of interactions, both older and younger speakers were reinforcing encounters which were not emotionally satisfactory and limited their abilities to build relationships that were more real, deep, and intimate. Pejorative interactional patterns between intergenerational dyads were so ingrained in the participants of their study that Coupland et al. (1991) linked it to cross-cultural communication issues, despite the fact that everyone in the study was from a similar background.

Research on attitudes toward the elderly show how younger people evaluate the elderly following ageist stereotypes. Younger people attribute unflattering characteristics (e.g., frail, weak, insecure) to older people (Giles et al. 1992a, b), perceive them as more vulnerable and less competent (Steward and Ryan 1982), and stereotype older speakers as unable to recall messages efficiently (Giles et al. 1992a, b). Studies argue that these salient formulations of stereotypical beliefs about older people are a reflection of "intergenerational boundaries" and have the potential of alienating older adults (Coupland et al. 1991; Harwood et al. 1995). Ryan et al. (1995) characterize these stereotypes as "biopsychosocial consequences" that cause "poor health status, depression, and social isolation" (p. 106). Studies in intergenerational communication between Hispanic elders and their family members have stressed the culture of familism, or *familismo*, which enhances intergenerational solidarity and support as well as a tradition of taking care of the elderly (Cruz-Lopez and Pearson 1995; Padilla 2002; Vega 1990). Ruiz and Ransford (2012) offer a different perspective by showing how Hispanic elders might sometimes feel disconnected from their younger family members. In study focus groups, elderly informants reported infrequent contact with younger family members as well as a shift in the paradigm of familismo since Hispanic elderly encouraged the younger generation to direct their attention to their nuclear families as opposed to parents and elders. Evidence also showed that Hispanic women, in particular, have adapted to this change by finding support in networks external to the extended family. Researchers warn about romanticized notions of familismo: "...as these elders' stories demonstrate, having family around, who 'could help' or 'should help' does not necessarily translate into actual or measurable assistance and support" (Ruiz and Ransford 2012, pp. 56–57). A more detailed discussion of how ESL programming impacts familismo and the social networking of older adult learners is presented in Chap. 7. In the following section, we focus on intergenerational relationships, communication patterns, and the role of language among Hispanic families.

Older Adult Learners and the "Right to Speak"

> Well...these days because I don't work, I don't go out as much, it is just me and my grandson at home most of the time because my daughter is always working. When you live in South Dallas it is easy to just go around and speak in Spanish: in Fiesta [a supermarket] they speak in Spanish, in the elote stand they speak in Spanish. Everywhere they speak in Spanish.

When we first met Clara, we were impressed by her ability to connect with other students and her ESL teacher. The teacher considered Clara to be an excellent language learner who was progressing relatively quickly. For over 15 years, Clara was a worker in a party balloon factory. She claims to have learned most of her English vocabulary through interactions with English speakers and/or bilingual coworkers. As a retiree, she spends more time at home and feels she is losing what she had learned. Clara described how her "social world is becoming smaller" to the point where her only conversational partners are her daughter and grandson. Whereas before she used to speak some English with her daughter, in the last few years they have reverted to speaking only in Spanish.

Similar to Clara, many of our study participants pointed out that living in a predominantly Spanish-speaking neighborhood is both a blessing and a curse. On one hand, friends and family also live in or near their neighborhood which helps them maintain and nurture these relationships. Likewise, Spanish-speaking businesses and medical providers are easier to locate and access. Yet, on the other hand, being confined to a small segment of a large metropolitan area means that there are relatively few opportunities to develop and nurture relationships with English-speaking interlocutors.

Patterns of L1 regression among older speakers (i.e., reverting to a speaker's first language in settings where the second language is common), like the one experienced by Clara, are common in ethnocultural enclaves (Clyne 1977). While older adult Hispanics start reverting back to Spanish, the younger generational cohorts in the family continue in the opposite direction as they strengthen their relationships with English-speaking peers.

Clara described how her relationship with her grandson had deteriorated. Dissimilar to how they once communicated with each other and freely "talked about everything," the language barrier was becoming an issue. As a result of these communication problems, she felt that she "could not enter into his world." He had "secrets that he would not tell" her and she no longer knew how he was performing in school.

Intergenerational communication barriers were echoed by many of our older adult ESL learners. José, a 66-year-old man, worked in a cement company before it was dissolved. During his working years, he was surrounded by other Spanish-speaking men who, as he explained to us, focused on making money for their expanding families and were not at all concerned with acquiring English. After he lost employment, José felt confined to his house and backyard due to the changing demographics of his neighborhood (i.e., English monolingual professionals bought and rehabilitated houses on his street). Since his wife was still working and his children worked long hours, he was the default babysitter for nearly all of his small grandchildren. Throughout a typical day, his primary interlocutors were his toddler and prekindergarten grandkids who luckily understood Spanish. Despite his profound love for his children, he described this environment as "isolating" since most exchanges were based on the forms of "baby talk" and most of his activities revolved around the children's essential needs. José commented how not having a job was making him feel that he was "not useful for his family" since they were going through economic hardships and he was not able to save as much for his retirement as he wanted. Learning English was a way to show his family that he was trying to help them and make him feel that he was "useful again."

In the case of José and Clara, we can observe how their opportunities to speak English were constrained by their caretaking activities. They both came to the United States in their late 40s and for most of the time after their arrival they had mostly interacted with Spanish speakers both at work and in their neighborhoods. Like others in the ESL program, Clara and José expressed how people around them held lower expectations of their learning English and made comments that vaguely referenced a biological determinism, such as, "You cannot learn a language when you are this old." When we asked Clara whether her grandson would try to teach her English, she commented, "He does not have the patience for that." At the same time, she also pointed out how her grandson was embarrassed about the way she spoke English, especially when they went outside together. This made her feel even more insecure about her language abilities. In the excerpt below, Clara describes her grandson's attitude toward her learning English:

> My grandson always says, "You don't understand grandma." But I want to understand! I really want to know what is going on! I want to learn English. I ask him, "Will you teach me?" and he says, "No, because you won't learn. You are too old. Why would you want to learn English? We can help you, too."

As we can see, Clara's grandson was operating with negative stereotypes which typecast older learners as incapable, ultimately denying older adult learners the *right to speak*. Clara counteracted this negative affective positioning by being assertive; she really wanted to know what was going on in her grandson's life and she felt that learning English was the way to understand his social world. Her grandson dismissed her needs by considering that she was "too old to learn" and that she did not need to learn the language because of the presupposition that there will always be bilinguals to help her. Clara felt that despite living in Dallas where Spanish-dominant communities and institutions exist, not speaking English was limiting her freedom. She also commented how, as she was getting older, she was becoming less self-assured about the chores and activities she could do by herself. For example, she feared taking the bus because she thought that she would get lost. Once lost, she thought she would not know what to do. She could not go to the doctor by herself because she was scared of not being able to explain what was going on with her. As long as Clara depended on the language ability of others, she was confined to the house and limited to the places she could go.

Clara's relationship with her grandson reflects the affective intergenerational mismatches studied in the literature of aging and sociolinguistics (Coupland et al. 1991; Giles et al. 1992a). Negative stereotypes are emotionally taxing to older learners and threaten their self-esteem which in turn shapes their ability to adapt in old age. When pressed to explain in greater detail the rationale behind the sentiment that older people are not fit to learn a language, older adults often refer to authoritative discourses (e.g., research studies, popular discourses, or "my teacher said that …"). Considering that even 30- and 40-somethings commented how they were deemed by peers to be "too old to learn," we cannot underestimate the power ageist discourses exert not only on older adults in retirement, but also on prime-of-life adults learning a second language.

Apart from bilingual family members, older learners describe stressful encounters with English-speaking interlocutors. They fear speaking English because native English speakers tend to truncate the time they need to express their ideas. Similar accounts in the literature of intercultural communication point out that during interactions with target language speakers L2 learners are expected to be more proactive and to seek understanding while native interlocutors are passive and detached (Bremer et al. 1996; Norton 2000). Our older L2 learners were able to relate to this "under-accommodative" way of speaking:

> The problem is that they [native English speakers] speak too fast, they look at you and talk to you as if you are understanding them when you are actually just seeing how their mouth moves and you are not understanding a word! And they don't stop for you even if they see an old man in front of them. They don't care! But sometimes it is me …. I don't understand them either because I am old, or I am absent-minded or because I cannot recall how to say words in English.

José, Clara, and their peers in the ESL program share several issues and communicative contexts. English interlocutors tend not to consider age a distinctive characteristic of a language learner and position elderly simply as normative interlocutors. In this sense, elders' environment is not providing comprehensible input that enhances interaction and language learning opportunities. Another corollary is that like José, many of our adult language learners approach interactions with English interlocutors with a self-defeating attitude and operate from their own ageist conceptions regarding their abilities to understand and speak the language.

Our older language learners also described how they were confronted with disparaging evaluations of their efforts to learn English, such as, "So many years in the country and they do not speak the language?" Attitudinal comments conventionalize the perception that learning a language is a simple matter of being in the target language country for an extended period of time. Mauricio, one of the most advanced students in the program, offers the following encounter:

> The other day my landlord came to my home and it was awful, a pipe had just broken and my kitchen was full of water. I was trying to talk to him in English with the words that my ESL teacher told me before coming to class, you know, words about plumbing. He kept on saying that I broke the pipe. I explained to him what happened and that I wasn't even in the house at the time that it broke. He didn't understand me. Then he said, "How can it be that after 20 years here you still don't speak the language?" And it is true, I should speak English better.

The longstanding notion that spending a long time in the target language society is sufficient to learn any language is misguided. This viewpoint assumes that older language learners have been offered several years of meaningful and quality exposure to the target language, as well as the institutional support to learn the language. In reality, however, many L2 learners have experienced extreme adversities and limited interactions with English speakers their entire adult lives (Norton Peirce 1995). Menard-Warwick (2005) discusses how the language learning trajectories of L2 elders "cannot be separated from the gendered responsibilities of their daily lives, from their personal histories of education, work, and family life" (p. 296).

José worked in a cement company where most of his coworkers were Hispanic and nearly all of his conversations were initiated in Spanish. Rarely did he ever have the opportunity to converse with English speakers, let alone create lasting friendships. While it was through work that Clara learned basic occupational English, in the last 5 years her relationships have been limited to her family members who tend to speak with her in Spanish. Mauricio had a good command of the language thanks to his supportive Anglophone boss who always encouraged him to speak in English. However, recently his illnesses and related depression have kept him closer to home. In old age, target language interactions can decrease in frequency, along with important language socialization experiences.

Clara also responded to role expectations within her own family structure, such as taking her grandson to the doctor, and buying him clothes, food, or school materials. Outside her intimate social networks, her relationships with English-speaking interlocutors were infrequent, but at the same time became more significant for her sense of well-being. Getting older has increased Clara's interactions with doctors and nurses, which has resulted in a greater need for English fluency. While before she could survive without speaking English by going to Spanish-speaking *clínicas* (medical facilities managed and served by Spanish-speaking doctors, nurses, and staff), she now needs to communicate directly with specialists who do not often know Spanish. Clara now feels that medical encounters were more difficult than ever:

> I go to the specialist and I feel dumb because the interpreter is on the phone and I have to go back and forth and explain things to the doctor. And when the interpreter is present I feel that the doctor is not listening to me and I cannot fully express how I feel ....

Like Clara, our older learners also expressed how, when interpreters were present, they felt ignored in the sense that the healthcare provider paid more attention to the interpreter than to them as patients. Overdependency on interpretations did not allow older adults to fully comprehend all healthcare information and to lose a degree of ownership over their own health. These situations had the indirect effect of silencing older Spanish-speaking immigrants and hindering their ability to manage conversations about their well-being.

In our focus group interviews, many disclosed painful experiences during doctor–patient interactions. While not everyone shared painful disclosures, when these stories were told, nonverbal gestures from the group suggested that others had experienced the same encounters themselves or had heard something similar from family members. Luisa, a 67-year-old woman, recounted the story of her most recent visit with her doctor:

> I was trying to explain to the doctor where I was hurting and what was happening to me, but he was not understanding to me. At some point, I asked him, "Do you speak Spanish?" He looked at me and he said, "I don't speak Spanish. We are in America." I understood what he said. When I left the room, I asked the receptionist about my medication. I knew she was going to treat me better because she spoke Spanish.

The doctor's non-accommodative response to Luisa shows an "unequal investment in social interaction" (Norton 2000, p. 85). Whereas, a cooperative response would have been "I don't speak Spanish, but I know somebody who does. The receptionist. Let's go talk to her." At the hospital, Luisa felt marginalized because she was positioned as a lower status immigrant and she felt that she was not given appropriate care as a result (Norton 2000). Luisa expressed how her lack of fluency in English and her age made her feel vulnerable with doctors. As a result, she refrained from initiating conversations in English and tended to self-evaluate her English competency lower than what it was in reality. Insecurity in the target language decreases motivation to learn and hinders fluency, pronunciation, and overall speech performance (Krashen 1985).

Investments

While our older adult learners believed that there was some truth to the idea that learning a language was more difficult at an older age, a small handful did not passively accept that assumption. They were attending the ESL program because they still had hope that acquiring English would be possible for them. Part of their fight to learn English was tied to their own *investments* (Norton Peirce 1995). This means a commitment to talking with people in English, enrolling in ESL classes, and taking themselves out of their comfort zone to produce English utterances on the fly. Doing so means, among other things, building confidence, living more autonomously, and alleviating the burden they know they are placing on their children and grandchildren.

For many of our older learners, the social and personal investments were concentrated in their families, especially their grandchildren. For Clara, learning English was a head start to communicating with her grandson now that she was spending more time at home. She also commented on how, through the ESL program, she was learning important information about schools, medical insurance programs, and other civic requirements for residency (e.g., how to pass the citizenship exam or how to do obtain a state ID/driver's license). Clara explains her investment orientation this way:

> When I finish my class I sometimes go to the library. The other day I asked about the computer classes because I wanted to learn. I need to learn it. If I learn English and I learn how to use a computer, I will be able to help my family.

By gaining English language skills, Clara is not only acquiring the needed linguistic bridge to her grandson, she is also building confidence and becoming more independent. English literacy means that she can also acquire other types of literacies: digital literacy (e.g., how to send and receive emails), governmental literacy (e.g., filling out official documents and forms), pharmaceutical literacy (e.g., reading prescriptions), and social media literacy (e.g., communicating inexpensively with family members abroad).

Before starting the literacy program, many of our older adults had tried to learn English in other ESL programs throughout the years, but their life trajectories were complicated by illnesses as well as losses of family members and friends. Mauricio, who had been suffering from depression since his wife was deported to Guatemala, explains how the ESL program was a vital space for him to feel integrated in a community:

> I am grateful to the teachers and to the people here because this course makes me feel that I am somebody and that I can learn how to speak English little by little. I proved to myself that I can do it. It keeps me awake. This class exercises my brain.

In the last year Mauricio had been experiencing some age-related cognitive changes which he described as "not remembering things sometimes" and "having problems paying attention." Mauricio explained how coming to class allowed him to be attentive and exercise his brain. Throughout the ESL program, he grew tremendously in his own self-efficacy (i.e., the self-knowledge of his capabilities) (Bandura 1984). Observing that people like himself manage the task of learning a new language increased his awareness of the learning process and his overall expectations for communicating in English in the coming years.

Older adult learners often view the enterprise of language learning as purely biological: either you have it or you do not. If after 12 weeks an individual has not learned enough English to survive, then they must not have what it takes to learn a second language and, therefore, they will never learn. When expectations of what ought to be learned in a given time period are too high, learners may feel discouraged and lose motivation. It is a downward spiral that may leave English L2 learners wanting to avoid ESL contexts since they exist as a place of failing to meet their own expectations, which may be unachievable from the beginning. For this reason, a large part of adult ESL curriculum touches on what is a normal progression through the process of learning a second language.

Like Mauricio, many others felt that coming to class was an investment in their own sense of self. During interviews, José framed his identity not as an older man, but as a respected worker in the cement company where he used to work. Learning English was a question of regaining autonomy and the control over his life that he used to have. He felt that by learning English he could have an important role in his family again.

> If I knew English I would feel better about myself. I would be able to find a job and help my family. But in the end, it is not even a question of finding a job. It is about coming to class and feeling content that you can do something for yourself and that I am valued here.

José was starting to feel that although he loved taking care of his grandchildren, his life was becoming monotonous without activities that were challenging to him. ESL classes provided José with a way to reappraise his own potential (Bandura 1984). By attending class, he was able to gain confidence and create friendships with new interlocutors. Even if he could not find a job at his age, he could at least come to terms with the long and arduous work of using a language that challenged and redefined his essential character and personal identity.

Aging in Place: ESL Classes as Safe Zones

During breaks from classroom instruction, our ESL students would regularly gather together to have lunch in the large multipurpose room located in the library. The children played together while younger and older adult learners gathered and casually discussed a range of topics: medical insurances and facilities, nearby schools (public, parochial, or charter), food items sold at different grocery stores, operating hours of nearby governmental sites, legal services for immigration papers, and reliable Spanish-speaking tax service providers, to name a few. As our learners began to know and trust each other, the conversations shifted to more intimate topics, especially among our older adult learners who, many times, self-disclosed family hardships related to deportations, health issues, family deaths, and continual solitude. Apart from observing the emotional bonds that flourished in what was a *safe space* for language learning, many participants, such as Luisa, made the connection explicitly:

> Last year I lost my sister. She was my best friend. I was devastated because I could not travel to Mexico. I wasn't going to come to class, but then Marisa called me and said, "Come to class! You will feel better!" The teacher was also so nice. I was crying in class and she came and asked me in Spanish "Luisa, are you ok? Are you ok?"

For two semesters Luisa struggled with the death of her sister to the point where she was rarely left home alone due to her depression. Attending class was both a place to learn English and space to cope with her sorrow. Research on socioemotional theory shows that as people grow older, their goals in life are less oriented toward seeking information and more on prioritizing emotional satisfaction and meaning (Cartensen et al. 1999). Our older adult learners regularly shared their feelings and expressed that their participation in the Saturday program lowered their sense of isolation. For the younger adult learners who were involved with raising their own children, the program's childcare services afforded time for themselves without the responsibility of watching their children.

Studies have shown how the ESL classroom can be a place for learning as well as a place for social interaction. For example, Horsman (1990) and Sylvester and Carlo (1998) found that learners were often coming to class in part because of the social interaction it offered with others. In the classroom, emotional bonding was created as people shared empathy regarding the difficulties of language learning. In comparison to the outside world, where our ESL learners felt fearful at approaching conversations with English speakers, the ESL classroom was an environment where older learners could experiment with English without feeling judged by others. Clara describes this experience here:

> When I try to speak with my grandson the only thing that he does is correct me. He makes me feel nervous because he is not patient .... Here I don't care because we all know each other and we are all in the same boat. We help each other as much as we can.

While speaking in English with her grandson was a threatening act, Clara felt freer to commit errors in the ESL classroom context despite her "murdering the language," as she jokingly claims. Many of our learners made similar comments, depicting the ESL classroom as a "welcoming and accepting space" that included "an environment in which students are willing to participate and honestly struggle with challenging issues" (Holley and Steiner 2005, p. 49). As ESL students observed how their peers positioned themselves as "fearful" of English language socialization outside of class, inside the ESL classroom they identified with each other and provided themselves with a reason to attend class. Mauricio commented: "I felt the same as the others. I thank the teacher for making us realize that we are not alone, that we are all in this together, that we can do it. It means a lot to us." For many of our older learners, the ESL program shifted their experience of second language learning to one where they felt supported and valued. These peer relationships challenged the rationale that acquiring English at an older age was an impossible endeavor. Rosaura, a 63-year-old woman, stated the following:

> Of course learning at an older age is hard, but we are trying and we see that we can do it. Coming to class every week, trying to speak outside a little either with friends or family—that is the key. And we can do it!

A "safe" and "transformative" space for language resocialization is important in the formation of a learner's identity. Older adult ESL students aided one another in recognizing shared experiences and building solidarity. Their alignment of affective stances allowed them to create new personal and self-as-learner identities. Mauricio, embodying what Norton (2001) calls an "imagined identity," discusses how English proficiency is interpreted as influencing future lifespan developments.

> When you learn English, you develop yourself intellectually. You grow as an individual.... If you have better knowledge of the literature, a better education, everything will start growing as you learn more and more English. So, it is a question of learning for growing.

What *knowing* English means for Mauricio has changed over the last year and will most likely be revised again in the coming months and years. An important step for many older language learners hinges on their ability to participate in English language activities outside the classroom. They envision how their increased proficiency will grant them more autonomy and control in their lives.

As the semester progressed, we could see how Mauricio and Luisa, both students who were going through difficult emotional issues outside of class, were doing much better than when the class began. Mauricio commented how the class was keeping him "active" and allowing him to "mentally escape" from the hardships of his life. Luisa was now making friends and inviting classmates to have lunch with her. Mauricio commented many times how grateful he was for the program. Mauricio described what it meant to be an older language learner:

> The sadness about growing older is how you get sick. You lose your strength. You can even lose your mind! And on top of that, you are in a country where you don't speak the language and you are getting older. It isolates you even more. And you still need to learn even if the words don't stick to your brain! Because you are old and everybody knows that it's harder when you get older .... I thank the library for putting such an effort on us. I really thank you.

Mauricio's story is similar to those of other older learners. The life changes that occur in retirement and old age are already prone to a sense of solitude, anguish, and age-related illnesses. For them, the additional burden of depending on their aging body and brain to learn something as complex as a new language requires them to cultivate tremendous mental and attitudinal resolve.

Finding a Place for Older Adult Learners

Studies that follow an ecological perspective of health and well-being integrate how age associated patterns of health are interrelated with behavioral and environmental factors (Golant 2003; Lawton 1986; Scheidt and Norris-Baker 2003; Wiles et al. 2011). From an "aging in place" perspective, we see how social spaces impact SLA among older adult immigrants. Using Bourdieu's (1977) notion of the "right to speak," we argue that ownership of the language development process is contingent on local material and social conditions, as well as the operation of cultural ageist attitudes. Older learners' social status in everyday interactions also affects the way they are perceived by others as legitimate speakers, and how negative stereotypes about old age abilities handicap their SLA efforts.

Two specific interlocutors, younger grandchildren and medical practitioners, were identified as a source of negative affect in English-dominant interactions. In these interactions, older adult learners were made to feel vulnerable and ashamed. Communication tends to be truncated by the pressure they feel to speak more fluently and acquire the language more rapidly. Many of our informants talked about how others shamed them for being "many years in the country and not speaking the language," denoting a moral evaluation that language learning should "always" occur "no matter what." By sharing their experiences about learning a language, our students started to put into perspective issues such as "time" and "speed" were not the only way to judge their SLA accomplishments.

When learners expressed the ageist attitude that "language learning at an old age is an impossible endeavor," they many times supported it with references to authoritative discourses of "experts" (e.g., newspapers, linguists, and teachers). Socializing in the ESL classroom; however, was important at a metacognitive level because many of our learners had not previously belonged to social networks that openly discussed the challenges to learning a second language. The ESL classroom, led by what they believed were "experts in applied linguistics," was really the first time they found other language learners who would talk about the difficult process of language acquisition. This new framework helped to supplant individualistic discourses based on the misinformed deficit models with holistic concepts from applied linguistics and sociology of typical L2 stages. In the place of the ESL classroom, we were less interested in circulating discourses about ideal speech practice. Instead, of significance to us were the exchanges and interactions within an ESL learning community that formalize the process of understanding and generating strategies for English language encounters. Importantly, these social interactions allow older adults to debunk many of the myths associated with learning a language in old age and to reinvest in their own language development.

For all of our older adults, learning English was becoming synonymous with different material and symbolic investments. For some of them, it was a way to reconnect with the younger members of their families, find a job, or gain ways to advocate for themselves and their families. By learning English, older learners were also figuring out their own cognitive "self-efficacy," that is, their ability to acquire new skills. They also were engaging with other aspects of their aging (i.e., losing memory or hearing). But more importantly, learning English allowed them to reinvent their identities and gain confidence in themselves as learners.

Our study shows how ESL programming can be a safe space for older language learners that alters their sense of social isolation and stigma through a "community of sentiment" with other learners. Peer relationships in the ESL classroom are central to language acquisition because these social interactions augment learners' self-esteem and motivation in ways that maintain language resocialization encounters. Research in gerontology has demonstrated that social integration (i.e., participation in social activities and social networks) is associated with diminished symptoms of depression (Glass et al. 1999), and in general more satisfaction in life (Yuri Jang et al. 2004). As social infrastructure, the ESL classroom can help older learners more fully participate in their everyday local spaces in both personally and socially meaningful ways. In our program, students were able to develop new interests, new sources of fulfillment, and a new sense of self-efficacy. The classroom space also promoted social inclusion in several ways: first, it created bonding between students; second, by learning English older learners were able to increase their access to resources outside their own family and outside nearby Spanish-speaking communities; third, as learners advanced through the program and they learned more English, they were able to reduce the amount of assistance necessary to carry out activities and advocate for themselves. Subsequent chapters further explore the ways the ESL space can provide the formative relationships needed for older adults to envision a new identity as a learner-self and to aspire to a future as a target language speaker.

References

Bandura, A. (1984). Recycling misconceptions of perceived self-efficacy. *Cognitive Therapy and Research, 8,* 231–255.
Bayles, K. A., & Kaszniak, A. W. (1987). *Communication and cognition in normal aging and dementia.* London: Taylor and Francis.
Block, D. (2007). *Second language identities.* London/New York: Continuum.
Bourdieu, P. (1977). *Outline of a theory of practice.* Cambridge: Cambridge University Press.
Bremer, K., Roberts, C., Vasseur, M.-T., Simonot, M., & Broeder, P. (1996). *Achieving understanding: Discourse in intercultural encounters.* New York: Longman.
Carstensen, L. L., Isaacowitz, D. M., & Charles, S. T. (1999). Taking time seriously: A theory of socioemotional selectivity. *American Psychologist, 54,* 165–181.

References

Clyne, M. (1977). Bilingualism of the elderly. *Talanya, 4,* 45–65.

Coupland, N. (1997). Language, ageing and ageism: A project for applied linguistics? *International Journal of Applied Linguistics, 7,* 26–48.

Coupland, N., Coupland, J., & Giles, H. (1991). *Language, society and the elderly: Discourse, identity and ageing.* Massachusetts: Blackwell.

Cutchin, M. P. (2003). The process of mediated aging-in-place: A theoretically and empirically based model. *Social Science and Medicine, 57*(6), 1077–1090.

Cruz-Lopez, M., & Pearson, R. (1985). The support needs of Puerto Rican elderly. *The Gerontologist, 22,* 254–259.

Darvin, R., & Norton, Bonny. (2015). Identity and a model of investment in applied linguistics. *Annual Review of Applied Linguistics, 35,* 36–56.

Giles, H., Coupland, N., Coupland, J., Williams, A., & Nussbaum, J. (1992a). Intergenerational talk and communication with older people. *International Journal of Aging and Human Development, 34,* 271–297.

Giles, H., Henwood, K., Coupland, N., Harriman, J., & Coupland, J. (1992b). Language attitudes and cognitive mediation. *Human Communication Research, 18,* 500–527.

Glass, T. A., Mendes De Leon, C., Marottoli, R. A., & Berkman, L. (1999). Population based study of social and productive activities as predictors of survival among elderly Americans. *British Medical Journal, 319*(7208), 478–483.

Golant, S. M. (2003). Conceptualizing time and behavior in environmental gerontology: A pair of old issues deserving new thought. *The Gerontologist, 43*(5), 638–648.

Harwood, J., Giles, H., & Ryan, E. B. (1995). Aging, communication, and intergroup theory: Social identity and intergenerational communication. In J. F. Nussbaum & J. Coupland (Eds.), *Handbook of communication and aging research* (pp. 133–159). Hillsdale, NJ: Lawrence Erlbaum Associates.

Hasher, L., & Zacks, R. T. (1988). Working memory, comprehension, and aging: A review and a new view. In G.H. Bower (Ed.), *The psychology of learning and motivation* (vol. 22, pp. 193–225). San Diego, CA: Academic Press.

Hepworth, M. (2003). Ageing bodies: Aged by culture. In J. Coupland & R. Gwyn (Eds.), *Discourse, the body, and identity* (pp. 89–106). Basingstoke: Palgrave, Macmillan.

Holley, L. C., & Steiner, S. (2005). Safe space: Student perspectives on classroom environment. *Journal of Social Work Education, 41*(1), 49–64.

Horsman, J. (1990). *Something in my mind besides the everyday: Women and literacy.* Toronto: Women's Press.

Yuri Jang, J. A. Mortimer, W. E. Haley, W. E., & Borenstein Graves, A. R. (2004). The role of social engagement in life satisfaction: Its significance among older individuals with disease and disability. *Journal of Applied Gerontology, 23*(3), 266–278.

Krashen, S. D. (1985). *The input hypothesis: Issues and implications.* New York: Longman.

Labov, W. (2001). *Principles of linguistic change. Volume II: Social factors.* Oxford: Blackwell.

Lawton, M. P. (1986). *Environment and aging.* Albany, NY: Center for the Study of Aging.

Menard-Warwick, J. (2005). Trajectories and sociopolitical context: Latina immigrants in adult ESL. *TESOL Quarterly, 38*(2), 65–185.

Norton, B. (2000). *Identity and language learning: Gender, ethnicity and educational change.* Harlow, England: Longman/Pearson Education.

Norton, B. (2001). Non-participation, imagined communities and the language classroom. In M. Breen (Ed.), *Learner contributions to language learning: New directions in research* (pp. 159–171). London: Longman/Pearson Education.

Norton Peirce, B. (1995). Social identity, investment, and language learning. *TESOL Quarterly, 1,* 9–31.

Padilla, A. M. (2002). Hispanic psychology: A 25-year retrospective look. In W. J. Lonner, D. L. Dinnel, S. A. Hayes, & D. N. Sattler (Eds.), *Online readings in psychology and culture* (Unit 3, Chapter 3). Retrieved June 3, 2016, from http://www.wwu.edu/_culture

Pavlenko, A., & Blackledge, A. (Eds.) (2002). Ideologies of language in multilingual contexts. Special issue. *Multilingua, 21*(2/3), 163–196.

Ruiz, M. E., & Ransford, H. E. (2012). Latino elders reframing familismo: Implications for health and caregiving support. *Journal of Cultural Diversity, 19*(2), 50–57.

Ryan, E. B., Sheree, D. M., MacLean, M. J., & Orange, J. B. (1995). Changing the way we talk with elders: Promoting health using the communication enhancement model. *International Journal of Aging and Human Development, 41*(2), 69–107.

Scheidt, R. J., & Norris-Baker, C. (2003). The general ecological model revisited: Evolution, current status, and continuing challenges. In Wahl, H.-W., Scheidt, R. J. & Windley, P. G. (Eds.), *Annual Review of Gerontology and Geriatrics. Focus on Aging in Context: Socio-physical Environment* (vol. 23, pp. 34–58). Springer Publishing Company: New York City, NY.

Stewart, M. A., & Ryan, E. B. (1982). Attitudes toward younger and older adult speakers: Effects of varying speech rates. *Journal of Language and Social Psychology, 1,* 91–109.

Stine, E. L., Wingfield, A., & Poon, L. W. (1986). How much and how fast: Rapid processing of spoken language in later adulthood. *Psychology and Aging, 1,* 303–311.

Sylvester, E., & Carlo, M. (1998). *"I want to learn English": Examining the goals and motivations of adult ESL learners in three Philadelphia learning sites* (Report No. TR9808). Philadelphia: University of Pennsylvania, National Center on Adult Literacy.

Vega, W. (1990). Hispanic families in the 1980s: A decade of research. *Journal of Marriage and the Family, 52,* 1015–1024.

Wiles, J. L., Leibing, A. Guberman, N, Reeve, J., & Allen E. S., Ruth. (2011). The meaning of "ageing in place" to older people. *The Gerontologist, 1,* 1–10.

Chapter 6
Building Emotions for Self-Identity and Learning

> The other day a member from our church invited my husband and I to a party and I told my husband "Come on let's go!" but he does not want to go because he does not speak English fluently ... neither do I! I know we feel embarrassed, but we have to do it! There is no other way to confront these fears than to throw yourself into the situation and see what happens. The problem is that my husband does not want to put himself out there because he is shy and feels uncomfortable. He has this attitude that he cannot do it and I think it is more an emotion than anything else. ....

During ESL program registration, Berta, a 67-year-old woman, was one of the first ones in line to enroll in English classes. Berta brought her husband, Braulio, with her. He remained throughout several semesters in the program, though he stopped coming to the program after the third week. Berta commented how Braulio was especially sensitive to being corrected in the classroom and how he would "freeze" when the teacher asked him to speak up in class. Berta described how Braulio was a different person when they both lived in Mexico. He was a sociable and energetic man who would talk to everybody and made friends easily. Moving to the United States changed his personality, leading to "a crippling anxiety" when he tried to socialize in English. Berta noted that she always encouraged him to talk with others, even if his English was not perfect. While Braulio never returned to ESL classes, Berta stayed enrolled and progressed through the program levels.

This chapter explores the "affective stances" (i.e., emotions, feelings, attitudes) (Besnier 1990; Englebretson 2007; McEwan-Fujita 2010; Ochs 1986) developed among our older adult second language learners toward their use of the target language, and how emotions shape their identity as language learners. As we will see, the strong bonds created in the ESL classroom alleviated older learners' fear of anxiety and shame related to their linguistic behavior. In the absence of these stigmas, older immigrants were free to recast their emotive stances which, in turn, allowed them to minimize the fears that block socialization with English interlocutors outside the classroom.

Affect and Language Learning

In order to understand the emotion work of older adults, it is important to examine the epistemological and ontological debate on the topic of "affect" in second-language acquisition literature. From the perspective of cognitive studies in second-language acquisition, "affect" refers to a set of inherent psychological traits in the individual (e.g., introversion or extroversion) or emotions (e.g., anxiety and confidence) that might inhibit or help the language learning process (Arnold 1999; Loschky 1994; cf. White 2003). Under the concept of "affective filter," widely used in cognitive SLA and developed by Krashen (1985, 1989), a successful language learner needs to have certain inherent psychological traits such as being self-confident, motivated, and less prone to anxiety (Krashen 1985, 1989, 1994). Conversely, a learner can be cognitively capable, but a lack of self-confidence and heightened anxiety may negatively shape learners' experiences in language acquisition (Horwitz et al. 1986). From a cognitive framework, the consequences of different affective stances are measured by analyzing the psychology of the learner and correlating these individualistic traits with the frequency of second-language communication.

Proponents of the socio-SLA paradigm (see Chap. 5) argue that emotional factors such as anxiety, motivation, self-esteem, or confidence are not invariant personality traits but are conditions that are socially constructed (Norton 2000). In her study of Canadian women, Norton (2000) found that many of the women she interviewed "tended to feel ashamed, inferior and uninteresting" (p. 122). Norton shows these feelings were ultimately connected to the discriminatory practices that language learners experience. In this regard, emotions should not be separated from the context where they occur and should not be treated as static, but rather as part of a fluid process that is discursively and situationally constructed. Norton also criticizes studies that mainly focus on explaining language acquisition as a cognitive process and not as a social practice. A wide range of scholars now point to the central importance of issues such as identity, social positioning, and language socialization (Block 2003, 2007, 2013; Norton 2000, 2001; Pavlenko and Blackedge 2002).

Norton (2000) highlights the need for a reconceptualization of Krashen's notion of "affective filter" to one that takes into account how affect is shaped by the context in which learning occurs. For Norton, learning a second language is not invariably "a skill that is acquired with hard work and dedication but a complex social practice that engages the identities of language learners" (Norton 2000, p. 132). Norton places the learner's identity as the cornerstone of second language development. From this perspective, identity should not be understood merely as an outgrowth of cognitive dispositions that exist *in vacuo*, but as an evolving process continually emerging through ongoing interactions with others (Ochs 1993).

Language Socialization and Affect

The language socialization framework identifies closely with sociocultural approaches of second language learning although the root of this approach develops from traditions in linguistic anthropology. In its origins, the language socialization approach involved the study of how children were socialized by older adults to acquire the target language (Bayley and Schecter 2003). Since the 1990s, this paradigm has also been employed to examine the socialization dynamics of adults. In the immigrant context, it is through participation in different types of contexts that the adult language learner becomes both linguistically and socially competent. Apart from grammatical competence, language socialization leads to the acquisition of broader social and symbolic knowledge, including sociopragmatic rules, cultural attitudes, social roles and ideologies, among other dimensions (Ochs et al. 1996; Schieffelin and Ochs 1986).

As we have seen in Chap. 5, the language socialization of older adults in the immigrant context is a difficult process that has profound implications for the learner's identity and self-concept. Expressions of "affect" and language learning appear commonly in the narratives of our older adults. They encoded "negative affective stances," such as the "shame" of not speaking English after being many years in the country, the "fear" of being judged by others or not being able to communicate in important situations (e.g., during encounters with doctors), and the "regret" of not being able to help their families because of their linguistic limitations (cf. McEwan-Fujita 2010; Ochs 1988; Ochs and Schieffelin 1989). Negative affective stances were observed in the recursive encounters with target language interlocutors in which learners were positioned as socially inferior (cf. Norton 2000). Due to their lack of language skills, older learners feel peripheral to social participation and develop a sense of social isolation. However, learners' affective dispositions can change and evolve. Learners may carve out identities as "worthy interlocutors," especially when they experience environments consisting of positive socialization (Norton 2000).

Within interactions, individuals mutually shape one another's affective behaviors through "affective alignments." These alignments can be in the form of either "congruent alignments" (e.g., when the interlocutor mirrors the other interlocutor's level of emotion) or "oppositional alignments" (e.g., when the interlocutor reflects emotions of hate, envy, or dismissal) that are incoherent vis-a-vis the receiver's emotions (Blader et al. 2010; Goodwin 2012). Blader et al. (2010) further categorize "congruent alignments" as "similar." This can include feeling sad for the receiver, or being "complementary" by cheering up the receiver (Blader et al. 2010, p. 36). It is through "congruent alignments" that security and acceptance is achieved. By showing an "emotional synchrony," learners are able to effectively express empathy toward each other (Davis 2004, cited in Blader et al. 2010, p. 36).

In addition to linguistic resources, interlocutors can also use nonverbal communication to convey emotional information. Facial expressivity, head nodding, posture as well as paralinguistic speech characteristics such as speech rate, pauses, or pitch can indicate congruent alignments (Goodwin and Goodwin 2000). Affective alignments can also carry sociocultural information in the form of attitudes and ideologies which can shape cultural understandings (McEwan-Fujita 2010; Ochs 1988; Ochs and Schieffelin 1984). Learners can be socialized to have specific types of emotional responses through recursive forms of socialization in positive or negative affective laden interactions (McEwan-Fujita 2010). In the context of immigrant language learning, negative affective interactions with English speaking interlocutors are common and can hinder the learner's self-esteem.

In this chapter, we analyze "affect" as an interactional and contextualized activity rather than an individualistic phenomenon. Adding this dimension to the study of language socialization of older adults allows us to understand a range of emotions and how learners come together to comprehend the social experience of learning a language at an old age.

Affective Alignments Among Older Language Learners

During interview focus groups, older ESL learners expressed affect in the form of "painful self-disclosures" (Coupland et al. 1991), such as the "frustration" about the fact that younger members in their families spoke better English than them, the "shame" of not being able to speak English fluently in order to be able to help their children, or the "anxiety" when they had to speak in public spaces. Implicit in these painful self-disclosures were other aspects of socialization within their families that included the reversal of the hierarchical structure of the family and the fact that their grandchildren, at such a young age, had already more access to important forms of capital (e.g., cultural, educational, social, economic) available in the United States. In the dialogue excerpt below, Berta and Blanca, share the experience of asking their grandchildren for help with their English:

Dialogue 1: Intergenerational Boundaries and Linguistic Insecurity: Building Bonds through Affective Discourses

Berta   I don't even dare asking my granddaughter for help [with English] because she is … how to say it … she is terrible! And she always laughs at me! She feels bothered when I ask her to help me.

Blanca   My granddaughter is the same. She would tell me "that is not how you pronounce this or that word" or "nobody will understand you if you speak like that" and not in a nice tone but in an angry tone! And I tell her "this does not happen in my ESL class; people don't laugh at me in my ESL class.

In this excerpt, we can see how Berta and Blanca found common ground with their feelings of insecurity when practicing English with their grandchildren, and they connected with the despair of not finding in their grandchildren an ally who could help them with their language learning. Like Berta and Blanca, other older adults expressed negative affective stances when they talked about intergenerational issues revolving around how not speaking the dominant language was leading to feelings of inferiority due to a loss of authority in their families.

When ESL students articulated comments about their experiences, these disclosures allowed them to find affiliative connections with other peers from the class and build "modes of reasoning" for attending English class (Jacoby and Ochs 1995). This identity work was a form of "affective care," where older adult learners tapped jointly into their emotional bonds to overcome the pressure of external peer groups who discouraged their SLA. For example, during our focus groups, older adults collectively recognized how part of their discouragement toward learning was not related to their own inherent personality traits but to how interlocutors made them feel during target language interactions. In the excerpt below, learners Rosaura (age 66), Lida (age 68) and Francisco (age 70) talk about this topic:

Dialogue 2: "I am scared that they will laugh at my English": Anxiety in Language Learning and the Development of Empathy

Investigator	How do you feel when you have to speak English?
Rosaura	When I go to the doctor or even in the supermarket, they speak so fast! And they are not very nice when they realize that you cannot speak well. Then on top of that, I want to speak but I feel that my tongue starts to get twisted! I cannot pronounce the words and I get very embarrassed.
Lida	That happens to me too. I know the words but I start to think that the person in front of me will laugh at me and I just cannot do it; I get paralyzed; I even start sweating.
Investigator	Can other people comment about this?
Francisco	I think we all feel like this.
Investigator	So, it is when you are in front of English speakers?
Lida	And family members and other Hispanics! They judge us because we don't speak English well. My family is the worst because they make me feel self-conscious. My nieces and grandchildren they correct me and what bothers me the most is that I don't understand them! And I want to understand what they are saying! I want to speak to them and tell them "stop laughing at me!"
ESL class	(group laughter)
Investigator	So, are these the main reasons why you learn English?
Lida	Yes! For ourselves and for our families! We need to help them and we need to help ourselves.
ESL class	(class nodding with their heads or saying "yes" quietly)

Lida and Rosaura connected feelings of anxiety about speaking English with physiological responses (e.g., "my tongue starts to get twisted," "my brain freezes," "I get paralyzed"). These "fight or flight" indicators in the language learner have been explained as an evolutionary neurobiological response in which "the brain evaluates the stimuli it receives via the senses from the language learning situation... and this appraisal leads to an emotional response" (Schumann 1999, p. 28). Lida highlights how these emotions occur in concert when she speaks with other family members. A low-level proficiency can also foster a degree of embarrassment even among those with whom elderly feel more intimate. When Lida states, "Yes! For ourselves and for our families!", the conversation takes a turn in which the anxiety is overridden by alternative emotive stances based on feelings of concern and responsibility for their loved ones, as well as a desire to gain autonomy for themselves. By vocalizing "Yes" or nodding with their heads, the class responds with a congruent alignment to Lida's comments leading to a type of "emotional contagion" (Hatfield et al. 2014). This interaction demonstrates a collective response of empathy toward Lida's emotions, as well as affirmation of older adults learners' shared language "investments" (cf. Norton-Peirce 1995).

As family members assimilate to an English speaking culture and its social practices, they enhance the boundaries which separate their cultural and linguistic practices with those of non-assimilated members of their families (Rumbaut 2005). When comparing English interlocutors with their own family members, our ESL learners commented how, in some instances, Anglo strangers did not create the same level of shame as their own family members (Ciriza et al. 2016). They expressed how bilingual family members who were more assimilated than them tended to be "too aggressive" or "had a negative tone" when correcting them.

In-group negative affective stances among Hispanic members can be described as instances of "fractal recursivity," which includes "the projection of an opposition, salient at some level of relationship, onto another level" (Irvine and Gal 2000, p. 38). To put it another way, ideologies about the importance of English linguistic competency in American society are projected among Hispanic members within members of their own community. Attitudes toward the perceived linguistic competency of other family members were enacted during familial contexts (e.g., reunions, family meetings, and birthdays) and have an affective impact on the language socialization of ESL learners.

In the classroom, however, older adults felt that the ways in which ESL instructors provided corrective feedback were not as face-threatening as the way in which their grandchildren corrected their errors. It is important to note how affiliative connections between ESL classmates occurred many times through nonverbal responses, such as nodding heads, padding each other on the back, but especially through laughter. In the classroom, laughter was many times the confirmation that there was an emotional resonance between the message conveyed by the speaker and the receiver's emotional stance. Affiliative laughter (Jefferson et al. 1987) created solidarity and empathy between learners, but also permitted students to identify intimate connections between their lived experiences as ESL learners and the experiences of others (Ciriza et al. 2016). For example, in Dialogue 2 group laughter occurs after Lida talks about the fact that she wants her family members to stop laughing at her when she tries to speak English. By laughing as a class, students worked together to destabilize the painful experience of being made fun of for their lack of language skills. They also gained security with one another by sharing a common struggle. As Thonus (2008) puts it, "metapragmatic display of laughter plays a role in moving new relationships along the familiarity–intimacy continuum" (p. 338).

Affective alignments did not occur only during interactions with the researchers in the focus groups. The solidarity and peer bonding created in the classroom led to lively and open discussions during the ESL class itself and during classroom breaks. Darlina and Roberto are married and both are in their late 60s. In the excerpt below, they entered in an interesting discussion about language learning and gender. The discussion was part of a critical thinking exercise, a debate in which men and women had to argumentatively support why their gender was better at doing different tasks (e.g., cooking, learning new things, remembering important information).

Dialogue 3: Shared Frustrations and Gender Roles

Roberto	I think that women have more aptitudes than men for language learning but men are more dedicated. It is scientifically proved that men expend more time in other things than the family, but women are more capable.
Darlina	[raising her voice] That is not true! I think that we are also very dedicated but what happens is that men do not realize that we have other priorities. Your priority is to study, Roberto, but I have to alternate studying with cleaning, with my own husband and my family. I am dedicated but I have more things to do! You are dedicated because "I" have to do the rest!
ESL class	[laughter]
Roberto	I never thought about it that way.
Marta	I agree with Darlina being at home does not allow us to grow.
José	My wife says the same thing and I understand. We are not the best, sometimes we need to help them more around the house.
Severino	Yes, I agree…we need to do more around the house and free space for them to come to class. I always encourage my wife to come.
ESL class	(nodding)

Roberto starts with a binary distinction between men and women, in which he describes women as having more intellectual aptitudes and men having more dedication. Darlina strongly argues against Roberto pointing out that she cannot be as dedicated as him because she has had to take care of him, his children, and do the chores around the house. When Darlina exclaims "I have to do the rest!" she is challenging the essentialism of conventional gender roles and what they represent for learning English. By expressing her frustration, she is deliberately opening up a hot topic in the classroom—namely, that gender is a product of social relations of power. This is further compounded by the fact that as an older woman, her comments appear to contradict conventional images of the domestic role of a traditional Hispanic woman. The group first laughs because of the way Darlina strongly emphasizes the point that she has to "do the rest." However, the group's laughter is followed by two serious comments by two men: Severino, a 67-year-old man, and José, who is 56 years old. Both men recognize that domestic expectations can be overburdening to women, and that men can assist more often in the house so that women are freer to attend the ESL program.

In many instances, we observed how laughter served to frame intense feelings of pain, fear, and injustice. Affiliative laugher functioned to break through long-standing conventional assumptions about older adult language learning. As we have seen, these assumptions include ageist stereotypes about the inability of older persons to acquire a new language to essentialist notions that position men as more competent students. A safe form of group laughter allowed difficult conversations to take place and to give weight to the social issues that impact older adults' lives.

Because these discussions happened in a classroom with both older and younger individuals, learners of various ages came to empathize with one another. As the semester progressed, we could observe how older men reconsidered, through affective alignments, standards of masculinity and femininity to become "inter-gender allies" (Ciriza et al. 2016, p. 9; Gordon 2004). It was through the group's emotional and reflective discussions that older men and women understood that, regardless of their backgrounds, they were all "in the same boat" of Hispanic learners. In this way, they all viewed themselves as committed and motivated learners on the same journey toward language resocialization. The solidarity and empathy built through the semester allowed students to feel that they could "reinvent themselves" and claim a "new public personae" (Ciriza et al. 2016, p. 9). As will be discussed in more detail in Chap. 8, it is through their identity work that older students come to reflect on their own feelings and recast gender norms in ways that minimize constraints on their learning.

Affective Alignments Between ESL Students and Their Teachers

Displays of affect were common in the classroom: ESL students showed concern when others were absent in class; they asked each other about their health or that of their families; and they helped each other navigate different social spheres in a new country (e.g., schools, hospitals, social services). Affiliative connections were expressed through verbal as well as nonverbal signs in the form of "haptics" (i.e., by touch or caressing) and "proxemics" (i.e., by using short distances of body contact, as well as smiles and laughter) (cf. Goodwin 2006). ESL teachers also displayed affiliation toward students by reorienting class discussions to relevant life events outside the classroom, such as family matters. Classroom exercises were also purposefully designed to where students could share their personal tastes, preferences, and attitudes to enhance mutual understanding. Often ESL teachers stayed after class to assist students with issues that they could not resolve by themselves, such as problems with their landlord and how to gain information to assist their navigation of the legal or school system.

Atoofi (2013) examines the affective behavior of teachers and students in the classroom. Teachers often "go beyond their immediate learning issues such as their reading, pronunciation, and writing," which underscores how "the teacher's concern encompasses a larger scope that takes into consideration students' overall feelings and relations with their class, teacher, and other classmates" (Atoofi 2013, p. 229). Atoofi (2013) also argues that the type of emotional work displayed by the teacher is bidirectional in the sense that both teachers and students affectively connect with each other during "on-going and moment-to-moment negotiation of affective practices with one another" (p. 234). In the ESL class, these affective alignments built a sense of "familial care" between teachers and students enhancing a sense of social inclusion important for positive language resocialization.

In line with research findings, our ESL teachers' attachment to their students was created through a variety of "social and emotional feedback" (Atoofi 2013, p. 234). The following interaction illustrates the type of emotional behavior between teachers and students in the ESL classroom. This specific vignette occurred during a class exercise focused on practicing past tenses in which students had to create a timeline of events and describe past life experiences. As part of the exercise, students had to present a poster to the rest of their classmates with either pictures or drawings that depicted different important events (e.g., the birth of their children, marriage, or starting a new job). The excerpt below shows the emotional response of Blanca, a 64-year-old mother, and her teacher. Blanca sheds tears as she presents her timeline, illustrating how emotional communication between teachers and students can be part of the learning process.

Dialogue 4: Affective Alignments between Teachers and Students

Blanca	Here is a picture of my daughter. She is very pretty and very smart. But 5 years ago my daughter went to the doctor and the doctor told her that she was very sick and, that she has cancer.
Teacher	Oh, my God! How did you feel?
Blanca	(starts crying)
Teacher	(goes to Blanca and hugs her) Come on class! Let's tell Blanca that she is a wonderful person!

In this vignette, we can see how the teacher decenters the linguistic task at hand, preferring to stop the conventional lesson in order to hug Blanca. Through an emotional display, positive affective positioning is created between the teacher and students in a way that legitimizes the student's familial context. Further affective alignment occurs when the teacher integrates the class as a whole, creating a space for them to share empathy.

The day in which this interaction took place, all the ESL program teachers consulted one another in a debriefing session. Blanca's teacher, Maria, was asked to share her feelings on the emotional sharing that occurred in the classroom. Maria was an ESL volunteer and worked full time as a secondary school teacher. Even as a volunteer, Maria said that older adult ESL students were connecting with her differently than her public school students. Reflecting on her emotional bonding with ESL learners, Maria noted that she empathized with older adults' difficult life trajectories because it matched the experiences of her own parents and family members. Maria also explained how for older learners like Blanca it was important to make the classroom environment as accommodating as possible to their affective needs. She used different strategies from giving them more one-on-one attention, putting them in groups with more advanced students, and being more conscientious with how she presented them with corrective feedback. In all, emotional bonds between teachers and students were a foundation for positive target language socialization that encouraged student participation and guided language instruction.

It was within this supportive classroom environment where ESL teachers encouraged older adult students to take the necessary risks associated with target language speech development. Lida, now in her 70s, describes how her teacher's positive attitude and instructional strategy in the classroom helped her confront fears related to speaking English and to begin socializing more fully in English:

> She [the teacher] talks about practical topics and in that way she keeps us interested. We talk about Obamacare, education and also about overcoming inhibitions and speak the language. She tells us that there are different ways to overcome inhibitions for example when you focus on a very interesting topic and you start practicing what you think but in English. Maybe you don't know about that topic but then another topic arises, and you can talk about that other topic and start giving your opinion that is when you start learning English.

Lida's comment sheds light on the different curriculum adaptations that ESL teachers perform to make the class relevant to older learners. By bringing real topics to the classroom (e.g., healthcare and education), Lida's teacher was able to foster communication in English which allowed students to "perder la pena," or to lose embarrassment over speaking a new language. Our ESL program teachers were not afraid to deviate from a traditional grammatical curriculum that can focus heavily on correcting linguistic errors. Instead, our ESL teachers understood that with a multigenerational, immigrant student body it was critical to integrate relevant contemporary materials that would be relevant to their daily lives.

Many of the ESL teachers deliberately provided students with psychological strategies to adapt more positively to speaking English in public. For example, teachers encouraged older students to use positive self-talk; facilitated whole classroom discussions about having a "risk-taking" attitude toward speaking English outside the classroom; and promoted a classroom attitude of acceptance regarding linguistic mistakes. ESL teachers were especially aware of older learners' unique language challenges. Brenda, one of our ESL teachers, shared the following story:

> I am more careful with older adults like Berta. I tend to do a lot of pronunciation exercises because I know that they like them, and I don't tend to overcorrect them. With Berta, I have decided to make her work with other outgoing more extrovert students that will help her, or students who will speak slower and are more patient. She is pretty relaxed right now ....

Brenda's commentary shows the reflective efforts ESL teachers undergo to create a classroom space relevant to older adult ESL learners. Brenda adopted a paced approach to teaching and used it to maintain an understanding of older adults' needs and to guide her teaching practices. This included focusing on pronunciation, not overcorrecting their errors, putting older students in groups with outgoing learners, and finding good language mentors who would pace their speech. This holistic pedagogical approach took into account both their cognitive as well as their mental needs (Atoofi 2013).

Overcoming Negative Self-stereotypes About Language Learning in the ESL Classroom

One of the most prominent affective stances among our older adult language learners was related to negative stereotypes about their elderly identities, which they interconnected with other discourses about themselves such as their self-worth and aspects of their personhood. The following dialogue illustrates how the ESL classroom allowed participants to modify these ageist discourses:

Dialogue 5: Cultivating Positive Aging Identities

Reynaldo	The problem is that I am too old to learn.... I look at my grandson and he learned English so fast, so fast! I question myself, Will I ever learn? Will I ever go out and not feel that if … lets' say, I take a bus and I get lost, would I know how to ask "Where am I?", "How do I get home?"
Berta	But you are here, you want to improve yourself. You are learning and you are a hard worker. You are not at home watching TV and wasting your time. Don't listen to what they say!
Reynaldo	Well that is true! At least I am trying! [laughter]

In literature on aging and communication, "implicit self-stereotyping" refers to the internalization of attributes related to age (Hummert et al. 2004). In the above excerpt, Reynaldo uses an implicit self-stereotype when he states "I am too old to learn the language," while Berta reorients Reynaldo's feelings by highlighting "but you are here, you want to improve yourself." This complimentary alignment becomes a "cheering up" moment which leads to a convergence of emotions between Reynaldo and Berta. Reynaldo aligns with Berta's feelings and adopts a less somber stance about his own learning as he smilingly notes the importance of his efforts over his age: "at least I am trying".

Teachers reflected on how older adult learners were especially self-critical with their performance, and pointed out how many times these negative attitudes led them to withdraw from speaking in English in front of the classroom. Older learners often use "age-related excuses" to not perform during public speaking exercises in the classroom (Hummert et al. 2004). For example, our older adults used the fact that they were "not recalling" words in English, "losing memory due to their old age," or thought that their "slowness" when learning new grammatical forms was related to their aging. Studies on aging have shown how negative self-stereotypes have implications for elderly learners and can potentially impact the individual who "may start to believe it and act accordingly" (Hummert et al. 2004, p. 107). In the ESL classroom, the internalization of negative self-stereotypes often led to feelings of frustration and anxiety among older learners. However, as the semester continued we observed how the affective bonding created in the classroom placated these feelings. When older learners uttered a negative self-stereotype their peers would often downplay these attitudes by giving an alternative explanation to age (e.g., "you are too tired today"). Other times, classmates simply looked to cheer up disillusioned peers (e.g., "you can do it!"). These behaviors allowed older students to affectively bond with their classmates by finding in them a "community of sentiment" that understood their hardships having a social—as opposed to a simple biological—etiology.

Fostering strategies aimed at helping older learners, such as speaking in a paced fashion, recasting errors in a positive tone, and encouraging students to produce in the target language without overfocusing on the errors, were just some of the ways in which an intentional safe classroom space was developed. These strategies reduced many of the older learners' fear of speaking in the classroom context. As discussed earlier, "affiliative laugher" (Jefferson et al. 1987) was also key in mitigating negative age-related stereotypes. The interaction below exemplifies this approach. In this example, students were completing a grammar exercise in which they had to make distinctions between the auxiliary "do" and the auxiliary "does," as well as the use of "s" in third person singular. In this case, the teacher is practicing this exercise with Berta.

Dialogue 6: Laughter during Corrective Feedback

Teacher	Where does the girl from the picture live? And where is she from?
Guadalupe	She live in Dallas (error 'lives')
Teacher	She *lives* in Dallas.
Guadalupe	She lives in Dallas and she from Guadalajara (error 'is')
Teacher	She *is* from Guadalajara, and where does she work?
Berta	She work at the library (error 'work')

Teacher	She *works* at the library
Berta	(laughs) she lives in Dallas, and works at the library (laughter)
ESL class	(group laughter)

In this excerpt, the teacher starts by correcting Guadalupe's grammar by recasting and reiterating the learner's statements but producing the correct statement. Despite being corrected, in the next turn Berta commits the same error again. Noticing her mistake, Berta laughs and self-corrects. The affiliative laughter, as well as Guadalupe's own laughter, shows an alignment of interactional moves which shows the importance of displaying a positive affect and a relaxed attitude in the classroom toward learners' mistakes.

By employing a pedagogy that is not overfocused on errors, learners were able to communicate more freely in the classroom. This positive atmosphere allowed both younger and older learners to not be paralyzed by the fear of committing errors. Using laughter as a tool, students could see through their errors to take in new linguistic information and maintain socialization with interlocutors. Positive affective stances prepare older language learners to confront the risky prospect of making language mistakes when communicating in English. In short, students become free to concentrate on communicating messages versus producing error-free speech.

Affective behaviors such as empathy and pride in the language accomplishments of others were also observed between younger and older dyads. The excerpt below presents the interaction between Mario, who is 27 years old, and Rosaura, who is 65 years old. Both are working on an English language grammar exercise.

Dialogue 7: Younger and Older Learners Working Together:

Mario	You just have to use 'Do' when the verb is in the plural form for example…
Rosaura	I know! I know! Don't tell me! 'Do they like bananas?'
Mario	Exactly! and then you use 'does' for 'he' and 'she'
Rosaura	Does she like bananas?
Mario	Exactly! You learn so fast Rosaura!
Rosaura	I told you! I went home and studied all night long!

We can see how Mario shows positive affect toward Rosaura, noting his confidence in Rosaura's language abilities. Within the ESL classroom, many younger learners became language mentors to older students and were willing to sit down with them to help with issues of language grammar, pronunciation, and vocabulary. In doing so, they were covertly enacting a more socially inclusive vision of language learning, one in which older learners could participate without fear of being negatively stereotyped as aging learners. Younger mentors became positive "sociolinguistic mentors" by promoting a more "inclusive vision" of intergenerational language learning than older adults may encounter in kin and non-kin networks (McEwan-Fujita 2010, p. 54). The intergenerational bonds created in the classroom facilitated language acquisition and positive language socialization with younger learners.

It was through this type of intergenerational socialization in the ESL program that students arrived to an understanding that both young and older learners faced similar problems acquiring English. At the end of one semester, Tomás, who is 73 years old, commented: "we all have issues pronouncing words, we all forget vocabulary words often, and none of us understand when they speak fast to us. It is not a question of age, it is a question of learning how to learn a new language." Like Tomás, self-criticism was redirected to an appreciation that they were all "learners." Deficiencies are certainly part of being a learner, but that is not the only defining characteristic of older adult learners. By observing younger learners, Tomás comes to the realization that older adults' linguistic issues are more related to expectations to produce error-free speech than their inherent cognitive disadvantages. Older learners like Tomás also felt that the classroom was allowing them to minimize their fears to socialize in English with other interlocutors outside the class. During our interviews, older learners discussed how they defended their right to speak with English interlocutors. Most notably, they connected their empowered position to the positive affective emotions developed in the classroom that supported their self-as-learner identity.

In this chapter, we have seen how understanding the learner's affect (i.e., the learner's motivation, anxiety, self-esteem, and confidence) is a key determinant to understanding language learning. Conventional views of emotions and language learning tend to conceptualize affect as a trait-based/individualized phenomenon. Emergent viewpoints of language learning argue that apart from learning how to use the language, speakers also develop in interaction an understanding of social actions, situations, emotions, and other sociocultural elements. Affect forms part of these broader sociocultural meanings that are inculcated through interaction and which shapes linguistic socialization. Importantly, learners co-construct affective stances toward their language learning and socialization.

In this chapter, we have discussed how in the ESL classroom "affective care" toward older learners was shaped (a) via solidarity and bonding with other ESL learners who understood their hardships, (b) the affective behavior of the teacher who shaped teaching practices to accommodate to the needs of older learners, (c) the relaxed atmosphere regarding corrective strategies, and (d) the intergenerational affiliative encouragement by younger learners.

Adult learners utilized affective stances to communicate cultural understandings about their hardships. Both empathy and solidarity were developed out of a collective recognition of affective care and frustration. A mutual sense of understanding and solidarity emerged as older adult learners narrated both the difficulties of their learning trajectories and their high affective investment to learn the language. This new sense of "group membership" and unity, which was being cultivated during the semester-long language classroom, was solidified through shared empathic understanding.

Our older adult ESL students found the classroom to be a place for learning that did not include the embarrassment and anxiety characteristic of English socializing with family or non-ESL peers. Women learners in our study, in particular, reflected on their frustrations and used laughter to delegitimize gender norms restricting their access to the classroom. In this way, collectively sharing affective stances allowed students to reinvent themselves in ways that made available new social and cognitive resources supportive of language acquisition. Despite the differences in their individual backgrounds, students aligned with the social position of others and created a type of shared mentality about what it means to be an immigrant language learner. This type of empathetic work occurred across gender and age boundaries. In doing so, older adult men and women were able to have a critical discussion about how gender roles constrain learning experiences.

Older immigrants often seek to minimize "errors" by withdrawing from language socialization. By building a classroom atmosphere based on positive affective stances, teachers can alleviate learners' fear, anxiety, and shame related to their linguistic behavior. In the classroom, teachers can employ pedagogical strategies that are socially inclusive to older learners and attend to their cognitive and social psychological needs. In multigenerational ESL programs, younger ESL learners can also become language mentors by helping older adults with their grammar, pronunciation, and vocabulary. In turn, this type of mentorship can be a positive model for intergenerational language socialization outside the classroom.

Classrooms can be places that transform negative stereotypes about old age learners when they are structured as a positive and responsive community of learners. This transformation must come from solidarity and recursive discursive practices that promote the type of risk-taking necessary for language development. Our narratives illustrate the important role emotion work plays both inside and outside the classroom.

References

Arnold, J. (Ed.). (1999). *Affect in language learning*. Cambridge: Cambridge University Press.
Atoofi, S. (2013). Classroom has a heart: Teachers and students affective alignment in a Persian heritage language classroom. *Linguistics and Education, 24,* 215–236.
Bayley, R., & Schecter, S. R. (Eds.). (2003). *Language socialization in bilingual and multilingual societies*. Clevedon: Multilingual Matters.
Besnier, N. (1990). Language and affect. *Annual Review of Anthropology, 19,* 419–451.
Blader, S. L., Wiesenfeld, B., Rothman, R., & Wheeler-Smith, S. (2010). Social emotions and justice: How the emotional fabric of groups determines justice enactment and reactions. In E. A. Mannix & M. A. Neale (Eds.), *Research on managing groups and teams: Fairness & groups* (pp. 29–62). Bingley, UK: Emerald Publishing.
Block, D. (2003). *The social turn in second language acquisition*. Edinburgh: Edinburg University Press.
Block, D. (2007). *Second language identities*. London/New York: Continuum.
Block, D. (2013). Critiquing applied linguistics: An introduction. *Applied Linguistics Review, 4*(2), 221–228.

Coupland, N., Coupland, J., & Giles, H. (1991). *Language, society and the elderly: Discourse, identity and ageing*. Massachusetts: Blackwell.
Ciriza, M., Shappeck, M., & Arxer, S. (2016). Emergent target language identities among Latino English language learners. *Journal of Latinos and Education, 15*(4), 287–302.
Englebretson, R. (2007). Stancetaking in discourse: An introduction. In R. Englebretson (Ed.), *Stancetaking in discourse: Subjectivity, evaluation, interaction* (pp. 1–25). Philadelphia, PA: John Benjamins.
Goodwin, M. H. (2006). Participation, affect, and trajectory in family directive/response sequences. *Text and Talk, 26*(4/5), 513–542.
Goodwin, M. H., Cekaite, A., & Goodwin, C. (2012). Emotion as stance. In A. Peräkylä & M-L. Sorjänen (Eds.), *Emotion in interaction* (pp. 16–63). Oxford: Oxford University Press.
Goodwin, M. H., & Goodwin, C. (2000). Emotion within situated activity. In A. Duranti (Ed.), *Linguistic anthropology: A reader* (pp. 239–257). Oxford: Blackwell.
Gordon, D. (2004). I am tired you clean and cook: shifting gender identities and language socialization. *TESOL Quarterly, 38*(3), 437–457.
Jacoby, S., & Ochs, E. (1995). Co-construction: An introduction. *Research on language and social interaction, 28*(3), 171–183.
Hatfield, E., Carpenter, M., & Rapson, R. L. (2014). Emotional contagion as a precursor to collective emotions. In C. von Scheve & M. Salmela (Eds.), *Collective emotions: Perspectives from psychology, philosophy, and sociology* (pp. 108–122). Oxford: Oxford University Press.
Horwitz, E. K., Horwitz, M. B., & Cope, J. A. (1986). Foreign language classroom anxiety. *The Modern Language Journal, 70*(2), 125–132.
Hummert, M. L., Garstka, T. L., Ryan, E. B., & Bonnesen, J. (2004). The role of age stereotypes in interpersonal communication. In J. F. Nussbaum & J. Coupland (Eds.), *Handbook of communication and aging research* (pp. 91–115). Mahwah, NJ: Lawrence Erlbaum Associates Inc.
Irvine, J., & Gal, S. (2000). Language ideology and linguistic differentiation. In Paul Kroskrity (Ed.), *Regimes of language: Ideologies, polities, and identities* (pp. 35–84). Santa Fe, New Mexico: School of American Research Press.
Jefferson, G., Sacks, H., & Schegloff, E. (1987). Notes on laughter in the pursuit of intimacy. In G. Button & J. R. E. Lee (Eds.), *Talk and social organisation* (pp. 152–205). Clevedon Canada: Multilingual Matters.
Krashen, S. D. (1985). *The input hypothesis: Issues and implications*. New York: Longman.
Krashen, S. D. (1989). We acquire vocabulary and spelling by reading: Additional evidence for the input hypothesis. *Modern Language Journal, 73*(4), 440–464.
Krashen, S.D. (1994). The input hypothesis and its rivals. In N. Ellis (Ed.), *Implicit and explicit learning of languages*. (pp. 45–77). London: Academic Press: London.
Loschky, L. (1994). Comprehensible input and second language acquisition. *Studies in Second Language Acquisition, 16*, 303–323.
McEwan-Fujita, E. (2010). Ideology, affect and socialization in language shift and revitalization: The experiences of adults learning Gaelic in the western isles of Scotland. *Language in Society, 39*(1), 27–64.
Norton, B. (2000). *Identity and language learning: Gender, ethnicity, and educational change*. London, UK: Longman.
Norton, B. (2001). Non-participation, imagined communities, and the language classroom. In M. P. Breen (Ed.), *Learner contributions to language learning: New directions in research* (pp. 159–171). Essex, UK: Pearson.
Norton-Peirce, B. (1995). Social identity, investment, and language learning. *TESOL Quarterly, 29*(1), 9–31.
Ochs, E. (1986). Introduction. In B. Schieffelin & E. Ochs (Eds.), *Language socialization across cultures*. Cambridge: Cambridge University Press.
Ochs, E. (1988). *Culture and language development: Language acquisition and language socialization in a Samoan village*. Cambridge: Cambridge University Press.

References

Ochs, E. (1993). Constructing social identity: A language socialization perspective. *Research on Language and Social Interaction, 26*, 287–306.

Ochs, E., Schegloff, E. A., & Thompson, S. A. (Eds.). (1996). *Interaction and grammar*. Cambridge, UK: Cambridge University Press.

Ochs, E., & Schieffelin, B. B. (1989). Language has a heart: The pragmatics of affect. *Special Issue of Text, 9*(1), 7–25.

Pavlenko, A. & Blackledge, A. (Eds.) (2002). Ideologies of language in multilingual contexts. Special issue. *Multilingua, 21*(2/3), 121–326.

Rumbaut, R. (2005). Sites of belonging: Acculturation, discrimination, and ethnic identity among children of immigrants. In T. S. Weiner (Ed.), *Discovering successful pathways in children' development: Mixed methods in the study of childhood and family life* (pp. 111–164). Chicago, IL: University of Chicago Press.

Schieffelin, B. B., & Ochs, E. (1986). *Language socialization across cultures*. New York, NY: Cambridge University Press.

Schumann, J. (1999). A perspective on affect. In Jane Arnold (Ed.), *Affect in language learning* (pp. 28–41). Cambridge: Cambridge University Press.

Thonus, T. (2008). Acquaintanceship, familiarity, and coordinated laughter in writing tutorials. *Linguistics and Education, 19*, 333–350.

White, L. (2003). *Second language acquisition and universal grammar*. New York, NY: Cambridge University Press.

Chapter 7
Practicing Safe Language Socialization in Private and Public Spaces

> Family is everything where I come from.... In my family, when you need something and need help, everyone helps and supports each other. Some people like to think you can do everything by yourself but you can't. You need the help of others. I learned that from my parents and that's how I raised my children and what I teach my grandchildren.... Their support has been very important so I can come to class every Saturday. It is hard but they motivate me. I think they like seeing me as a student.

Ana is fortunate to be part of a family network that helps her to attend Saturday ESL classes on a regular basis. Ana shared with us that she has tried many times to learn English by enrolling in language classes. She struggled though, having to juggle multiple part-time jobs and raise her children. Ana described to us that she would often attend the first couple ESL classes but would find herself skipping days as the semester wore on because of family and work responsibilities. Now 58 years old, Ana is upbeat about her effort to learn English and cites her family's support as important to her ESL class participation. She insists that it is necessary for her to make strides to speak English given shifts in language usage in the family.

> All my grandkids speak English more and more....and I want to be able to know what they are saying. All their homework is in English and they talk to their friends in English with all their phones. Sometimes they talk to me in English to help me but it is difficult to understand everything they are saying.

Ana draws attention to the changing linguistic expectations in many immigrant homes. Younger generations are practicing more English-speaking in the home and older adults are having to manage a communicative gap with their children and grandchildren. Ana describes her frustration with wanting to communicate with her grandchildren and participate in aspects of their lives, such as school-related events, but it is quite challenging. The increased use of social media has further complicated the issue as older adults are left out of the social mediums that attract younger generations.

When Ana arrived to the United States, the household's first language was Spanish. Her children first learned to speak in Spanish and through their schooling received English language instruction. This is increasingly changing, however, as more family members are bringing English into the home. In some ways this has made life a bit easier for Ana.

> My children and even grandchildren help me all the time with something in English that I don't understand. Sometimes it can be something in the mail or a note from my doctor. They will read it to me slowly to help me understand what it says. This is great because when I first arrived to the United States I was essentially on my own.

In other ways, though, the introduction of bilingualism into the household has led to some detours in learning English. Interestingly, she describes that while more family members speak English with her, these are not the type of conversations that help her successfully practice English.

> I feel like when people talk in English at home I don't really participate. They speak it so well that I feel bad interrupting or asking them what they are saying. I do catch a couple words but really I just let them talk with each other. It's ok but I need to be learning English with others and with the help of an instructor in a classroom, like this one. Really, my grandchildren shouldn't have to teach me English.

While Ana does have access to some English language socialization within the family, she points out that it is not always an ideal learning situation. Fears and concerns block her participation with individuals she considers to be proficient English speakers. Ana notes that not all English-speaking spaces are the same and that she looks to the interactions within the ESL classroom as perhaps being more beneficial given the guidance of instructors.

Ana's story speaks to the complex, and sometimes contradictory, nature of language acquisition for Hispanic older adults. The family can be a significant source of social support, as younger generations mediate English language socialization with actors outside the home. At the same time, the growing incidences of bilingualism in the home, as younger family members acculturate to English-dominant institutions, can generate gaps in communication between generations and withdrawal from English socialization. Indeed, as Ana expressed, having young children be the English language experts can be unsettling to older adults and transform traditional family arrangements.

This chapter explores the private and public spaces that structure the production of language resocialization capital. For many Hispanic older adults, the domestic sphere has been transformed as English has been introduced by younger family members. While this offers older adults an opportunity to socialize in English, these interactions do not always provide nonthreatening opportunities for practicing a second language. In many cases, children and grandchildren are positioned as linguistic "caretakers" for older adults. Role reversal of language caretakers within a household may lead to poor socio-pragmatic and linguistic input for older adults. With this in mind, we take a look at kin and non-kin work done to explore the ways in which ESL classroom socialization offers resources that support older adults speaking English at home. Similarly, we consider how ESL experiences encourage English socialization in public spaces, such as at their workplaces. At heart, we emphasize that ESL socialization affords Hispanic older adults a "safe" space to practice their linguistic communicative competence and to reengage in their bilingual homes and public settings.

Navigating Communication Domains in a Multilingual Society

The acquisition of a second language among older adult immigrants is associated with a range of factors. Scholars have found that for the United States immigrant population in general higher English proficiency is linked to early age migration, higher levels of education, years of formal education in the United States, marriage to a native born, time spent living in the United States, and a long-term commitment to staying in the United States, such as owning a home (Espenshade and Fu 1997; Stevens 1999). These factors are understood to be predictors of English proficiency because they indicate immigrants' exposure to and possible engagement with English in multiple sociolinguistic contexts.

Although older adult immigrants' language learning is propelled by practical communicative needs, the social identity of learners mediates access to English in multiple contexts (Pavlenko 2000). Age, race, ethnicity, gender, and nationality influence the social spaces in which learners find themselves. So the need to communicate in the target language is not the same across various experiential domains. In this respect, scholars have linked SLA proficiency to the effects of cognitive, cultural, and discourse domains (Borgatti 1994; Langacker 1987; Young 1999). Competence in a second language is related to a learner's ability to acquire language knowledge and skills in specific domains. Second language learners come to use sanctioned speech, vocabulary, registers, and cultural references relevant to specific domains (Centeno 2007; Savignon 1983). Older adult immigrants encounter domains with different linguistic competencies, some that may have a greater or lesser requirement for English. Given that access to the target language may be spatially distributed across various social groups, older adult immigrants face having to move between linguistic worlds without much support. Blommaert et al. (2005) refer to this as a form of "truncated multilingualism," whereby second language learners struggle to manage the specific language requirements of multiple life domains. Because they have less access to formal language education, immigrants arriving at a later age are even less initiated into the norms of target language domains.

Older adult immigrants' need to use a second language can vary dramatically across domains because they may be likely to speak their first language at home with family members. This may be unlike when they are in more public settings and must negotiate interactions dominated by English. Pancho, who is 58 years old, highlights this division between "private" and "public" domains, how it dictated his English socialization, and helped to delay his participation in language classes.

> I can speak Spanish at home with everyone so I just didn't think I needed to learn English. It is difficult sometimes at work or when I'm trying to talk to someone who only speaks English at a store. But I can ask my children or grandchildren to translate. But now even at home my grandchildren speak English more and so many things involve knowing English.

Gal (2005) describes the "private" as domestic spaces that primarily include kin and significant others. At times neighbors may fall within the private sphere within close knit communities that are ethnically concentrated and monolingual. The private domain is generally protective of first languages in these cases. Various informal and formal settings are considered public domains, such as workplaces, schools, hospitals, stores, and other settings. Pancho describes his reliance on family to maintain first-language communication and to mediate for him in public, English-dominant, interactions. He also brings to light the reality of a multilingual society and how social domains are not purely monolingual in nature. Multiple languages are operating in the home, for example, as younger minority members are increasingly proficient in speaking English. This shows the complex landscape that older adult immigrants traverse and some of the impetus for their participation in ESL classes.

In this chapter we delve into the private and public domains of our older adults to identify how these sites structure their needs and ability to learn English. Importantly, we seek to reveal the dynamic interplay between these domains and the experiential space of the ESL classroom. As a defined location with a range social capital resources, such as instructional guidance and peer support, the ESL classroom works as a unique space for learning. Experiences within the ELS classroom often have consequences for older adults' home and work lives in ways that reinforce second language learning in those domains.

Family Language Socialization and Role-Strain

Conventionally, scholars have tied the preservation of immigrants' first language to the domestic sphere, seeing the home as a monolingual space. Early on scholars understood the emergence of a bilingual society as meaning that as immigrants came to acquire English, their first language would be relegated to interactions with close friends and family. As was mentioned in Chap. 3, familial bonds provide a wide range of resources that support elderly immigrants' transition to a new society, but they may also isolate them from linguistic and behavioral norms outside the family that would mitigate the pressures of acculturation (Gallo et al. 2009). For many immigrants, particularly those who are recent arrivals, there may be less need to use English within the household or in concentrated ethnic communities if the first language is preferred in that context. Pancho's story reflects this reality as he has been able, to a large extent, to not speak English at home and manage his public English interactions with the aid of English proficient family members. Maria's home experience is similar to Pancho's, in that she describes being shielded from the need to use English beyond a basic level.

> My family helps me when I go shopping or go to the doctor. My children speak English, so they interpret for me.... I know some words and how to introduce myself. But at home everyone speaks Spanish so I don't have to worry when I'm home or talking to friends. It is harder with my grandchildren who speak less Spanish.

On the one hand, Pancho and Maria emphasize how family protects the use of their first language and in certain ways decreases the need to use English. But they also present a more complicated image that disrupts the monolingual character of the home and suggests how older adult immigrants' are increasingly living in bilingual households. Domestic spaces may conserve immigrants' mother tongue, but they are also structured by the presence of multiple generations in the household. Research tends to show that English use increases from the first immigrant generation to later ones (Alba et al. 2002). Conversely, among some ethnic groups, proficiency and adoption of the first language decreases with later generations (Schrauf 1999). Since many older adult immigrants live in multigenerational households, they can expect to encounter more English with members of the next generation, such as with their children and grandchildren.

This intergenerational language effect is driven by changes in the language socialization process of immigrant households. Immigrant adults, who are traditionally regarded as the primary agents of socialization but lack target language proficiency, transfer the responsibility of language socialization to other institutions, such as schools. A consequence is that a social asymmetry emerges whereby younger members acquire a higher set of linguistic and symbolic resources than recently arrived immigrant parents who find themselves without authority in the dominant societal language and do not have the material and cultural resources to resocialize into the target language (Auerbach 1989; Luykx 2005).

The reversal of the "typical age-based distribution of power" alters the traditional role of immigrant parents as the authority figures of the household, placing them in a linguistically subordinate position in relation to their children. As Auerbach (1989) notes, the fact that children's English literacy proficiency may be more developed can lead parents to feel "that respect for them is undermined and children feel burdened by having to negotiate" (p. 171). In a study of Mexican immigrant families, Partida (1996) points out how families depict the process of acculturation as accompanied by "strained family relations, isolation, misunderstandings, poor communications and the clashing of values, morals, cultures and ideals" (p. 244).

Many of our participants reflected on how changes in first-language usage in the household led to stress on family relationships with their children. At 56 years old, Paola's adult children are much more proficient in English now than they were when they were young. As children they primarily spoke Spanish, but as they entered school and by the time they were in their teens Paola's children spoke more English. Paola discussed her children's shift to speaking more English than Spanish and how that impacted their relationship.

> When they were little they only spoke Spanish. It's what was spoken in the house. When they went to school they learned more English, which was difficult for me to learn. But you know, it's easier for children to learn since they are still growing. I remember they began to speak less Spanish in the house and to lose words. It sometimes felt like they were in a

different world. They could watch things on television in English or talk to friends and I wouldn't know what they were saying. I would ask, but I don't know if they were telling me the truth. I feel the same way with my grandchildren now, but maybe it's even worse because they speak a lot more English even as little children.

Dependence on the linguistic ability of younger others becomes an aspect that marks the linguistic socialization of older family member. Paola shows that language gaps can disrupt the conventional authority of immigrant parents as they are unable to fully control behavior of children done in English-dominant spaces (Tse 1995, 1996; Valdes 2005). The description given by Paola refers to one of two worlds, where English proficient children are able to escape the observation of monolingual parents.

Thus a central issue is the cultural and communicative gap between older adults and younger interlocutors that emerges from the generational effects of assimilation. Over time, children and adolescents that migrate to the new country tend to ethnically self-identify more with the external dominant culture than with their family's internal cultural–linguistic practices. Some refer to this process as "dissonant acculturation" (Rumbaut 2005). Children are more often taught by the external culture to value English speakers as role models and this can lead to the devalued status of parents and elders. This might play out in young children turning more to their peers and to an American value orientation and problematizing the definitions of family previously adopted (Gil and Vega 1996). Scholarship shows that this parent–child dynamic is not always helpful to older second language learners. From the perspective of language socialization, a breakdown in parental authority can lead to fears about speaking in English, and perhaps even in the first language, to authorized English expert children and to poor language input by children experts (Rumbaut 2005).

While growing emotional and communicative distance is often part of a child's own development in becoming an independent individual, in the context of acculturation and intergenerational language barriers, studies have shown negative effects related to debilitated bonds within the family (Partida 1996). In a review of the literature of communication problems between families in immigrant contexts, Usita and Blieszner (2002) cite a range of problems, such as resistance by children to share confidential information and frustration by caretakers in their inability to effectively express their thoughts to children and grandchildren. This is significant given that Hispanic older adults, particularly women, continue to have higher self- and social expectations for filial piety in the form of caretaking (Kao and Travis 2005). In this way, Hispanic older adults experience acute counter pressures stemming from intergenerational communication barriers and family obligations related to the caretaking of younger language expert family members.

While Paola's story emphasizes the challenges she confronted as a parent raising her bilingual children, she also describes a similar process occurring now as a grandparent. As a monolingual older adult, Paola suggests that the language gap is "even worse" with her grandchildren who have more quickly adopted English as a preferred language. In terms of multigenerational immigrant families it is important to investigate how language is used in interaction with elderly people and how this language socialization shapes the communicative problems of older adults.

Overcoming Elderspeak Through Affiliative Kin Work

Referred to as "elderspeak," the way communication occurs with older adults can have a positive or negative impact on target language development. It was important in our study to explore the ways elderspeak within the family impacts older adults' language socialization and also defines conceptions of aging in society. We look into how younger family members accommodate to the perceived English language deficiencies of elderly immigrants and the extent to which such adaptations of speech condition older adult SLA.

Problems arise for older language learners who seek to develop linguistic abilities with their family members. From the perspective of the elderly, they often describe how their children or grandchildren criticize or over-correct elderly speech, or they lack the patience to teach them English. Many times younger speakers might also dictate the language they want to speak in the family, English or Spanish, despite the parent's lack of understanding or the family's unwritten law that "Spanish should be the language spoken at home."

Returning to Pancho's story, we see that older adults rely on younger family members to assist in language translation and mediate public interactions. Though this provides a measure of social support, Pancho notes that the nature of language socialization across generations often comes at the cost of elder's self-assurance.

> My grandchildren correct me when I say something wrong or mispronounced something in English. Sometimes I tell them that it's more difficult for me since I didn't grow up here [in the United States] or go to school. I get embarrassed because they [the grandchildren] sometimes get frustrated with me because of my English.

Cross-generational communication can include face-threatening acts in which older adults feel ashamed and blame themselves for not being able to master the language. In their study of Japanese mother–daughter communication, Usita and Blieszner (2002) highlight poignant comments from the daughters who indicated frustration and embarrassment when adult second-language-learner parents used "wrong words and expressions" (p. 274). Younger language brokers interviewed by McQuillan and Tse (1995) also confessed to being embarrassed of parents for their lack of English skills.

These interactions index larger sociological problems between young and old. When younger interlocutors correct older adults they are positioning themselves as displaying more knowledge of the language than their parents and caretakers. This can create a hierarchical arrangement of teacher–student. Repeated face-threatening and negative affective dispositions not only engender hindrances in the acquisition and social use of English, but also alters the very nature of the parent–child or grandparent–grandchild relationship as roles become reversed.

From a linguistic socialization perspective, mutual support, family trust, and acceptance are significant factors. It is important for older adults to be able to make mistakes without being judged and for young "experts" to make accommodations that supply not only vocabulary, grammar, and register but also confidence and satisfaction. Instances of mutual support and positive mentorship can occur during the language socialization between family generations. Usita and Blieszner (2002) observed how as daughters became older they consistently strove to improve their mother's English by teaching them pronunciation skills and attentively listening to their mothers when the meaning of their message was unclear or when they had communication problems so as to make them feel more at ease. These strategies also served to foster closeness between parent and child and enhance positive relationships within the family.

In our study, the ESL classroom was shown to help mediate the communicative gaps between generations and provide ways of shoring up familial resources for responsive second language socialization. Our older adult participants spoke about the development of self-confidence in speaking English and how the ESL classroom helped to structure this process. Ana recalls her high level of anxiety and fear during the first few days of class. She describes feeling overwhelmed and uncertain with her decision to enroll in ESL classes.

> I don't like to speak in English in front of other people because I know very little. Especially in the beginning...before I started taking classes. I was very nervous. You know...I didn't know what to expect. I was worried that this would be too difficult for me or that I would be wasting my time. But now I love it. I love my classes. I love my teachers and classroom companions....Now I want to come to class and I'm sad when it's over. I also feel more confident speaking English with others and even my grandchildren at home.... In class I never felt stupid or bad for making a mistake. We all make mistakes here but we don't make fun of each other. We are here to learn.

Classroom bonds with peers play a critical role in the self-identity of older adult learners. These bonds contain some of the few individuals in the lives of older adult immigrants committed to their language resocialization. Although many family members assist in older adults' language needs, the ESL classroom appears to offer unique social dynamics that may be absent at home. An ESL context creates a safe space where participants understand that making mistakes and learning go hand in hand. As Ana says, the fact that "we all make mistakes ... we are here to learn" sets the tone for how others will respond to errors in speech. In this way, the classroom space is different from the private space of older adults' home environment where language experts may be willing to help but are not attuned to the various affective and interactional needs of second language learners. Self-confidence is therefore tied to social and affective dynamics associated with ESL classroom interaction.

Scholars highlight the significance of adaptive strategies of immigrant families to cope with the social challenges of assimilation, particularly as it relates to older adult immigrants who benefit from families that take an active role in elder immigrants' transition to United States (Delgado-Gaitan 1990; Perreira et al. 2006). In this vein, Auerbach (1989) argues that immigrant family's literacy practices should be bidirectional, wherein older adult learners and younger language experts help each other. Looking at parent and child relationships, Auerbach (1989) describes an ideal scenario where "the children help their parents with homework, act as interpreters for them, and help them in the outside world. Parents in turn often foster their children's first-language competence and help in areas where they feel competent" (p. 171). In other words, family members respond to elderly needs in a comprehensive way.

As was mentioned, however, younger family members' language expertise may not always translate to successful language resocialization for older adults. These encounters may include uncomfortable role reversals and face-threatening interactions that undermine older adults' self-confidence and risk their future engagement with the target language. What we observed among our participants was how ESL classroom participation helped older adults develop a self-as-learner identity around the self-conception of being a student. In turn, this new student identity was instrumental in building affiliation and mutual understanding with younger generations in the household who possess similar biographical experiences. The ESL classroom can be a way to build kin work between older adult learners and younger expert interlocutors on their shared student identity.

Viewed generally, "kin work" includes the multitude of strategies used by family members to support each other's daily living (Alicea 1997). In an immigrant context, kin work suggests the common activities done by older adults and family interlocutors that promote elders' acculturation and transition to the new country, such as in preserving their first language and mediating second language needs.

> When I come home after class my grandchildren are always interested in what happened. They ask me what books I'm reading and what homework I have. They really want to know about my homework. They like the idea that I have homework like them. It's fun because we both talk about what we are doing in our classes.

As the excerpt above illustrates, older adults talk about intergenerational affiliation, or being "like them," by discursively emphasizing their role as an ESL student. A type of affiliative talk emerges and is described as vital to constructing mutual appreciation and understanding across the gulf of generations. Affiliation also leads to a different way to structure intergenerational communication. Here Ana emphasizes that by sharing common experiences as students, such as doing homework, talking in English is now a "fun" pursuit.

Pancho more directly spoke about how affiliation produced from sharing a common identity directly impacts English language socialization between older adults and younger family members. As his story shows, children and grandchildren have memory of the stress and pressures associated with being a student. This biographical experience can inform their interactional decisions with other students, such as choosing to be empathetic toward their parents and grandparents currently taking ESL classes.

> My children have been encouraging me coming to class. They remember how it was being a student and so they really support me.... I have noticed my grandchildren try to help me with my homework and talk to me in English. They now do it a bit more slowly. They say, "'abuelo' [grandpa] this is how my teacher teaches us." And my granddaughter talks slowly and repeats to help me remember what a word means.

We see that older adults' identity work as a student is important not only for their own self-confidence but also in promoting positive language socialization with family. Young expert interlocutors refashion their communication style by referencing their own experience in school, trying to model the "best practices" of classroom teachers. Communication strategies, such as pacing one's speech and emphasizing through repetition, are adopted by some children and grandchildren as a more effective way to support their elder family members. The family role reversals endemic in many immigrant families due to uneven English language proficiency is moderated through affiliation based on a shared learner identity. Our findings show that building on commonality is a way to engage in kin work that creates opportunities for positive ESL socialization among multigenerational family members.

Public Language Socialization Through Family Alliances and Inner Speech Development

As was mentioned in Chap. 3, those older adult immigrants who live in ethnic communities with a concentration of first-language speakers gain support and linguistic protection. This also helps immigrants' transition and settlement into American society as social, material, and political resources are available in older adults' first language. United States Census data shows that older Hispanics with low English proficiency are more likely to reside in geographical locations with at least three times the proportion of Hispanics as compared to the nation overall (Mutchler and Brallier 1999). This is to say that elderly Hispanics with lower levels of English proficiency also tend to live in neighborhoods where the primary language is Spanish and where there are fewer opportunities to speak English. There are differences among Hispanic groups in the United States in terms of the composition and linguistic landscape of their neighborhoods. The sample of older adults in our study that includes individuals primarily from Mexico and some from El Salvador, Honduras, and Guatemala represent immigrant groups who tend to live in geographically concentrated, Spanish-speaking neighborhoods.

In an English-dominant society such as the United States, public spaces are typically monolingual English domains. In this case, workplaces, government offices, schools, and hospitals are places where Spanish is constrained and individuals are encouraged to use English. We do not want to overstate this point, since institutions and organization provide channels of communication, such as organizational documents and websites, in Spanish. This is particularly the case in metropolitan areas with high numbers of racial and ethnic minorities and with an influx of migrants, such as in the cities of Dallas, Miami, and Los Angeles. Still, immigrants' first language can retain a minority status as the presence of multiple generations, new social media, and a global economy can open these monolingual settings to English. This suggests that many Hispanic older adult learners find themselves in a bind, in that their communities help to protect their first-language usage but also do not fully prepare them to communicate in public settings dominated by English.

Similar to the domestic domain, our participants shared how their ESL classroom experience shapes their public English language socialization. Our older adults describe two major ways in which the ESL classroom space structured pathways for English speaking in public spaces, such as at work. Here older adults point to the construction of familial and peer-based alliances and the development of inner speech as frameworks aiding them in public English socialization.

We consider that older adults' self-perceptions as second language learners and their interactions within English socialization are embedded within in larger social contexts that include peers and family members. Older adults may be entangled in a mix of social and linguistics pressures that problematize learning English. Community and family interlocutors, for example, may dissuade older adults' engagement in English through first language concentrated interactions and interpreter-focused target language mediation. As Pancho mentioned earlier, family often intercedes on behalf of older adults in publics settings, such as in supermarkets and other English-dominant institutions, thus reducing the impetus to use English.

Taken broadly, the ESL classroom established a network of social support that older adults used to build alliances for the purposes of public English speaking. Most notably, ESL classroom interaction assisted during the beginning period when older adults acclimated themselves to speaking English in public. Many participants noted that while they used to be anxious about speaking any English at all in public and were quick to rely on family to intercede for them, their ESL classroom experience helped them address these initial roadblocks to public socialization. Student-to-student interactions were a way for older adults to become more comfortable with and positive about English socializing. In turn, older adults transferred these feelings and attitudes to domains outside the classroom to try out their skills. Juan, who has been enrolled in ESL for two consecutive semesters, describes the process

> Now that I have been in class for a while I feel more comfortable trying English when I go out. Here we practice with each other and talk to each other and I want to do that when I go out to the store. My family still helps me but I try to talk too. Sometimes it is just a few words but with my family there I feel like I have the support I need when I don't know what else to say. But my family is impressed by how much I have learned and how I speak more English with others now.

From a sociolinguistic perspective, the experiential space of the ESL classroom can be a testing ground for public domain English-use. Juan notes that classroom socializing and activities were a bridge that helped him transition to larger public domains. As opposed to a "truncated multilingualism" where linguistic competencies are segregated to different domains and older adults are peripheral actors in English-dominant spaces, our ESL older adults were able to transfer knowledge and experience across language settings.

Along with other participants, Juan says this has also changed family relationships from a unidirectional to a bidirectional arrangement. While in the past older adults described their role in public encounters as primarily one of dependence on family translators, now many participants emphasize their increased activity in English-dominant interactions. In this way, older adults developed a "right to speak" based on a more balanced alliance with family English language experts. For Juan, family members are now better at recognizing his need to practice his English language knowledge in public settings. A new trust that family members will support Juan's efforts and provide instrumental aid when needed was formed.

Changes in older adults' public English socializing was also related to the development of their internal or self-directed speech. Research shows that inner speech is important for the self-regulation and management of various language tasks (Goodman 1981). Perhaps not surprising, greater interiorization of language has been associated with higher levels of language usage and proficiency (Pavlenko 1998). Evidence shows that inner speech, whether in the form of vocalized self-talk or mental self-talk, evolves out of exposure to and participation in social speech (Lantolf and Thorne 2006). Put simply, self-talk is an outgrowth of social interaction, making inner speech highly related to the practice of communication with others. For many of the reasons already mentioned throughout this book, older adult immigrants have fewer pathways to develop interior English speech. Earlier age-at-migration correlates with higher levels of interior second language use, such as in talking to oneself in English, writing self-notes, thinking of English vocabulary, computing math, and even praying (Larsen et al. 2002). This is due to the fact that younger immigrants have greater access and exposure to formal instruction and social speech conducted in English than older adult immigrants.

Carlos, a 56-year-old mechanic, made conscious choices to develop his inner speech as a way to speak more English at work. Carlos works for a small car repair shop and he worries about being laid off because of growing competition. He sees learning English as a way to help secure his job because it would make him a valuable employee in being one of the few English speakers at his workplace.

> English is very important at work because you want to have as many clients as possible. My boss speaks some English but no one else does. People today don't have a lot of money to fix their cars and sometimes the shop doesn't get much business.... But younger customers speak English and we need to know that.... I try to show my boss that I can understand some English and can help translate. I used to be nervous to speak English at work but I feel better after taking some classes because I now tell myself, like people say here, "you do understand something".... And I practice what we learned in class, like how to pronounce words.

Perhaps most interesting about Carlos' account is the explicit way the ESL classroom shaped his inner speech. In a way, the voices of his classroom peers became his own inner voice and were a means to initiate self-talk about English speaking. Our participants' language behavior involved the obvious interconnection and overlap of psychological and social dimensions. ESL peer social support was a foundation for self-directed speech and a path to public English socializing. In the absence of family members to assist in translating, older adults discursively carried their ESL peer allies into public domains when they are more isolated from direct language resources.

Our analyses show that the concept of "allies" is central to how older adults structure their second language learning and underscores the way ESL classroom spaces generate social and human capital for language acquisition. We see that older adults' identity as a second language learner is conditioned by the social spaces they inhabit. The ESL classroom can provide ways to address the challenges, and identify the advantages, associated with elder minorities living in ethnically concentrated communities that may preserve their first language but insulate older members from the target language. From the issues related to language use in multigenerational households to the difficulties in finding supportive pathways to public speaking, older adults spoke about the transformational power of the ESL classroom. Experiencing safe English exchanges was a stepping stone for older adults to begin socializing in English within other spaces. With the backdrop of ESL interactions, older adults felt more confident and assured that familial and public English speaking would be nonthreatening and beneficial. ESL peer interactions provided a model of "ally work" that capitalized their self-esteem and knowledge-base. They then carried back these resources to their family relationships and to their workplaces. In the next chapter, we continue our focus on ally work and its impact on older adults' English resocialization. We pay special attention to the gender dynamics that structure social networking within the ESL classroom and the ways social capital is distributed among women and men in their efforts to learn English.

References

Alba, R. D., Logan, J., Lutz, A., & Stults, B. (2002). Only English by the third generation? Loss and preservation of the mother-tongue among grandchildren of contemporary immigrants. *Demography, 39*(3), 467–484.

Alicea, M. (1997). "A chambered nautilus": The contradictory nature of Puerto Rican Women's role in the social construction of a transnational community. *Gender and Society, 11*(5), 597–626.

Auerbach, E. (1989). Toward a social-contextual approach to family literacy. *Harvard Educational Review, 59*(2), 165–182.

Blommaert, J., Collins, J., & Slembrouck, S. (2005). Spaces of multilingualism. *Language & Communication, 25*(3), 197–216.

Borgatti, S. P. (1994). Cultural domain analysis. *Journal of Qualitative Anthropology, 4*(4), 261–278.

Centeno, J. C. (2007). Considerations for an ethnolinguistic framework for aphasia intervention with bilingual speakers. In A. Ardila & E. Ramos (Eds.), *Speech and language disorders in bilinguals* (pp. 195–212). Nova Scotia Publishers.

Delgado-Gaitan, C. (1990). *Literacy for empowerment: The role of parents in children's education*. New York, NY: Falmer.

Espenshade, T. J., & Fu, H. (1997). An analysis of English-Language proficiency among U.S. immigrants. *American Sociological Review, 62*(2), 288–305.

Gal, S. (2005) Language ideologies compared. *Journal of Linguistic Anthropology, 15*(1), 23–37.

Gallo, L. C., Penedo, F. J., Espinosa de los Monteros, K., & Arguelles, W. (2009). Resiliency in the face of disadvantage: Do Hispanic cultural characteristics protect health outcomes? *Journal of Personality, 77*(6), 1707–1746.

Gil, A. G., & Vega, W. A. (1996). Two different worlds: Acculturation stress and adaptation among Cuban and Nicaraguan families. *Journal of Social and Personal Relationships, 13*(3), 435–456.

Goodman, S. H. (1981). The integration of verbal and moto behavior in preschool children. *Child Development, 52*(1), 280–289.

Kao, H.-F. S., & Travis, S. (2005). Effects of acculturation and social exchange on the expectations of filial piety among Hispanic/Latino parents of adult children. *Nursing and Health Sciences, 7,* 226–234.

Langacker, R. W. (1987). *Foundations of cognitive grammar* (vol. 1: Theoretical Prerequisites). Stanford: Stanford University Press.

Lantolf, J. P., & Thorne, S. L. (2006). *Sociocultural theory and the genesis of second language development*. New York: Oxford University Press.

Larsen, S., Schrauf, R. W., Fromholt, P., & Rubin, D. C. (2002). Inner speech and bilingual autobiographical memory: A Polish-Danish cross-cultural study. *Memory (Hove, England), 10*(1), 45–54.

Luykx, A. (2005). Children as socializing agents: Family language policy in situations of language shift. In J. Cohen, K. T. McAlister, K. Rolstad, & J. MacSwan (Eds.), *Proceedings of the 4th international symposium on bilingualism* (pp. 1407–1414). Somerville, MA: Cascadilla Press.

McQuillan, J., & Tse, L. (1995). Child language brokering in linguistic minority communities: Effects on cultural interaction, cognition, and literacy. *Language and Education, 9*(3), 195–215.

Mutchler, J. E., & Brallier, S. (1999). English language proficiency among older Hispanics in the United States. *Gerontologist, 39*(3), 310–319.

Partida, J. (1996). The effects of immigration on children in the Mexican-American community. *Child and Adolescent Social Work Journal, 13*(3), 241–254.

Pavlenko, A. (1998). Second language learning by adults: Testimonies of bilingual writers. *Issues in Applied Linguistics, 9*(1), 3–19.

Pavlenko, A. (2000). Access to linguistics resources: Key variable in second language learning. *Estudios de Sociolinguisitica, 1*(2), 85–105.

Perreira, K., Chapman, M., & Stein, G. (2006). Becoming an American parent: Overcoming challenges and finding strength in a new immigrant Latino community. *Journal of Family Issues, 27*(10), 1383–1414.

Rumbaut, R. (2005). Sites of belonging: Acculturation, discrimination, and ethnic identity among children of immigrants. In T. S. Weiner (Ed.), *Discovering successful pathways in children's development: Mixed methods in the study of childhood and family life* (pp. 111–164). Chicago, IL: University of Chicago Press.

Savignon, S. J. (1983). *Communicative competence: Theory and classroom practice*. Reading, MA: Addison-Wesley.

Schrauf, R. W. (1999). Mother tongue maintenance among North American ethnic groups. *Cross-Cultural Research, 33*(2), 175–192.

Stevens, G. (1999). Age at immigration and second language proficiency among foreign-born adults. *Language in Society, 28*(4), 555–578.

Tse, L. (1995). Language brokering among Latino adolescents: Prevalence, attitudes, and school performance. *Hispanic Journal of Behavioral Sciences, 17*(2), 180–193.

Tse, L. (1996). Who decides?: The effects of language brokering on home-school communication. *The Journal of Educational Issues of Language Minority Students, 16,* 225–234.

Usita, P. M., & Blieszner, R. (2002). Immigrant family strengths: Meeting communication challenges. *Journal of Family Issues, 23*(2), 266–286.

Valdes, G. (2005). Bilingualism, heritage language learners, and SLA research: Opportunities lost or seized? *The Modern Language Journal, 89*(3), 410–426.

Young, R. (1999). Sociolinguistic approaches to SLA. *Annual Review of Applied Linguistics, 19,* 105–132.

Chapter 8
Language Resocialization and Gender Allies

> At my age it is difficult to learn a completely new language.... But I know that I need English to be able to communicate with my children and even grandchildren. The thing is that my daughter has friends who speak entirely in English. So when we are all together I'm only able to say a few words because I can't follow the conversation. Not so much my husband.... He speaks only Spanish and doesn't care to learn English.... I'm the only one interested in learning English at this point in my house. But here are my ladies [pointing to three women sitting next to her] who want to learn and that has been a good thing to share with others.

Sandra speaks as a mother (and grandmother) as a way to define her interest in and pursuit of learning English. Much of her focus is on maintaining good communication with her daughter and also finding ways to be involved in her child's social life. Sandra draws a distinction with her husband who has chosen not to take language classes. In this way, her women peer-students in the ESL classroom have been a positive group to share the experience of learning English.

Sandra's story is echoed by another classmate, Pedro, a 59-year-old former construction worker. He describes similar reasons why he has enrolled in language classes, but also emphasizes how his experience is somewhat different from Sandra's.

> I want to learn English to grow personally and improve my communication with others. None of my friends really speak English.... They don't think that they need to because they speak Spanish at work and at home. They think it is silly to be a student at my age. But I know that it will be good for me to learn English for work and to be able to interact more with younger people in my family.... You don't see many men here [in the ESL program] and that's too bad. It's hard for me to explain to my friends why they should come to classes like this.

Pedro has a similar passion for learning English, and he echoes Sandra's comment about the lack of men in the ESL program. While Sandra spoke more specifically about her husband choosing not to learn English, Pedro highlighted how few men generally pursue English-language classes. Speaking from the perspective of a male peer, he describes the losses Hispanic older men incur as a result of not engaging in target language socialization. Pedro notes that language learning can have a significant positive impact in the areas of family and work, particularly the interactions in these arenas. So while Sandra and Pedro share much in common as ESL students, their stories emphasize the gendered character of language learning and alert us to the different challenges Hispanic immigrants face as older adults.

As was mentioned in Chap. 2, life transitions are distinctively marked for Hispanic immigrants of older age. At the center of second language acquisition are critical issues tied to identity, competence, power, access, and agency (Duff 2002; Norton and Toohey 2002). In the above interview excerpts, Sandra and Pedro introduce the importance of gender social positioning as a mediating force. For Sandra, bonds developed with other women in the ESL classroom support her language learning endeavors. Pedro speaks in terms of the loss of other men with whom he can socialize in English. In this way, it is important to consider how gender identity unevenly shapes language resocialization experiences.

Changes to older immigrants' lives—a new job, health issues, or challenges related to a new language—can lead to significant adjustments to a persons' self-identity. These shifts in older immigrants' personal lives may be linked to their gender identity, which can debilitate or promote their language learning. For example, when women and men believe that their sense of femininity and masculinity is dependent on achieving certain goals and behaving in particular ways, it can affect how they approach second language acquisition. Transitions to a new language, in particular, may be different for women and men who must contend with gender ideologies—and their related interpretive and behavioral practices— that inform their choices as women and men. When speaking of gender ideology, scholars refer to the "notions, norms and models which guide conduct and allow for its justification and rationalization" (Wetherell et al. 1987, p. 60). For example, the assertion that women are "naturally" more nurturing and communicative than men can create a situation where women shoulder more responsibility in maintaining communication among family and non-kin English speakers.

At the same time, particular events can lead women and men to transform their views of their gender identity—that is, the way they interpret femininity and masculinity. In this way, new experiences and relationships may open up new opportunities for older immigrant women and men to participate in language resocialization. Men sometimes feel they must minimize failures or deficiencies in their lives, such as perhaps disappointments and frustrations related to their English competency. Among men peers, participating in language classes may be dismissed as childish—or as Pedro notes, it is viewed as "silly"—and something outside the norm. The novel experiences created in an ESL classroom, however, can provide a way to reimagine what one is capable of achieving and offer means to invest in second language learning. As Sandra explains, the bonds created in the ESL classroom supported her language learning efforts. Pedro demonstrates how he too looked to his peers, referencing them as he conceptualized himself as a learner.

This chapter examines the gender identity work of older adult learners as a way to capture how language resocialization is conditioned by everyday gendered practices. We suggest studying *identity work*—"anything people do, individually or collectively, to give meaning to themselves or others" (Schwalbe and Schrock 1996, p. 15)—to demonstrate both the agenic and socially circumscribed nature of second language acquisition. To the extent that successful language resocialization involves new identities (Norton 2000), then a closer look at the everyday social positioning of older adults in language learning contexts is important for understanding the "voices constructed by learners in a target language" (Ehrlich 1997, p. 440). How gendered selves concretely manifest in ESL classroom discourse and how social positioning shapes ESL learning in this context can shed light on the constraints and opportunities for successful language resocialization.

Social Positioning, Gender Identity, and Language Learning

Our study of Hispanic older adult immigrants is situated in trends of applied and social linguistics that understands language learning as a deeply social, cultural, and temporal activity. Drawing from language socialization literature (Duff 1995; Ochas 1988), we center the identity work of our Hispanic elders and assume that this self-making activity conditions learning and language socialization in situ. This process impacts Hispanic elders' ability to gain membership and competence in the target language community. By examining classroom discourse and interaction we are able to see the social positions enacted by Hispanic elder women and men that influence their ESL classroom experience, self-as-learner identity, and resources available for language resocialization.

Scholars define social positioning as "an event of identification, in which a recognizable category of identity gets explicitly or implicitly applied to an individual" (Wortham 2004, p. 166). Speakers' identities are developed and assigned within social interactions and in reference to language interlocutors. Blackledge and Pavlenko (2001) describe identities as dynamic and involved in a process of negotiation among language users. Torras' (2005) study on the linguistic identities of Spanish speakers, for example, shows that individuals negotiate through codeswitching when speaking to either monolingual or bilingual speakers. The idea here is that a sense of self-identity and recognition of context informs language knowledge and practice.

Social linguistic and sociological research suggest that self-identity is connected to participation in situated discursive practices (Davies and Harré 1990). Here, we follow a view of discourse as "an institutionalized use of language-like sign systems" (Davies and Harré 1990, p. 45). Individuals are located in contexts that carry ideas and norms of going concern that inform the ways individuals define themselves and others. Within these settings people make choices of how they will discursively participate. An individual's "history as a subjective being"—a speaker's biography—also plays a role in how they come to interpret discourses in their environments (Davies and Harré 1990, p. 48). However, as Blackledge and

Pavlenko (2001) point out, contexts do matter because "certain identities may not be negotiable because people may be positioned in powerful ways in which they are unable to resist" (p. 250). Various studies have examined how identity is shaped by dominant discourses operating in classroom settings. Black (2004), for example, studied British primary school classrooms and examined how teachers positioned some students as highly competent and others as less competent. The dominant narrative that categorized students into different levels of competency was observed to impact students' self-definitions and performance outcomes. In this way, McKay and Wong (1996) argue that researchers need to investigate how learners are "both positioned by relations of power and resistant to that positioning" (p. 579).

Watson-Gegeo (2004) reminds us that people learn languages in social, cultural, and political environments that have consequences for how people hear, use, and give significance to the target language. With respect to immigrant learners, recent research (Menard-Warwick 2005) points to how immigrants must overcome the constraints of poverty and social prejudice that limit language learning. Along these lines, Davies (2001) has focused on gender as a key factor which shapes immigrants as English language learners. Of importance to these scholars is how gender discourses impact the agency of learners. In other words, definitions of femininity and masculinity carry self-conceptions that may impede or enhance language socialization. Moreover, the choices made by immigrant women and men can further exacerbate or moderate the challenges they face.

Patricia is 52-years old and immigrated to the United States from Mexico over 10 years ago. She recalls how she was not prepared to leave her country and felt deeply ambivalent about how this transition would impact her life.

> I was completely scared…. I really wasn't sure how I was going to be able to make a life in a place where I couldn't speak the language and didn't know many people. At the time my daughter was still in school…she now has a child of her own. I would tell my husband that I was worried for her [Patricia's daughter] because she didn't know too much English either. My husband wasn't as worried as me. He would say that's what school's for. I still knew that we [Patricia and her husband] needed to learn English in order to help our daughter and to improve ourselves…. He used to not pay attention to me when I would say that I wanted to go to take English classes. He said that it would do no good and that the family needed me at home. It took me a long time…but I'm happy to be taking classes and learning English. My husband still thinks it's silly for me to come to these classes but I don't care at this point…at my age.

Characteristic of the immigrant experience, fears and anxieties of having to navigate a new language and social interactions are considerable obstacles. Having a daughter helped to frame Patricia's concerns about second language acquisition. In this way, her biographical story as a mother created a sense of urgency and motivation to learn English. Simultaneously, she highlights how being a woman carried expectations that impeded her pursuit of ESL classes. In this case, the association of domesticity with femininity resulted in pressures delaying her participation in English classes. Particularly interesting is how gender and age intersect to reframe Patricia's self-definition and language learning efforts. As Patricia explains, past concerns seem to fade with age, opening the door to taking English classes.

Patricia's story illustrates how immigration, age, and gender intersect to shape decisions over language resocialization. Immigrants' biographical histories and larger societal discourses about femininity are important for the development of immigrants' self-identity as language learners. In our study, we paid close attention to the ways in which Hispanic older adults spoke about how gender discourses in various settings, such as family and community, impacted their language resocialization. Importantly, we also examined the extent to which the ESL classroom setting provided alternative narratives that could redirect women and men's gender positioning. In this case, we were interested in knowing if and how the ESL classroom could transform gender identity and gender relations in ways that facilitate language learning.

Gendered Literacy as Gendered Labor

Hispanics' older age places them at a disadvantage to access the two primary ways of learning a second language—namely, formal study in a school setting and informal interactions that include mixed languages. Hispanic older adults are largely restricted from formal schooling, except in cases where they enroll in ESL courses at local community colleges, libraries, and other institutional settings. Even in these situations, affordability, time, and transportation issues pose barriers to participation. Informal, public domains where the target second language is spoken are, therefore, crucial to language acquisition. Not all Hispanic groups have equal access, however, to the types of informal, particularly non-kin, social networks that include mixed language usage and socialization. Older immigrants, who rely heavily on monolingual familial networks, are at a disadvantage for not having interaction with target language interlocutors. Because these Hispanic older adult immigrants do not always benefit from either formal or informal settings, language learning is a problem for them. We document how gender dynamics also structure access to interlocutors and the type of language resocialization adopted. This is particularly captured in the case of our Hispanic older adult immigrants who speak little English.

We last encountered Dora's story in Chap. 3, where she reflected on her racial identity after moving to the United States. Here Dora talks about her identity as a mother and grandmother, as well as the ways in which family roles shaped her access to language socialization.

> My family is everything to me. I do what I do for them…I want them to be happy and successful in their lives…. When I first came to the United States I knew that it would be important for me to learn some English, but I had a lot of responsibilities and didn't have time to learn. Raising two children, taking care of the house, taking care of my husband and even now helping as the grandmother ("la abuela")…who has time to learn a new language? I see it with my children who have children of their own. Lucky for them they grew

up in this country and learned English from school and friends. I didn't have that opportunity so it has taken me a long time to start taking classes like this [referring to our ESL program].

Dora confirms the central role of Hispanic women as sustainer of the family structure. For some time, the role of *la abuela* (the grandmother) has been studied as "the backbone of family endurance and the symbol of cultural survival" (Zepeda 1979, p. 5). Dora identifies as a woman who has been responsible for a variety of tasks in the family over the years, most recently as a nurturing elder.

She also illustrates the struggles related to competing life demands. Scholars describe these competing demands as a form of "double-jeopardy" (Dowd and Bengtson 1978), while others use the notion of "triple-risk" (Melville 1980) to emphasize the intersectional quality of being an elderly minority. In either case, age, gender, ethnicity, and other social factors compound the disadvantages experienced by elderly minority women and men. In the case of Dora, it delayed her from participating in formal English classes.

Sofia is a bit more direct in her account of how "women's work" is defined in the family and impacts access to language socialization.

> I hear it all the time from my husband and other men…that we [women] don't need to be going to school to learn English. My husband thinks I should always be at home taking care of the kids and him and preparing food. I am more than a domestic servant. For a long time I would think about attending classes but then decided not to because I felt I needed to be doing other things…. Because you [the ESL program] offer childcare, people can focus on learning English.

Here Sofia draws attention to the differing constructions of femininity and masculinity in the family. She mentions the way men in general, and her husband in particular, perceive women's role to be primarily domestic in nature. Feminist scholars have raised questions about the traditional roles assigned to women in the family and how it impacts women's trajectories in various social arenas, including their participation in target language communities (Ramdas 1985). In this respect, Ramdas (1985) argues that "there must be a clear recognition of the role played by men in preventing women from going out of their homes" (p. 103). Perhaps unlike Sofia, Dora does not have the direct support of her husband but she notes that having childcare offered by the ESL program can be helpful to many families. To the extent that Hispanic elderly women's literacy practices are linked to family networks and filial obligations, it is important to address how gender discourses and relations within the family impact their participation in formal language schooling which exists outside the home.

Another key theme that emerged from our interviews relates to differences in the type of language skills relevant to women and men. A pattern that we observed was the way in which women relied on both spoken and written English, while men more singularly used spoken English. Here again, the gender division of labor and the confinement of women to the domestic sphere structured women and men's language needs and learning.

We shared Francisco's story earlier in the book and his reasons for enrolling in English classes. He said, "I don't have to speak English much at work.... But the boss is American and I know that it would be good for me to learn more English. That's why I'm here taking English classes." The men we interviewed stressed the importance of *talking*, of making themselves present and understood in the public settings where English is spoken. David, a 55-year-old construction worker, echoes this pattern when he describes his goals for learning English.

> I've seen people lose their jobs and it was really bad several years ago during the economic crisis. I didn't have work for a while. I think that it is important to know some English because it can help you get a job. All the managers know some English and it's because they need to speak to their bosses in English. You don't have to be perfect but just being able to say a few words and be able to understand what someone is saying can help you.

David points to the value of learning English in terms of occupational success and places significance on the ability to speak English in the workplace. For many of our Hispanic men, the public arena was a focal point that establishes a rationale for learning English and also their attention to public English speaking.

While Hispanic women also shared an interest in improving their spoken English, they tended to emphasize the importance of a more comprehensive set of literacy skills that included reading and writing. In this case, Hispanic women's orientation toward literacy was linked to the fact that they tended to do the majority of the literacy-based work of the household. Patricia recalls the range of language tasks that she confronted when she was young and recently arrived to the United States.

> It was very difficult to do simple things like contact a doctor and attend to my kid's schooling. I didn't know what she [her daughter] was bringing home. I couldn't read the homework and so I couldn't help her. I felt so bad that I couldn't help her in school like I wanted. And I wanted to talk to the teachers but they only spoke English. As a grandmother I also want to help my granddaughter with her homework or to read to her.

Patricia nicely captures the sentiment of many other women we interviewed. They provided a detailed inventory of various English language situations that require skills related to reading, writing, and speaking English. Gordon's (2004, p. 446) study of second language students documents how immigrant women are more involved in "negotiating domestic events," such as interacting with professionals at their child's school and making medical appointments. Researchers have found that these events demand more complex English than what is needed in typical monolingual immigrant settings. For Patricia, language learning is an extension of, and conditioned by, the domestic sphere she manages. Interestingly, she describes the intergenerational character of her concerns and how these issues are carried through to later age. While men in our study did express an interest to read and write better in English, women tended to emphasize a broader range of desired language skills. In this way, both women and men tied their interests in language learning to their biographical context. A gendered division of labor that separates the public (occupational) world of men and the domestic (household) realm of women structured their language needs, goals, and practice.

Negotiating Competence in a Gendered Setting

Our participants also suggested that major challenges to their participation in language resocialization include negotiating competence, identity, and power relations as a learner. The transitions that interested us in the lives of our older adults are those related to their immigration at a later age. These transitions can make older adults particularly susceptible to feeling anxious, confused, frustrated, or concerned about their ability to be part of their new country. Changes for elderly immigrants also constrain pathways we focus on in our research: the development of a self-as-learner identity, the promotion of relationships for language resocialization, and the role of place as a context for language learning. Diego, a 55-year-old father of two children, describes the pressures of life transitions on his self-identity as a second language learner.

> It is hard to commit to taking English classes. Everyone thinks that you are simply too old to learn English. My friends tell me that I'm already married, with children and old. They say that maybe if I came to this country [United States] when I was younger, but now I'm too old to try to speak English. It gets you to think the same way and it makes it hard to motivate oneself to take classes. You think you're too old to be good at it [English]

Diego notes several life transitions, such as marriage, having children, and immigrating at a later age, as working to define him as "too old" to learn English. Each of our participants has unique life circumstances and struggles, but they all highlight a concern for being a competent member of an English-speaking community. A common identity shared by our older adult ESL students was of being less competent than others and being a less legitimate English language user. Furthermore, the way in which women and men experienced and managed this identity varied. Variations depended on the local classroom context and relationships beyond this setting.

Set against the backdrop of the life changes of immigration, older adult immigrants grapple with related transitions in family, work, and other life domains. Coordinating these life areas in the context of a new language is difficult. Margarita is 61-years-old and immigrated from Honduras. She talks about the stress that comes from living in a new environment and the ambivalence of navigating new cultural and social interactions.

> I can tell you that I was scared. I was already older and had a life before. Having to move to an entirely new country changes one's world completely. I hardly knew any English, just a few words. It was hard dealing with so many things at once and having to talk to people who don't speak Spanish. What is good about this [ESL] class is that it is a place where I can focus on learning specific things. That helps me move forward and not feel so scattered. I can practice with people, other women like me....it makes me feel more confident to continue trying.

Participating in ESL classes is a stabilizing force in Margarita's life, since it allows her to "focus" on important aspects of language learning. In turn, this has the effect of building self-confidence in learning English that was difficult to construct in other settings. Part of this new sense of confidence is tied to language practices with other women in the classroom with whom she identifies.

If we listen to Carlos, a 52-year-old ESL student, his account shows the influence of gender on his language practice. In contrast to Margarita, Carlos appears to emphasize the relative absence of men with whom he can identify in language socialization.

> I really enjoy coming to class and speaking with my classmates in English. I'm not very good and make a lot of mistakes, but we are all the same in that way.... It makes me sad to not see too many men in the class. I think there are 4 of us [ESL men]. More men should join because men, especially young men, are often the ones that don't participate in these types of opportunities. But how else are we going to improve ourselves and be involved in this country.... I would like to practice English with other men ...not that I have a problem with speaking with the women here...but sometimes it is a bit strange and so I sometimes don't talk and wait for someone else. I don't see a lot of men in my family and friends speaking English so it motivates me when I see men in the classroom because I don't feel silly.

Being competent in English is tied to the language practices done with others. The fact that there are fewer men than women in the classroom leads to a degree of situational ambivalence. While Carlos still finds positive socialization with other classmates, he experiences added feelings of "sadness" and "strangeness" along the way that impact his security to speak. These emerge from gender relations in the classroom and limit valuable socialization with other men who stand to benefit from ESL literacy programs. Carlos' observation of men's lack of participation confirms research showing that women are the primary participants in literacy programs (Rockhill 1987). Furthermore, Carlos notes the loss of intergenerational communication and the potential benefits of having young and old students sharing with each other.

Social positioning literature shows that learners engage in "reflexive positioning" when developing a linguistic identity. Reflexive positioning occurs when learners claim identities for themselves, such as being linguistically competent, when in interaction. Both Margarita and Carlos spotlight how gender relations within the classroom differentially structure pathways to claiming an identity of competence and assurance in the target language for both older adult women and men. Their testimonies also suggest that literacy program interventions would benefit from mixed age and gender classrooms.

Building Speech Community Membership Through Gender Ally Work

Along with developing a self-identity based on language competence, scholars note that a certain degree of legitimacy is needed for learning. Second language learners find themselves outside of official and legitimate target language contexts. To the extent that language learning is a situated process, tied to everyday social interactions, successful language resocialization requires movement toward fuller participation in a given target language community (Lave and Wegner 1991). Lave and Wegner (1991) refer to this process as "legitimate peripheral participation," in which nonspeakers begin to gain access to sites of target language speech and grow in their involvement and understanding. This builds a sense of "legitimacy," according to Wenger (1998), since learners come to view themselves as belonging to a language community through more participation. Wenger (1998) defines the notion of legitimacy in language learning this way:

> In order to be on an inbound trajectory, newcomers must be granted enough legitimacy to be treated as potential members.... Only with legitimacy can all their inevitable stumbling and violations become opportunities for learning rather than cause for dismissal, neglect, or exclusion (p. 101).

Gaining a sense of legitimacy aids in fostering continued language practice and involvement during the learning process. This part of identity formation, which includes seeing oneself as a true member of a speech community, is essential for understanding older adult's language-learning practices.

We observed that our older adult learners negotiated speech community membership within the classroom. They sought to use the classroom as a proxy for "legitimate" membership to an English-speaking community that was distinct from their home and community interactions. Maria discusses how she conceptualizes membership in the classroom as tied to one's motivations and hard work, something that she says not everyone possesses.

> Women are more dedicated to the study of English and to improving ourselves. We are more interested in learning English.... There are lots of reasons for this. Sometimes men are exposed to English at work and women are not.... So you have to really want to come here [ESL class] and work hard.... We are learning English, even though we are older and people don't think we can.

Maria suggests that women and men have different motivations for enrolling in English classes. We can also see how Maria's emphasis on the challenges to learning English becomes a way to distinguish herself from those that do not take ESL classes. Noting that one has to "really want" to learn English, despite one's age, is a way of creating a new identity as a learner. As she says, "We are learning English," while others are not. In this way, a sense of group membership is established through contrast to non-ESL individuals.

Interestingly, women and men worked as allies toward this form of language group identification. The following focus group conversation between Maria and Pedro demonstrates how cross-gender bonds reinforce students' ESL member identity.

Maria   Yes, I have experience because once we started with 30 people and then ended with two. So then they closed the class because the majority of us didn't keep coming. I don't know what you know but we Hispanics, my husband, is very macho. Yes. So they [husbands] question why we go to class! So the majority of

	the classes are in the evening, from 6 or 7 to 8 and my husband says, "Who will prepare dinner?" As if they have a broken arm or something! [class laughs together].... It doesn't matter what age you are. You can always learn.
Pedro	Yes. We need to encourage people to attend even though family members and husbands may not want them to. Those are old ideas that women can't go outside the home.
Maria	This semester we are sticking together and I call them to make sure they come to class.

Pedro confirms Maria's sentiments by saying, "Yes." In response to Pedro delegitimizing a "machista" ideology that confines women to the household, Maria notes how she has taken an active role in recruiting and maintaining women's involvement in the ESL class: "This semester we are sticking together and I call them to make sure they come to class." As was discussed in Chap. 6, the affiliative laughter exhibited by the class also moves to destabilize gender norms that inhibit ESL participation.

Analyzing our older adult ESL students' perspectives showed that gender, age, and culture played an active role in how they negotiated their identity as a second language learner. The classroom provided a setting in which students could develop membership in an English-speaking community that broke with conventional gender norms and opened a way for people of older age (Maria: "doesn't matter what age you are"). As a strategy, women and men worked together as allies to fashion a sense of legitimacy in the classroom.

Age, Gender, and Language Capitalization

As we have seen in previous chapters, older adult immigrants who come to the United States experience related changes in education, employment, and residence. These rapid transitions mean that minority elders are left negotiating their social integration in tenuous living circumstances. Rosa sketches a hypothetical scenario tied to health concerns about her husband who, like Rosa, is in his early 60s.

> We are getting old and I get nervous sometimes about if my husband gets sick and we would need to take him to the hospital. I know of friends who have had a difficult time talking to doctors who don't speak Spanish.... I don't want that to happen to me. I want to be able to ask the doctor questions so that he [Rosa's husband] is taken care of. It is very important for me to be learning English because of our age and needing to be able to stand up for ourselves.

Concern about communicating in old age to health practitioners was a real worry discussed by our older adult ESL students. Their health issues were compounded by the fact that many ESL students described how they would need to continue working through old age. Several participants stated that they lost whatever state pension they might have accumulated in Mexico and given their illegal status they know they will not be earning any Social Security benefits from the United States government. Even if they become citizens, there will not be much to count on in old age. Retirement, in the traditional sense, is not something they are planning to enjoy. Daniel explains it this way: "Since we will always have bills to pay, we will always be working." Few older adults that we spoke to had a plan to return to Mexico. The majority see themselves as living the rest of their lives in the United States. This raises questions about elder immigrants' ability to navigate institutional settings, such as hospitals and social service centers, in the absence of language capital resources.

Scholarship shows that building language skills occurs as immigrants move to fuller participation in the target language community (Lave and Wegner 1991). Key to increased participation and language learning success is engagement in activities that involve interactions with more experienced target language speakers. From this perspective, older adults' success in language resocialization is tied to their growing participation in English language settings and interactions. However, gaining access to these communities of practice is not always a smooth process and involves conflict based on social power relations (Lave and Wegner 1991). As Lave and Wegner (1991, p. 42) point out, "hegemony over resources for learning and alienation from full participation are inherent in the shaping of the legitimacy and peripherality of participation in its historical realizations." For elderly immigrants who are located within monolingual networks of family and local community, participation in target language interactions can be difficult to achieve due to lack of available social and cultural capital. In short, the network of people and skilled interlocutors needed are not always available within an immigrant ethnic context.

Because participation in official English language domains is not always an option for our older adult ESL students, they developed innovative strategies for locating social and cultural capital resources for their own language learning. One strategy included identifying ESL classroom instructors as language education experts that could more skillfully guide the language learning process. For example, one of our ESL instructors is a university professor in the field of education and students would seek him out to ask questions specific to their own language acquisition. Students would ask, "Are we going to learn English if we continue to come to this ESL program?" and "You know our level of English; will we someday learn the basics and be able to communicate with English speakers to accomplish basic tasks?" "If so, when is this going to take place?" Keeping in mind that older immigrants are restricted due to age and finances from formal schooling, our students engaged in language practice by utilizing one of the few language experts available to them. Students are reflecting on their own language acquisition by trying to identify critical milestones, levels, and goals that will guide them more successfully in their language resocialization.

Another strategy adopted by students was to take suggestions from ESL instructors on how to continue their language practice beyond the classroom. Students responded to the idea that building a network of classroom peers could serve as a way to practice their English speaking with one another. Dora was particularly excited about this idea, explaining here how she took this idea and ran with it:

> When we were told by "el profesor" [the professor] to make friends in class and to exchange phone numbers I immediately turned to the person next to me and asked for her number. I did it on the first day. It is great because we call each other, and others as well, and we talk about class and what we are doing. Sometimes we practice over the phone or help each other with the homework for the week. We have become good "amigas" [girlfriends].

Again, it can be seen that Dora is emphasizing the ESL instructor as an expert by assigning the title of "el profesor" and taking his suggestion "immediately." She relies on his expert perspective in order to make better decisions related to her language learning. Women further benefited from expert instructors inquiring about key issues, such as citizenship, high school certification, and schooling for children. In this way, Dora and many other women in the classroom were able to benefit from expert speakers, developing both social (peer support) and cultural (expert information) resources for language practice. By locating and deploying available resources, ESL women empowered themselves and gained a degree of ownership over the language-learning process.

Older adult men, however, made less use of these strategies as compared to women in the classroom. Francisco, for example, describes a more limited type of social bonding: "I sometimes have lunch during class with others here. We go grab some food nearby, have a good time talking, and then come back to class." Unlike many women in the class, Francisco's relationships do not appear to generate the same kind of social capital. Strategies such as language practice and information sharing were not part of men's classroom peer relationships. As Dora notes, women rely on groups of "amigas" to form the basis of their network system, while men perhaps do not build similar social connections with other men who are fewer in number in the program. ESL students' gender identity played a role in how and whether they identified peers to be part of the social network. A form of gender segregation structured language capital resources and its uneven distribution among women and men.

When thinking about how literacy programs might assist older immigrants' efforts toward language resocialization, we suggest identifying the ways in which everyday social and cultural capital resources are developed in local sites. More initiatives and research in recent decades are paying attention to the important role that social relationships and self-identity play in second language learning. It is perhaps especially relevant in the case of Hispanic older adult immigrants for researchers and practitioners to consider the ways gender relations structure already limited language capital resources. Our observations show that women and men gain access, legitimacy, and membership to target language communities in different ways. Opportunities for concrete resources, such as language practice, instructional information, and peer support, are tied to the subtle gender relations experienced by ESL learners.

Studying gender identity work generates insights on transitions specific to elderly minority immigrants and their accumulation of human capital. Older adult immigrants experience unique transitions related to changes in work, health, and family. Reflecting on our participants' varied experiences *as women* and *as men* helps us to identify key dimensions of Hispanic immigrant elders' linguistic development. First, transitions related to immigration may make women and men differently sensitive to particular programmatic strategies in dealing with second language acquisition. Changes in older adults' formal and informal networks may differ for older women and men. This, in turn, can lead to differential access to language resocialization experiences. Second, the timing and sequencing of life transitions are important when considering how Hispanic older adults navigate the immigrant landscape. The pressures of learning a second language at a later age can alter how women and men perceive the consequences of acculturation. For example, ESL women note how learning English is critical for maintaining connections with family. They also spoke about the importance of the social support among classroom women. Men, on the other hand, pointed to issues related to men's lack of urgency and participation in second language learning. In either case, Hispanic older immigrants' responses to second language acquisition have consequences for their role in various social arenas, such as work, family, and community. Third, the nature of older immigrants' language learning is often tied to significant others' responses. This means that working effectively with older women and men may require that services and programming be provided to individuals in their life. Fourth, the duration of and participation in language resocialization can vary among older women and men. Thus, developing strategies that move older immigrants through second language classes may require sensitivity to the gendered nature of acculturation.

References

Black, L. (2004). Teacher-pupil talk in whole-class discussions and processes of social positioning within the primary school classroom. *Language and Education, 18*(5), 347–360.

Blackledge, A., & Pavlenko, A. (2001). Negotiation of identities in multilingual contexts. *The International Journal of Bilingualism, 5*(3), 243–257.

Davies, B. (2001). Literacy and literate subjects in a health and physical education class: A poststructuralist analysis. *Linguistics and Education, 11*(4), 333–352.

Davies, B., & Harré, R. (1990). Positioning: The discursive production of selves. *Journal for the Theory of Social Behavior, 20*(1), 43–63.

Dowd, J. J., & Bengtson, V. L. (1978). Aging in minority populations: An examination of the double jeopardy hypothesis. *Journal of Gerontology, 33*(3), 427–436.

Duff, P. A. (1995). An ethnography of communication in immersion classrooms in Hungary. *TESOL Quarterly, 29*(3), 505–537.

Duff, P. A. (2002). The discursive co-construction of knowledge, identity, and difference: An ethnography of communication in the high school mainstream. *Applied Linguistics, 23*(3), 289–322.

Ehrlich, S. (1997). Gender as social practice: Implications for SLA. *Studies in Second Language Acquisition, 19*(4), 421–446.

Gordon, D. (2004). "I'm tired. You clean and cook": Shifting gender identities and second language socialization. *TESOL Quarterly, 36*(3), 437–458.

Lave, J., & Wegner, E. (1991). *Situated learning: Legitimate peripheral participation*. Cambridge, England: Cambridge University Press.

References

McKay, S., & Wong, S. (1996). Multiple discourses, multiple identities: Investment and agency in second-language learning among Chinese adolescent immigrant students. *Harvard Educational Review, 66*(3), 577–608.

Melville, M. (Ed.). (1980). *Twice a minority: Mexican American women*. St. Louis, MO, Mosby.: C. V.

Menard-Warwick, J. (2005). Intergenerational trajectories and sociopolitical context: Latina immigrant women in adult ESL. *TESOL Quarterly, 39*(2), 165–185.

Norton, B. (2000). *Identity and language learning: Gender, ethnicity and educational change*. Harlow: Pearson Education Limited.

Norton, B., & Toohey, K. (2002). Identity and language learning. In R. Kaplan (Ed.), *The Oxford handbook of applied linguistics* (pp. 115–123). Oxford, England: Oxford University Press.

Ochs, E. (1998). *Culture and language development: Language acquisition and language socialization in a Samoan village*. Cambridge, England: Cambridge University Press.

Ramdas, L. (1985). Illiteracy, women and development. *Adult Education and Development, German Adult Education Association, 24*, 95–105.

Rockhill, K. (1987). Gender, language and the politics of literacy. *British Journal of Sociology of Education, 8*(2), 153–167.

Schwalbe, M. L., & Douglas, M.-S. (1996). Identity work as group process. *Advances in Group Processes, 13*, 113–47.

Torras, M. C. (2005). Social identity and language choice in bilingual service talk. In K. Richards & P. Seedhouse (Eds.), *Applying conversation analysis* (pp. 107–123). Houndsmills: Palgrave Macmillan.

Watson-Gegeo, K. (2004). Mind, language, and epistemology: Toward a language socialization paradigm for SLA. *Modern Language Journal, 88*(3), 331–350.

Wenger, E. (1998). *Communities of practice: Learning, meaning, and identity*. Cambridge, England: Cambridge University Press.

Wetherell, M., Stiven, H., & Potter, J. (1987). A preliminary study of discourse and employment opportunities. *British Journal of Social Psychology, 26*(1), 59–71.

Wortham, S. (2004). From good students to outcast: The emergence of a classroom identity. *Ethnos, 32*(2), 164–187.

Zepeda, M. (1979). Las abuelitas. *Agenda, 9*, 10–13.

Chapter 9
Conclusion: Aging, Second Language Acquisition, and Health

Our qualitative approach to studying older adults in a multilevel ESL program highlights how mastering a second language strongly interacts with the learner's affective positioning, impression management, and social capital distribution. Our older adult cohort participated in research to refine our understanding of language *attrition* during the aging process and address the relatively limited literature currently on the *acquisition* of their language skills and capabilities. When linguistic amelioration does happen to be the focus of these studies, the subjects are usually monolingual and the stimuli are administered in the subject's native language. Late-life second language acquisition is a field of investigation that remains systematically understudied (Bayley and Schecter 2003). Although a learner of a second language may live in their native country and study a foreign language through different means and with various resources, our work has delved into acquiring a second language in the immigrant context in the United States, specifically native speakers of Spanish who have immigrated as adults. The first step toward a deeper understanding of this phenomenon began by examining the configurations of minority aging and the relationship between aging and the acculturation process typical of the immigration experience.

Both late-life aging and acculturation as socio-affective phenomena have the potential to produce feelings of isolation and loneliness. The lack of sociopragmatic and linguistic skills in the target language adds to the challenges older immigrants face to access specific services and integrate their lives into their surrounding environment. Experiences vary among individuals. Kinship support structures, financial dispositions, citizenship status, workplace networks, country of origin relationships, prior educational attainment, and bilingual competence all play a significant part in promoting social integration and quality-of-life trajectories (Padilla et al. 1982). Yet, despite the circumstances that may favor some learners to some degree over others, the task of living and working in a second language while confronting the challenges of aging confounds a person's emotional health and membership claims to vital social groups in their community.

Through our work in the ESL program at the public library, we observed how the classroom at the very least functions as a vinculum for pertinent issues in the learner's life: language, social networks, emotions, immigration, education, aging, gender, and family to name a few. The narratives that we have highlighted in this book testify to the deeply complex and emergent dispositions of older adults' lives as immigrants. Through the categorization of Spanish monolingual speakers, older adults have been positioned in a peculiar social space that makes them vulnerable to the consequences of social isolation and diminishes their opportunity to benefit from institutional support and services. Their need could not have been more apparent than during their informal conversations with classmates and ESL instructors during our Saturday morning meetings. In fact, their marginalization and health risks were the impetus for the current case study and our continued support of public ESL programs. We grew emboldened to investigate the practices that effectuate positive affect, models of personhood, and reciprocal interactions as they transitioned to new and dynamic relationships as emergent English language speakers.

The transition, as we have imagined it, means recognizing the dynamism of their, and their immediate family members', relationship with emblems of authenticity in the acculturation process. The social and capital resources that are structurally afforded to younger Hispanic children and adolescents are quite different for immigrants who are in (or near) old age. The modes of engagement appear within reach for the immigrant youth who by and large experience dominant regimes of socialization through the education system. The expectations of youth to change and adapt oftentimes overshadows the transitions older adults encounter, confront, and accept. We cannot forget the forces one fights to live in a society that is dominated by a person's second language or how challenging it can be to embody contesting learner modes as a student of the English language. Older adults thus experience the tectonic shifts in their conception of self, emotional dispositions, family relationships, social networks, and pragmatic norms which are tied to the ideas of politeness and morality (Paykel 1974).

In the remaining sections of this chapter, we discuss three issues that draw attention to the dynamic relationships between the subjectivities of second language learning for older adults and the sociopolitical structures that help shape them. Based on these themes, we offer nine recommendations for adult ESL programs that serve late-life L2 learners. As we have recognized throughout the book, individuals negotiate their own expectations and type of participation with English language learning. For this reason, our programmatic and pedagogical suggestions are intended as broad dimensions of applied language teaching and not as a strict prescription that supplants the effective teaching techniques widely considered in adult ESL education.

The Role of Place in L2 Learning

As with all second language acquisition processes, the learner mediates their own performed identity work with the constraints established through institutional norms of comportment and interpersonal interactions. Since older adult learners do not progress through the incremental grade levels of a normalizing school system, their individual construction of self survives in a precarious balance of avoiding/ engaging with *places* that mandate not only English, but the various styles and registers routinely employed in activities of a particular place. Given that our adult language learners were repeatedly concerned with their language anxieties in medical interactions, the hospital, outpatient offices, clinics, and other informal health centers their narratives can serve as an itinerant reference point for our discussion of English *language interactions* and *place* (Cutchin 2003).

Reflexively, we can understand the ESL classroom itself as a place that regularizes linguistic and pragmatic behaviors to which ESL students will have to negotiate self-identities. The ESL classroom levies its own demands and constraints on an individual to perform a certain sociolect of English ("beginner English," "foreigner talk," "learner-directed English") during scheduled activities with a clearly articulated opening, closing, modeling, and expectation for student participation. By recognizing that the ESL classroom exists as only one of many life domains, students will begin to develop a sense of mastery and ownership of at least one English-dominant domain: the ESL classroom. The target language norms in a learning environment may not initiate older adults into the larger society in the same way as a K-12 school might for children and adolescents; however, the process of mastering the norms of adult ESL may help adult learners identify emergent patterns in both private and public domains.

Both private and public spaces significantly structure the level of engagement, target language input, and opportunities for socialization (Pavlenko 2000). The domestic setting, which we have associated with private spaces, commonly involves family members and close friends. The older adults in our study described progressive patterns of bilingual language use in their households with a trend toward English dominance among younger speakers. While older adults' interactions with younger family members in English may provide a degree of authentic linguistic input that they might not hear in different settings, the pragmatic norms established within the household do not seem to reinforce the ones they would experience with other native speakers of English, especially those from their own age cohort. Indeed, children and grandchildren, who were positioned as linguistic caretakers and impromptu translators, may have lowered their motivation and attempts at performing English in a wider range of domains. It has been documented that adults can make considerable progress toward mastery of English in contexts where they are required to use the language in personal, social, professional, or commercial interactions.

The ESL learners who immigrated later in life found themselves fulfilling the well-defined role of childcare provider for their grandchildren while their own children worked. Filial obligations, as a mode of participation within the kinship system, altered older adults' acculturation process and ability to interact with native speakers of the target language (Hamilton and Sandelowski 2003). Age-based cultural expectations were reported to produce psychological and social stressors that barred many immigrants from resources that have been documented to increase L2 learning and acculturation. As such, public domains (supermarkets, clinics, libraries, stores, and workplaces) become the prime locus of English language learning, though interlocutors are commonly not as accommodative and supportive as close friends and family members in native language contexts.

Since both the private and public domains offer older adult learners less than ideal conditions for their development of language socialization capital, the ESL classroom surfaced as a "safe" space to (a) discuss the English language metalinguistically and meta-pragmatically; (b) recalibrate their expectations in private and public domains; and (c) strategize future encounters with interlocutors as they occur in their daily interactions. The classroom teachers in the ESL program openly discussed the varying aspects of language resocialization which produced reflection on their language-learning process in addition to inspiring students to share their struggles and empathize with other classmates' issues.

Older Adult ESL Learners and Language Socialization

A review of the applied linguistic and SLA literatures points to a need for L2 learners to participate in the target language speech community. Among large immigrant enclaves, integration and participation are not fully realized which ultimately lowers the overall quantity and quality of interactions with native speakers of the target language. The rate of acquisition and eventual attainment depends on a learner's level of language socialization. In addition to observing and performing target language norms, an individual is required to navigate the complexities of meaning-making as it relates to institutional and interpersonal power. Creating English-speaking friendships, referred to as "recruiting target-language interlocutors" in the literature, is deemed the most effective resource for second language learning. When a native speaker of English converses with an ESL learner, they tend to accommodate their perceived linguistic level, and in doing so, modify their speech so that the learner may understand what they are trying to convey. These kinds of interactions function as a type of scaffolding. The native speaker: makes reference to the learner's prior knowledge of English; gives the learner more time to formulate sentences; teaches new vocabulary by using gestures and other extralinguistic information; pauses, asks questions, recasts sentences, and encourages more communication; and challenges the learner with new words and phrases given that as a native speaker of English they have a wealth of knowledge to share.

To the extent that recruiting interlocutors has been shown to be the best resource for a second language learner, it is a model that is quite difficult to replicate in the classroom. Every student would need to have their own native-speaking tutor/instructor. For this reason, we encourage our students to recruit a native-speaking interlocutor outside of the classroom, a task that sounds easy enough but proves to be a difficult hurdle for older adults. The issue hinges on access to native speakers and having a desirable background that would be of interest for English speakers. Many European language learners in the United States, for instance a French engineer who is learning English, appear to control the necessary captial to gain access to target language speech communities and cultivate relationships with individual speakers that nurture their acquisition process. Immigrants from humbler backgrounds struggle to recruit interlocutors who might provide consistent modified input and impromptu lessons about cultural norms and the consumption of relevant media. Levels and modes of participation thus sit at the center of the adult L2 socialization process (Wenger 1998).

As with issues of access to safe spaces, the language socialization process with older adult learners finds traction in the ESL classroom. Although developing relationships with an extended array of interlocutors in a non-ESL context would be ideal, the ESL classroom walks learners through the initial steps by practicing normative behaviors in an instructive context. The weekly meetings functioned as a space that invited learners to ask questions and make comments about social interactions they had experienced outside the classroom as well as observations that confounded their expectations of decorum and turn-taking. We encouraged their metalinguistic insights and desire to analyze the new cultural practices in relation to their own. The acculturation process, which is open to interpretation based on each individual's ideological disposition, is accelerated through the relationships L2 learners develop with English speakers. Our discussion on the right-to-speak is conjoined to (a) the macro-social essentialism of Spanish-speaking immigrants and (b) the agentic negotiation of self-as-learner identity construction. The reciprocation between a learner's dynamic understanding of self and the available contexts for building meaningful relationships is the essence of language socialization and in turn the ultimate predictor of successful SLA.

Identity Work and SLA

Language resocialization commits an individual to establishing new identities and ideological positions as they negotiate new language-learning contexts. The transition to new target language *selves* is entangled by socially constructed, though politically real, signifiers related to aging, ethnicity, immigration history, gender, Spanish language repertoire, and education. Identity work in a second language is also coupled with a person's sense of self as a learner (Holstein and Gubrium 2000). In the ESL context, learner identities that were created decades ago when they studied in elementary school in their countries of origin informed their learner identities as an older adult. For some individuals, the old perceptions that they had as a student were positive, for others they were not. Many of our older adult ESL learners displayed behaviors that conveyed feelings of shame, insecurity, and pessimism. These sentiments were also articulated during our focus groups and interviews. Self-conceptions tend to lead to dispositions about the project of learning English and as a result impact their behavior toward recruiting interlocutors, consuming target language materials, and seeking out situations that take them out of their comfort zone in order to practice English in spontaneous conversations.

The relationship between gender identity work and language socialization emerged in the data as a significant directive for participation in English language speech communities as well as in the ESL classroom. At every level in our ESL program and during every semester, the vast majority of our students were women. When this fact was articulated during the various focus groups, student responses were diverse and contradictory. In some groups, the women made the claim that men were simply not interested or motivated while during other years of the program different groups of women claimed that it was the *women* who were not interested in talking in English outside of their home. References to men working with English-speaking colleagues and bosses were frequently made to explain they were more advanced in their acquisition of English. What we found vital to the discussion was how discourses about gendered selves influenced the agency of the learner. Each semester we could observe how particular definitions of masculinity and femininity contributed to engagement with native-speaking interlocutors and language socialization in general.

When the perceived gender ideologies of the target language society challenge a learner's own sense of identity, the motivation to learn the target language and the prospect of performing a new gendered self may diminish (Davies and Harré 1990). Several older men in the ESL program commented on how other men who have never formally studied English viewed ESL class as a "waste of time," "child's play," and a bit "silly." Since they have known primarily women to attend class, the practice of meeting once a week in a library to work on English language skills was interpreted as perhaps a feminine activity. To contend with language acquisition, some students would first need to negotiate gender ideologies and redefine what are considered "normal" and "acceptable" displays of masculinity and femininity. Women, for example, will have to contend with essentialist notions of being more nurturing and social than men which situates them as the prime interlocutors among English-speaking family members, younger family members' teachers, medical practitioners, and the public in general. Men, on the other hand, will need to find ways to develop network structures that we observed to have benefited women older adults. The unfamiliar experiences in a typical ESL classroom, which enact communicative teaching methods such as role playing and information-gap activities, can provide both men and women a safe path to reimagine newly forged identities and gender conceptualizations.

L2 Pedagogy for Older Adult Learners

The acquisition of our first and second languages are fraught with errant notions of what occurs in our brains, what is meant by a disciplined approach to language learning, and what needs to happen in an ideal context. Our contribution to the field of L2 acquisition among older adults adopts socio-constructivism as a guiding principle of both analysis and pedagogy. As with any learner, they operate within several overlapping polities that direct possible entry points into qualitatively distinct varieties of interactional experiences. Developing relationships with trustworthy interlocutors is tied to their speech community's sociopolitical status and access to social networks. Enhancing a learner's sense of ownership and agency, the following recommendations below intend to help all L2 learners overcome many of the challenges outside of the classroom, such as increasing motivation and "investment" to enhance learner agency and dealing with the interpersonal obstacles they may experience in their lives. Based on these critical issues, we provide broad recommendations of action for older adult learners that are intimately linked to concepts of identity, competence, power, access, and agency. The main objective of this section is to illustrate how a holistic pedagogy may be developed around older adults' stories and backgrounds, the circumstances that shape their relationship with the target language, and the possibilities of implementing a more student-focused, communicative-oriented ESL program.

Recommendation 1: Awareness of Ageist Discourses

Being "old" is associated with divergent significations cross-culturally that set levels of expectations and responsibilities for older students' daily lives (Escobar et al. 2000). Building awareness of the roles older adults assume in two different societies (where they grew up and where they live now) sheds light on the constructivist nature of aging behaviors. While some institutions may not allocate resources to the elderly based on a belief they may not be fully utilized, older adults themselves may alter their own behavior and identity to fulfill a cultural expectation of what it means to be a good and respectable older person. When older adults begin to recognize that certain covert ideologies exist, they will feel more empowered to break the mold and initiate target language encounters.

Elder speech, which has been described as "second baby talk," is commonly practiced when younger interlocutors speak with older people. As with any type of speech register, the use of elder speech can be interpreted as condescending or a gesture of respect. It may be difficult to walk this fine line as an ESL instructor since many features of elder speech are shared with foreigner talk and student-directed speech. Since inhibition to attention is a real psychological phenomenon in the aging brain, ESL instructors are encouraged to slow down instruction both in speech rate and pauses during activities. The appropriately paced delivery will offer older adult learners more comprehensible input and better scaffolding as long as the intonation remains respectful and not infantilizing.

Recommendation 2: Intentional Development of Social Capital

It is not only the older generations that believe "learning" occurs through rote memorization, repetition, and continuous application of a clearly defined rule. The ideas from applied linguistics that prioritize interaction, social relationships, and self-identity are not intuitive for most L2 learners. Although these concepts may appear to be too complex for L2 learners, they are comparable in cognitive load to the grammar rules for English question formations (see Chap. 4, *do-support*, tag questions, embedded questions).

Recommendation 3: Gender Roles and Language Socialization

Our whole-class discussions about gender roles and identities were some of the most engaging and insightful topics we encountered throughout the semester. Older adult students tended to make relevant connections among other adult immigrants' decision to not study ESL. Women and men have been shown to access ESL resources in different ways. In addition to finding and registering for ESL classes at the library, learners have articulated the ways they have created relationships with coworkers, supervisors, and church members. Their access and membership to larger target language speech communities should be deconstructed and shared with other classmates as well as encouraged by the ESL instructors.

Recommendation 4: Metacognition

Our experience teaching ESL testifies to students' openness and curiosity when it comes to metacognitive and metalinguistic lessons. They seem to find it useful to *think about learning* and *talk about language* as they have experienced it, and not just how they should be experiencing it according to an ESL grammar textbook (Lantolf and Thorne 2006).

Furthermore, when peers notice the ways in which others complete a challenging task, they begin to configure new strategies for addressing other language and communication issues. Older adult learners often view language learning as an endowed skill that is not nurtured and practiced but simply utilized if cognitively available. Setting expectations of normal rates of improvement based on hard work and productive interactions go a long way in ameliorating learner identities.

Recommendation 5: Bonding, Trust, Solidarity, Camaraderie

As older immigrants mediate the transition to a new country and language, they tend to lack relationships with others who find themselves in similar situations. During our ESL classes, and the focus groups themselves, adults demonstrated sensitivity and empathy for each other's plights. They were surprised to hear that someone else had similar issues with the language and daily life. The genuine camaraderie that circulated between generations, language proficiency levels, and pre-immigrant backgrounds solidified their ESL group identity and in turn their learner identities. Each vulnerability was no longer viewed as an idiosyncratic character defect. The relationships that were forged during ESL class meetings represented the initial steps toward the building of a social network of English language learners. If they were able to do it in the ESL classroom, they will also have the potential to orient other interlocutors toward their English language project (Usita and Blieszner 2002).

Recommendation 6: Recruit Interlocutors

Whereas explicit instruction of English grammar rules still dominates most ESL landscapes, older adult learners may better utilize class time strategizing the recruitment of English-speaking interlocutors, even if it begins with their bilingual grandchildren. Successful language learning requires years of continuous exposure and interaction with target language speakers. If 3-h, weekly ESL classes constitute the primary English input that a learner is receiving, as is the case in high school foreign language courses, the target language will not be acquired in short order. Thousands of hours of quality input and interaction is the key ingredient to successful L2 learning at any age. Recruiting several English-speaking companions is the only feasible way of achieving this threshold of linguistic input. Even if an ESL class were to meet 25 h a week, an L2 learner would still benefit from practicing with interlocutors. Therefore, the ESL classroom should be converted into their "language socialization headquarters" where students share language-learning stories, social connections, second-language-friendly social spaces, authentic media and materials, and language connections between their native and second languages. For example, one male student convinced a church member to exchange L2 language lessons where he would teach his friend 30 min of Spanish for 30 min of English. Since other members of his church also asked him to do the same, he offered to put ESL classmates in contact with them to develop a similar relationship.

Recommendation 7: Recruit Classmates as Interlocutors

Communicative Language Teaching is a method in ESL where explicit grammar is viewed as unproductive, and instead, learners participate in student-centered activities that highlight the need to simply communicate meaning through any modalities necessary (Spada 2007). As two learners attempt to accomplish a task together, they inevitably encounter communication breakdowns where they simply cannot figure out the intended message from their conversation partner. They are in a sense "negotiating the meaning" of their interlocutor's message; as it turns out, the process of doing so is beneficial to both listener and speaker. As with authentic English conversations out in the "real" world, a learner will need to know how to manage turn-taking sequences when they are not understanding denotational and/or connotational meanings (e.g., "Oh, really?"; "Um, I don't think I understand."; "Do you mind saying that again?"; "So sorry, I am struggling. English isn't my first language."). It is unfortunate that many textbooks ignore common conversation strategies, such as the quotative *like*, idiomatic expressions, phrasal verbs, turn-taking norms, winding-down interjections, various closings, and speech fillers. In performing communicative activities, older adult learners are in a sense learning how to recruit potential interlocutors. In fact, many older adult learners in our program ended up recruiting each other as English language interlocutors and made plans to see movies and attend other free events together.

Recommendation 8: Value Older Adults' Contributions and Talents

As we have highlighted from the literature, a dominant practice of teaching in general categorizes students based on language proficiency which in turn influences a learner's identity and overall performance in the class. Older adults are sensitive to these and larger societal discourses about old age and the elderly. The ESL classroom ideally functions as a network of social support for older learners; however, the alliances are generally formed once the instructor leads students in a practice of respect and valorization. Our research indicates that language "allies" within the classroom setting enhances the overall language-learning experience for everyone involved and aides in creating a counter-narrative that views older adults as valued peers. It is an effective practice to consult them first on Spanish language and Mexican/Central American issues and position them as authorities on ethical and historical quandaries. Low risk encounters in the ESL classroom encouraged older adults to venture into other social spaces. Participation in communicative activities builds confidence for conversations in English-dominant spaces. The ally work maintained with ESL peers improved self-esteem and efficacy in conversations that at one time produced anxiety and fear. Socio-SLA research shows how reflexive positioning, when learners claim identities for themselves such as demonstrating to be being linguistically capable, is a prime motivation for language socialization in a learner's second language.

Recommendation 9: Advocacy

The commentary offered by the adult students in the program is supported statistically: most Spanish monolingual immigrants have not attended an ESL class or any type of formal instruction of English since immigrating to the United States. Adult learners belong to social networks that are predominantly Spanish monolingual, and thus, they have the opportunity to educate others about the processes of second language learning. They know that it requires (a) extensive interaction with English speakers, (b) the willingness to exist socially outside their comfort zone, (c) knowledge of the discriminatory forces that are working against them, (d) more motivation than IQ score, and (e) reflection on both home- and target language practices. As they can attest, older adult learners are also capable of learning English and making positive contributions to the classroom environment. For this reason, using part of the time during the class meeting to think about how and to whom they should inform about SLA is well worth the time. It also positions them as local experts on the language-learning process since they will have discussed pertinent metalinguistic and metacognitive issues with their instructor.

Final Thoughts: Aging, Place, and Health

In our contribution to the topic of aging in an L2 immigrant context, we have discussed the dialectics of minority aging identities through the pressures of macro-social demarcations and the challenges of micro-linguistic interactions and performances. As language learners of English are already socially excluded from numerous socialization sites in the Dallas-Fort Worth metropolitan area, the data that we gathered over the course of several years at an ESL program indicates that older adults face additional obstacles to learning English and accessing a range of quality-of-life resources. This is particularly the case for non-English speaking older adults who will have to find ways to successfully communicate with health care practitioners, social service workers, and other professionals. Second langauge socialization sites with psycho-social benefits can reinforce language resocialization. This, in turn, can help to address unequal access to quality-of-life resources in English-dominant institutions and promote the health and well-being of aging immigrant minorities.

In documenting the ways in which individual English language learners navigate these larger sociopolitical forces, the role of place emerged as a central way to generate capital used for communicaiton and second language acquisition. *Place* (a) determined access to language-learning practices (at home, in the classroom, in their community); (b) reified or challenged inequalities that intensify later in life; (c) shaped L2 learners' social identities; (d) regulated entry to socially meaningful institutions for immigrants; and (e) authorized target language socialization experiences. In working toward social inclusion, both within their own kinship structures as well as in the city in general, the participants shared ideas and affective positions that coalesced into a collective narrative of minority aging in the United States.

The ESL classroom changed the isolated experience of L2 learning in private contexts into a community of sentiment. While the potential of L2 acquisition in age-advanced learners tends to focus on cognitive aptitude, our study reveals that motivation and learner identities were strongly driven by their affective positioning. When older adult ESL students discovered that peers were struggling with similar issues of self-efficacy, they identified with their dispositions toward the target language and culture, thus forming part of a speech community centered on shared sentiment. Through the encouragement of peers and ESL instructors, they began to embody new learner identities and pragmatic modes that enhanced L2 socialization and acquisition. The transition to a new country and deeper integration in English-dominant social networks requires valuable forms of human capital to assuage the demand of minority aging. In highlighting the significance of place as a functioning auspice of human and linguistic capital, participants developed strategies for intervention in public and private discourses. In addition to communicative language teaching methods, effective approaches to older adult ESL teaching build on these holistic principles.

Teaching strategies for older adult ESL learners profit from acknowledging the dynamic nature of their lives and how their emergent learner identities influence the L2 acquisition process. We can cultivate this dynamism by connecting learning objectives to meaningful personal goals. One example of this connection would involve building lessons on subject-specific vocabulary on topics of direct relevance to their day-to-day lives. Similarly, by recognizing that older adult learners also negotiate membership with different speech communities, an efficient use of class time would refine their observation skills of that set of pragmatic and linguistic behaviors that are practiced by native speakers of English of all ages. The classroom as a safe space can serve as local praxis for recruiting potential English-speaking interlocutors. By structuring the ESL classroom around the students' affective positionings, the instructor is lowering the stress level, stimulating curiosity, and strengthening positive associations with the project of socializing in a learner context. The ultimate objective of the ESL classroom as a contesting and emergent social space indelibly revolves around the formative development of interactional styles for participation in various social fields of communication.

References

Bayley, R., & Schecter, S. R. (Eds.). (2003). *Language socialization in bilingual and multilingual societies*. Clevedon, UK: Multicultural Matters.

Cutchin, M. P. (2003). The process of mediated aging-in-place: A theoretically and empirically based model. *Social Science and Medicine, 57*(6), 1077–1090.

Davies, B., & Harré, R. (1990). Positioning: The discursive production of selves. *Journal for the Theory of Social Behavior, 20*(1), 43–63.

Escobar, J., Hoyos, N., & Gara, M. (2000). Immigration and mental health: Mexican Americans in the United States. *Harvard Review of Psychiatry, 8*(2), 64–72.

Hamilton, J., & Sandelowski, M. (2003). Living the golden rule: Reciprocal exchange among African Americans with cancer. *Qualitative Health Research, 13*(5), 656–674.

Holstein, J. A., & Gubrium, J. F. (2000). *The self we live by: Narrative identity in a postmodern world*. New York: Oxford University Press.

Lantolf, J. P., & Thorne, S. L. (2006). *Sociocultural theory and the genesis of second language development*. New York: Oxford University Press.

Padilla, E. R., Olmedao, E., & Loya, F. (1982). Acculturation and the MMPI performance of chicano and anglo college students. *Hispanic Journal of Behavioral Sciences, 4*(4), 451–466.

Pavlenko, A. (2000). Access to linguistics resources: Key variable in second language learning. *Estudios de Sociolinguisitica, 1*(2), 85–105.

Paykel, E. S. (1974). Life stress and psychiatric disorder: Applications of the clinical approach. In B. S. Dohrenwend & B. P. Dohrenwend (Eds.), *Stressful life events: Their nature and effects* (pp. 135–149). New York: Wiley.

Spada, N. (2007). Communicative language teaching: Current status and future prospects. In J. Cummins & C. Davison (Eds.), *International handbook of English language teaching* (Vol. 1, pp. 271–288). New York: Springer.

Usita, P. M., & Blieszner, R. (2002). Immigrant family strengths: Meeting communication challenges. *Journal of Family Issues, 23*(2), 266–286.

Wenger, E. (1998). *Communities of practice: Learning, meaning, and identity*. Cambridge, England: Cambridge University Press.

Index

A
Acculturation, 135
Acculturation knowledge, 60. *See also* Crystallized intelligence
Active interviewing, 23, 24
  with Hispanic older adult second language learners, 27–28
Adaptive strategies, significance of, 112
Adult ESL learners, 136
  and language socialization, 138–139
  L2 pedagogy for, 141
  teaching strategies, 146
Advocacy, 145
Affect
  and language learning, 88
  and language socialization, 89–90
Affective alignments, 89
  between ESL students and their teachers, 94–97
  among older language learners, 90–94
Affective behaviors, 99
Affective care, 100
Affective positioning, 135
Affective stances, 87
  negative stances, 89
Affiliative kin work, 111–113
  adaptive strategies, significance of, 112
  classroom bonds, 112
  development of self-confidence, 112
  intergenerational affiliation, 113
  refashioning communication style, 113–114
Affiliative laughter, 92, 99
Age and language capitalization, 129–132. *See also* Language capitalization
Age factor, 18
  procedural memory, 19
Age-related conceptions, 47
Age-related excuses, 98
Aging
  and applied linguistics, 72–74
  and language learning, 11
  and procedural memory, 6
Aging Hispanic population
  cultural and linguistic diversity, 5
  DREAM Act, 6
  Great Recession, 6
  implications for various issues, 5
  major demographic changes, 7
Aging immigrants, 32
  in culture and family, 37–39
Aging in place, 70
  ESL classes as safe zone, 81–83
Ally work, 127–128
American English, pragmatic rules, 53
Applied linguistics, and aging, 72–74
  biopsychosocial consequence, 74
  painful self-disclosure, 73
  sociolinguistics of aging, 73
  supportive talk, 73
  unflattering characteristics, 74
Artfully agenic, 8
Awareness of ageist discourses, 141–142

B
Basic questions, articulating, 49–50
Biopsychosocial consequences, 74
Building bonding, 90–91

C
Camaraderie, 143
Case study
  Hispanic immigrant communities, 21
  interviewing strategy, 23–27. *See also* Interviewing strategy
  language socialization, 21
  mixed methods approach, 20
  post-puberty learners, 19
Chomsky, Noam, 55

Classroom
  exercises, 95
  overcoming negative self-stereotypes, 97–101. *See also* Negative self-stereotypes, overcoming
  as positive group, 119
Cognition, research in SLA and, 55–56
Cognitive aptitude, 48
Cognitive slowing, 47
Communication domains, 107–108
  experiences in classroom, 108
  learners' ability, 107
Communicative gap, managing, 105
Concept of affective filter, 88
Congruent alignments, 89, 90, 92
Creative interviewing, 26
Critical period hypothesis, 6, 19, 55–56
Cross-cultural communication issues, 74
Crystallized intelligence, 60–62
  life experience, 61
  in SLA, 62
Cultural and linguistic diversity, 5
Cultural factors, 43
  communicative bond, 43
  ethnic minorities, 43
  self-as-learner identity, 44

D
Declarative knowledge, 18
Deficit-model, 64–65
Do-support declarative clause, 51, 59
DREAM Act, 6

E
Elder immigrants, 2
Elder speech, 141–142
Elderspeak, overcoming, 111–113
  adaptive strategies, significance of, 112
  classroom bonds, 112
  development of self-confidence, 112
  intergenerational affiliation, 113
  refashioning communication style, 113–114
Embedded questions, 52
Emotional health, 135
Emotional synchrony, 89
Emotions, among older language learners
  affiliative laughter, 92
  argumentative support, 93
  emotional bonding with learners, 96
  feelings of anxiety, 92
  fractal recursivity, 92
  frustration, 94
  negative affective stances, 91
  social and emotional feedback, 95
  between teachers and students, 95
English as second language (ESL) program
  family literacy program, 22
  language resocialization, 13
  language socialization, 8
  positive affective positions, 12
  speech competence, 21
  statistics, 6
  work-based classes, 7
Exit events, 33

F
Familism, 37
  alternative family arrangements, 38
  positive effects of, 38
Family alliances
  adults' self-perceptions, 115
  English-dominant society, 114
  sociolinguistic perspective, 115
Family language socialization, 108–110
  age-based distribution of power, 109
  conserving immigrants' mother tongue, 109
  cultural and communicative gap, 110
  intergenerational language effect, 109
  language gaps, 110
  pressures of acculturation, 108
  raising bilingual children, 110
Family literacy program, 22, 23, 47
Family network, 105
  bilingualism, 106
Filial obligations, 138
Finding place, for old adult learners, 83–84
  ageist attitude, 83
  debunking myths, 84
  negative affect, 83
  self-esteem and motivation, 84
Fluid intelligence, 58–60
  do-support clause, 59
  qualitative and quantitative inputs, 60
Fostering strategies, 98

G
Gender
  and language capitalization, 129–132. *See also* Language capitalization
  social positioning, 120. *See also* Social positioning
Gender identity, 120, 121–123
  immigrant experience, characteristics, 122
  immigrants' self-identity, 123
  self-as-learner identity, 121
Gender roles, 142
Gendered labor, 123–125
  informal interactions, 123

Index 151

Gendered literacy, 123–125
　negotiating domestic events, 125
　women's work, 124
Gendered settings, negotiating competence in, 126
　building self-confidence, 126
　legitimacy aids, 128
　machista ideology, 129
　positive socialization, 127
　reflexive positioning, 127
　wanting to learn English, 128
Great Recession, 6

H
Health risks, 136
Healthy cognitive aging, 65
Hidden American immigration consensus, 2, 3
High-frequency structures, 50
Hispanic immigrants, 3
　aging immigrants, language matters for, 4–5
　language resocialization, 3
　paradox, 3
　trajectory of SLA, 4

I
Idea of institutional ethnography, 28
Identity work, 10, 17, 21, 23, 24, 91, 113, 120, 121, 131
　and SLA, 139–140
Idiomatic question, 50
Immigrant effect, 22
Immigrant experience, characteristics, 122
Immigrants' self-conception, 3
Immigration, 33
　effects of racial discrimination, 35
　elder minority language acquisition, 11
　fear of deportation, 35
　illegal immigrants, 34
　language socialization, 13
Implicit linguistic competence, 18
Implicit theory of interviewing, 24
Impression management, 135
Inassimilable others, 35
Information-processing model, 18
Inner speech development
　English-dominant society, 114
　model of ally-work, 117
　participation in social speech, 115
Institutional disadvantages, 11
Intelligence
　crystallized intelligence, 60
　fluid intelligence, 58–60
Interactionalism and environmental factors, 56

Intergenerational boundaries, 70, 74, 90–91
Intersections, 35
　of aging and immigration, 33
　multiple intersection of aging, 33
Interviewing strategy, 23–27
　active interviewing, 23, 24
　challenge of interviewer, 24
　creative interviewing, 26
　implicit theory of interviewing, 24
　interpretive judgments, 25
　social turn, 27
　traditional interviewing, 24
　vessel-of-answers approach, 26
Investments, literacy program, 72, 79–80
　age-related cognitive changes, 80
　civic requirements for residency, 79
　regaining autonomy, 80

J
Judged by others
　fear, 89
　feeling, 81
Judgments, interpretative, 25

K
Kin work, 113. *See also* Affiliative kin work

L
L1 English-speaking toddlers, 49
L2 learning, 57
　general perceptions, 48
　language aptitude in, 57
　psycholinguistics and neurocognition, 48
　role of place in, 137–138
　social constructivism in, 71–72
Language acquisition, 57, 135
Language attrition, 57, 135
Language capital, building through place, 43–44
Language capitalization, 129
　insights on transitions, 131, 132
　nature of learning, 132
　scholarship, 130
　social security benefits, 129
　suggestions from instructors, 130
Language learning, 121–123
　and affect, 88
　immigrant experience, characteristics, 122
　immigrants' self-identity, 123
　self-as-learner identity, 121
Language resocialization, 10, 121
　later life, 8
Language socialization, 142
　adult ESL learners, 138–139

Language socialization (*cont.*)
    and affect, 89–90
    paradigm, 121
    peer-based social control, 20
Late-life language learning, 17, 135
    language aptitude, 57
    motivation and expectations, 22
    paucity of research on, 57
Late-life SLA research, challenges and issues with, 62–64
    compensatory strategies, 63
    functional vs. life experience, 62
    overall factors, 63
    social turn in SLA, 64
Latin American immigrant groups, 34
Legitimate peripheral participation, 128
Lexicon, 49, 53, 54
Life transitions, 33
Linguistic behaviors, 12
Linguistic caretakers, 12, 106
Long-term memory, 60–62
    life experience, 61
    in SLA, 62
Low-wage occupations, 36

M
Machista ideology, 129
Macro-social demarcations, 145
Memory
    long-term memory, 60
    working memory, 58–60
Metacognition, 142–143
Mexican migrants, 36
Micro-linguistic interactions, 145
Minority aging
    familial social exchange, 39–41
    micro-processes of, 32
    structure of, 34–37
    troublesome statistics, 36
Modern symbolic racism, 3
Morpho-syntax, 49, 53
Mother–daughter communication, 111
Motivation, 72
Multilingual society, 107–108
    experiences in classroom, 108
    learners' ability, 107
Multilingual society, 6

N
Narrative linkages, 28
Negative self-stereotypes, overcoming, 97–101
    laughter during corrective feedback, 98–99
    positive aging identities, 97–98
    younger and older learners working together, 99–101
Neighborhood contacts, 41–42
    Cubans migrants, 42
    ethnic enclaves, 42
    immigrant enclaves, 41
    migration experiences, 41
Neurocognition, 48
Neurolinguistic research, 48
Non-monolingual socialization, 42
Nonsampling errors, 25

O
Older adult second language learners, 18–22
    active interviewing, 27–28
    right to speak, 74–79 *See also* Right to speak
Oppositional alignments, 89
Over-accommodative way of speech, 73

P
Painful self-disclosures, 90
Pedagogy, for adult learners, 141
Phonology, 49, 53, 54
    phonological loop, 54
Place in L2 learning, 137, 145, 146
    classroom as safe zone, 138
    filial obligations, 138
    language interactions, 137
    private and public spaces, 137
Poststructuralist theory, 71
Pragmatics, 49, 53, 54
Procedural knowledge, 18
Psycholinguistics, 48
    linguistic areas researched in, 53–54
Public language socialization, 114–117
    adults' self-perceptions, 115
    concept of allies, 117
    English-dominant society, 114, 115
    minority status, 114
    sociolinguistic perspective, 115

Q
Qualitative approach, 135
Qualitative conceptualization of self, 9
Qualitative methods
    how-to guidelines, 26
    of interviewing, 24, 25. *See also* Interviewing strategy
    response effects, 25
Quality-of-life resources, 145
Question formation in English, 49

Index 153

Stage 1 questions, 49–50
Stage 2 questions, 50
Stage 3 questions, 50–51
Stage 4 questions, 51
Stage 5 questions, 51–52
Stage 6 questions, 52–53

R
Recommendations
  advocacy, 145
  awareness of ageist discourses, 141–142
  bonding, 143
  camaraderie, 143
  gender roles, 142
  intentional development of social capital, 142
  language socialization, 142
  metacognition, 142–143
  recruiting classmates as interlocutors, 144
  recruiting interlocutor, 143
  solidarity, 143
  trust, 143
  valuing older adults' contributions and talents, 144–145
Refashioning communication style, 113–114
Reflexive positioning, 127
Response effects, 25
Right to speak, 8, 12, 70, 71, 72
  English-speaking interlocutors, 78
  ethnocultural enclaves, 74
  negative stereotypes, 76
  overdependency on interpretations, 78
  under-accommodative way of speech, 77
Role strain, 108–110

S
Safe zone, ESL classes as, 70–71, 81–83
  emotional bonding, 81
  imagined identity, 82
  safe space for language learning, 81
  transformative space, 82
Second language acquisition (SLA), 1, 48, 70
  in adult L2 learning, 71–72
  epistemological changes, 70
  and identity work, 139–140
  late-life, 47–48
  question formation in English, 49–51.
    See also Question formation in English
  research in, and cognition, 55–56
  self-confidence and self-esteem, 20
  social turn in, 21
  socio-constructivist approaches, 70

Second language acquisition theory, social turn, 11
Second-language learner, 31
  rethinking friendship and family relationships, 32
Second language socialization, 11, 42
Self-as-learner identity, 10, 44
Self-conceptions, 122
Self-confidence, 112, 113, 126
  in SLA, 20
Self-criticism, 100
Self-disclosure, 73
Self-esteem, in SLA, 20
Self-handicapping strategies, 73
Self-identity
  risk-taking attitude, 96, 101
  seeking to minimize errors, 101
Self-monitoring, 58
Social capital
  distribution, 135
  intentional development of, 142
Social competence, 107, 121. *See also* Language capitalization
  communicative competence, 21
  negotiating competence, 126–127
  speech competence, 21
Social constructivism. *See also* Right to speak; Socio-SLA
  negative stances, 69
Social exchange, 39–41
  age-based expectations, 41
  English interlocutors, 40
  environmental changes and limitations, 40
  pressures of acculturation, 39
Social identity, 121
Social networks, 41–42
  Cubans migrants, 42
  ethnic enclaves, 42
  immigrant enclaves, 41
  migration experiences, 41
Social positioning, 121–123
  immigrant experience, characteristics, 122
  immigrants' self-identity, 123
  self-as-learner identity, 121
Social support systems, 2
Social turn, 84
Sociolect of English, 137
Sociolinguistics of aging, 73
Socio-SLA, 71–72
  poststructuralist theory, 71
  right to speak, 71
  traditional cognitive notions, 72

Solidarity, 143
Spanish-speaking immigrants, 64
Speech community membership, 127–128
Structural factors, 43
    communicative bond, 43
    ethnic minorities, 43
    self-as-learner identity, 44
Subject–verb agreement issues, 59
Supportive talk, 73
Syntactic movement, 59

T
Traditional interviewing, 24
Transition, 136
Transnational social networks, 34
Truncated multilingualism, 107, 115
Trust, 143

U
Under-accommodative way of speech, 73, 77

V
Valuing older adults' contributions and talents, 144–145
Vessel-of-answers approach, 26
Vocabulary knowledge, 54. *See also* Lexicon

W
Wh-questions, 51
    inversion in, 52
Women learners, 101
Women's work, 124
    competing life demands, 124
    negotiating domestic events, 125
Working memory, 58–60

Y
Yes/no question, 50, 51
Young immigrants' acculturation, 36
Younger interlocutors, 73
Younger mentors, 99–100

CPSIA information can be obtained
at www.ICGtesting.com
Printed in the USA
BVOW06*0505130617
486752BV00004BA/42/P